Creating a New Kind of University
Institutionalizing Community-University Engagement

Edited by

Stephen L. Percy
University of Wisconsin–Milwaukee

Nancy L. Zimpher
University of Cincinnati

Mary Jane Brukardt
Eastern Washington University

ANKER PUBLISHING COMPANY, INC.
Bolton, Massachusetts

Creating a New Kind of University
Institutionalizing Community-University Engagement

ISBN 1-882982-88-6

Composition by Lyn Rodger, Deerfoot Studios
Cover design by Dutton & Sherman Design

Anker Publishing Company, Inc.
563 Main Street
P.O. Box 249
Bolton, MA 01740-0249 USA

www.ankerpub.com

Library of Congress Cataloging-in-Publication Data

Creating a new kind of university : institutionalizing community-university engagement / edited by Stephen L. Percy, Nancy Zimpher, Mary Jane Brukardt.
    p. cm.
  Includes bibliographical references and index.
  ISBN 1-882982-88-6
  1. Community and college—United States. 2. Education, Higher—Social aspects—United States. 3. Education, Cooperative—United States. I. Percy, Stephen L. II. Zimpher, Nancy L. III. Brukardt, Mary Jane.

  LC238.C74 2006
  378.1'03—dc22

                                                        2005025631

Table of Contents

About the Authors

The Editors

Stephen L. Percy directs the Center for Urban Initiatives and Research at the University of Wisconsin–Milwaukee (UWM) and is also the chancellor's deputy for The Milwaukee Idea. He has been a campus leader in forging community-university partnerships between UWM and Milwaukee communities, including the implementation of a five-year Community Outreach Partnership Center funded by the U.S. Department of Housing and Urban Development. He is coprincipal investigator and project director for a $3 million Carnegie Corporation grant for Teachers for a New Era, and director of the Knowledge Management Component at the Helen Bader Institute for Nonprofit Management at UWM. A member of the UWM faculty since 1988, he currently serves as professor of political science and professor of urban studies with research interests focused on urban policy, organization of local governance, and policy evaluation. He is also author of numerous books, and articles, including *Disability, Civil Rights and Public Policy: The Politics of Implementation* (University of Alabama Press, 1989), which received the Outstanding Book Award by the Gustavus Meyers Center of Human Rights in the United States. He served on the Governor's Blue Ribbon Commission on State and Local Relations for the 21st Century. He is a recipient of the UWM Alumni Association's Distinguished Public Service Award.

Nancy L. Zimpher became the president of the University of Cincinnati in 2003, after serving for five years as chancellor of UWM. Her career also includes the deanship of the College of Education and executive deanship of the Professional Colleges at The Ohio State University in Columbus, Ohio. An author and editor of books on higher education and teacher education, she served as president of the Holmes Partnership from 1996–2001 and as a member of the Executive Board of the National Council for Accreditation of Teacher Education. She currently chairs the Commission on International Programs for the National Association of State Universities and Land-Grant Colleges (NASULGC) and has served as a member of the American Council on Education's Leadership and Institutional Effectiveness Commission. She serves on the boards of NASULGC and the American Association of Colleges for Teacher Education. Dr. Zimpher has participated on numerous state and regional as well as civic and community commissions and boards. She cochairs the Ohio Board of Regents' Articulation and Transfer Advisory Council and is the Inter-University Council representative to the Ohio Board of Regents' Funding Commission. She has served on several statewide commissions and councils, including the Ohio Board of Regents/Ohio Board of Education Joint Council, the Wisconsin Governor's Task Force on Technical Education, and the Wisconsin State Superintendent's Blue Ribbon Commission of the Arts and Education. She is a recipient of numerous awards, including the Council for the Advancement and Support of Education's Chief Executive Leadership Award, the Distinguished Research Award from the Association of Teacher Educators, and the Wisconsin Department of Public Instruction State Superintendent's Friend of Education Award. She is also included in the Ohio Women's Hall of Fame.

Mary Jane Brukardt serves as associate to the president at Eastern Washington University, in Cheney, Washington, facilitating strategic planning for the university. A writer and consultant to higher education for more than two decades, she also served as senior writer for Chancellor Zimpher at UWM and was director of communications for The Milwaukee Idea. With Nancy Zimpher and Stephen Percy she coauthored *A Time for Boldness: A Story of Institutional Change* (Anker, 2002). Other publications for which she has provided editorial support include *Crossing Boundaries: The Urban Education Imperative* (2004), a joint report from the American Association of State Colleges and Universities and the National Association of State Universities and Land-Grant Colleges; *A Call to Leadership: The Presidential Role in Internationalizing the University* (2004), a report of the NASULGC Task Force on International Education; and *Calling the Question: Is Higher Education Ready to Commit to Community Engagement?* (UWM, 2004), coauthored with Barbara Holland, Stephen Percy, and Nancy Zimpher. She has also edited a philanthropic journal and a two-volume history of The Johnson Foundation and Wingspread. She has received awards for print publications and web site development from the Public Relations Society of America and from the Council on Foundations.

The Contributors

Armand W. Carriere is former associate deputy secretary for university partnerships at the Department of Housing and Urban Development in Washington, DC. He currently works with the Worcdester UniverCity Partnership in Massachusetts. He lives with his bride of 32 years and several cats.

Anthony Ciccone is professor of French and director of the Center for Instructional and Professional Development at UWM. He also directs the UW-System Wisconsin Teaching Scholars Program and is a recipient of a 2005 Hesburgh Certificate of Excellence. He currently teaches a freshman seminar on comedy and graduate courses on college teaching and second-language pedagogy.

David N. Cox is executive assistant to the president of The University of Memphis. He holds the rank of professor in the Division of Public Administration. In 1998–1999 he served as director of the Office of University Partnerships for the U.S. Department of Housing and Urban Development. He currently serves as chair of the board of the Association for Community-Higher Education partnerships and is a member of the National Review Board for Engaged Scholarship.

Deborah Fagan has served as communication director for The Milwaukee Idea for the past five years. She has also worked in marketing communications for a variety of nonprofit organizations and is a former reporter for the *Milwaukee Journal*. She is the recipient of several writing awards from the Wisconsin Hospital Public Relations and Marketing Society and the International Association of Business Communicators.

Rita Hartung Cheng is professor of accounting and provost and vice chancellor at UWM. She was involved in creating and staffing the university's Helen Bader Institute for Nonprofit Management and has taught both credit and noncredit certificate programs in nonprofit management. Her research interests are in nonprofit and governmental accounting.

Barbara Holland became director of the National Service-Learning Clearinghouse in 2002 after serving as a visiting director of the Office of University Partnerships at the U.S. Department of Housing and Urban Development. She also serves as a senior scholar with Indiana University–Purdue University Indianapolis's Center for Service and Learning, as adjunct professor of the University of Western Sydney, Australia, and as executive editor of *Metropolitan Universities* journal.

Elizabeth Hollander is executive director of Campus Compact, a national organization of more than 900 college and university presidents committed to higher education's civic mission. She has coauthored chapters for *Civic Responsibility and Higher Education* (American Council on Education/Oryx Press, 2000) and *Learning To Serve* (Springer, 2001), and was a principal writer of the *Wingspread Declaration on the Civic Responsibility of Research Universities* (Campus Compact, 1999) and the *Presidents' Declaration on the Civic Responsibility of Higher Education* (Campus Compact, 1999).

Susan Kelly served as dean of the School of Continuing Education and associate provost for outreach and e-learning at UWM. In 2004 she accepted the position of provost with Argosy University, a national 13-campus proprietary university, specializing in graduate studies. Currently, she is a senior consultant with Hong Kong-based NextEd Ltd., advising on international education startup initiatives and sourcing U.S. degree programs for universities in China and Southeast Asia.

Gregory S. Jay is professor of English at UWM, where he is also director of the Cultures and Communities Program. He has published extensively on issues of curriculum reform and is author of *American Literature and the Culture Wars* (Cornell University, 1997).

Sandra Elaine Jones is assistant director of the Cultures and Communities Program at UWM. In 2004 she received her Ph.D. with a dissertation titled, "Handing on the Creative Spark: Black Women's Reading Practices, a Speculative History."

Jennifer Meeropol is the project associate at Campus Compact, where she oversees the Indicators of Engagement Project. She is coauthor of *The Community's College: Indicators of Engagement at Two-Year Institutions*

(Campus Compact, 2004) and of the forthcoming publication, *One with the Community: Indicators of Engagement at Minority-Serving Institutions.*

Ellen K. Murphy is professor emerita of nursing in the College of Nursing at UWM. She served as secretary of the university from 1999–2003. Her publications concentrate on legal issues in healthcare. She served as the president of the Association of Operating Room Nurses and currently serves on the Public Policy Council of the Wisconsin Nurses Association.

Linda M. Post is department chair of curriculum and instruction at UWM. She also codirects the Metropolitan Multicultural Teacher Education Program. She is a member of the Milwaukee Partnership Academy Board and the Implementation Team. In addition, she is codirector of the Urban Network to Improve Teacher Education (UNITE). She received her Ph.D. from Syracuse University.

Marleen C. Pugach is professor of teacher education in the Department of Curriculum and Instruction at UWM, where she directs the Collaborative Teacher Education Program for Urban Communities. She was the 1998 recipient of the Margaret Lindsey Award for Distinguished Research in Teacher Education from the American Association of Colleges for Teacher Education.

Alfonzo Thurman is dean of the School of Education, chancellor's deputy for education partnerships, and professor of administrative leadership at UWM. He also serves on the board of directors of the Milwaukee Partnership Academy and is president of The Holmes Partnership, a national education association.

John Wanat is past provost and vice chancellor at UWM and also holds an academic appointment as professor of political science. He previously served as vice provost and executive associate vice chancellor for Academic Affairs at the University of Illinois–Chicago and was on the faculty of the University of Kentucky.

Jon F. Wergin is professor of educational studies at Antioch University's Ph.D. program in leadership and change. He previously served as professor of Educational Studies at Virginia Commonwealth University and was senior scholar with the American Association for Higher Education from 1994–2005. He is the author of numerous books, including *Departments That Work* (Anker, 2003). He is a member of the National Academy for Higher Education Leadership.

Foreword

I vividly recall the excitement I felt when Nancy Zimpher was appointed chancellor of the University Wisconsin–Milwaukee (UWM), and called for the implementation of "The Milwaukee Idea." My excitement increased when I was asked to deliver a keynote address as part of the celebration of her inauguration in March 1999. I returned from the celebration with the optimistic conviction that something of genuine national significance was unfolding for the engaged university movement and for American higher education in general: namely, that a truly comprehensive effort to create a truly engaged, truly democratic university was being launched. *Creating a New Kind of University: Institutionalizing Community-University Engagement* indicates that my optimism was not misplaced.

Over the past five years, UWM has worked effectively to do just that—"create a new kind of university"—by engaging every one of its schools and colleges to realize the institution's core mission of service to the local community and indirectly, therefore, to American society whose basic social units must be "neighborly communities" (Dewey, 1927, p. 213). To a significant extent, the UWM story is that of a mission-driven strategy to achieve institutional alignment and excellence. Institutional alignment is at the very center of UWM's work with its community and its city. In effect, Zimpher and her colleagues developed and implemented a strategy to create a harmonious integration of all the different components of the university so that they increasingly functioned in ways likely to help achieve the university's primary mission.[1] To put it mildly, that is not an easy thing to do.

Far from being harmoniously integrated, American universities are remarkably specialized and fragmented, internally and externally, ferociously competitive, filled with conflict, and astonishingly unintegrated institutions. A call by a new president or chancellor for mission-driven alignment is surely not a sufficient condition to reverse the deeply ingrained, seemingly immutable fragmentation and "silo-ization" that characterize most American universities. A concrete "how-to-get-there-from-here" implementation strategy is the sine qua non for progress in this and all other efforts to produce serious and significant change. In effect, UWM put into place what I would term "a democratic, university-community partnership implementation strategy." In my judgment, Zimpher and her colleagues made just the right choice.

Working with communities to help solve universal problems (e.g., substandard schools, inadequate health care, urban poverty) manifest in a university's local environment holds enormous promise for creating institutional alignment. As the UWM case indicates, the resources and expertise of every university unit are needed if solutions are to be developed for these highly complex, multifaceted, continuously evolving, globally significant problems. And as the UWM case also indicates, creating and sustaining collaborative, university-community partnerships to improve both the community *and* the university requires continuity, adaptability, and, most centrally, a genuine commitment to a genuinely collaborative democratic process. As the editors note in the first chaper, "Community collaboration is at the heart of the engagement movement and yet it is the most difficult part to get right—as UWM continues to learn." An ever-increasing number of universities, it is worth emphasizing, are involved in a similar learning process.

In October 2004, I attended the third in a series of conferences sponsored by the Kellogg Forum on Higher Education for the Public Good, held at the Johnson Foundation's Wingspread Conference Center in Racine, Wisconsin. The conference on "Higher Education Collaboratives for Community Engagement and Improvement" assigned participants to one of several working groups. The draft report of the faculty and researcher working group[2] echoes many of the themes identified in *Creating a New Kind of University*. For us, as well as administrators and faculty members at UWM, democracy is the heart and soul of a successful community-university partnership. The faculty research group committee identified three "democratic Ps"—democratic purpose, process, and product—as crucial components for success. The following sections of the report summarize our argument:

> *1) Purpose.* A successful partnership is characterized by democratic and civic purposes... [Before World War I], the democratic mission served as *the* central animating mission for the development of the American research university, including both land-grant institutions *and* [private] urban universities. "It is not possible to run a course aright when the goal itself is not rightly placed," Francis Bacon wrote in 1620. An abiding democratic and civic purpose is the rightly placed goal if higher education is to truly contribute to the public good.

2) Process. In accordance with the purpose discussed above, a successful partnership should be highly democratic, egalitarian, transparent, and collegial. Higher educational institutions should go beyond a *rhetoric* of collaboration and conscientiously *work with* communities, rejecting a [unilateral], unidirectional, top-down approach, which too often describes the actual practice of university-community interaction. The higher educational institution and the community, as well as members of both communities, should treat each other as ends in themselves, rather than as means to an end. That is, the relationship itself and the community partners and their welfare (not developing a specified program or completing a research project) should have preeminent value. The collaborative should be significant, serious and sustained, beneficial to both the institution of higher education and the community, and lead to a relationship of genuine respect and trust.

3) Product. A successful partnership strives to make a positive difference in both the higher educational institution and the community. Contributing to the wellbeing of people in the community (both in the here-and-now and in the future) through structural community improvement (e.g., effective public schools, neighborhood economic development, strong community organizations) should be a central goal of a higher education collaborative for the public good. Research, teaching, and service should also be enhanced as a result of a successful partnership. Indeed, working with the community to improve the quality of life in the community may be one of the best ways to improve the quality of life and learning within a higher educational institution.

The brilliant and inspiring phrase at the core of Abraham Lincoln's Gettysburg Address might also serve as a useful guide to help get university-community partnerships "right." Successful partnerships should be: *of the people*—that is, emerge from real community-identified problems and concerns; *by the people*—that is, research to solve those problems should be conducted both by members of the community and the university; and *for the people*—that is, substantive improvement in the quality of life and learning in the community and on the campus should result from the collaborative research and work.

To a significant extent, these principles were applied by UWM as it implemented its partnership strategies. The important role of democratic principles is discussed in the chapters by Elizabeth Hollander and Jennifer Meeropol, David Cox, and Armand Carrier, which provide a national context for the activities at UWM. Cox, for example, highlights the democratic ethos and purpose found in today's engaged university movement by quoting a powerful statement by William Rainey Harper, the first president of the University of Chicago, made in 1902 at Nicholas Murray Butler's inauguration as president of Columbia University. For Harper (1905), a great urban university, "which will adapt itself to urban influence, which will undertake to serve as an expression of urban civilization, and which is compelled to meet the demands of an urban environment . . . will ultimately form a new type of university" (p. 158).

In that same address, in effect, Harper (1905) invoked John Dewey's fundamentally pragmatic proposition that major advances in knowledge strongly tend to occur when human beings consciously work to solve the central problems confronting their society:

> The urban universities found today in . . . [the] largest cities in the country . . . and in [Europe] form a class by themselves, inasmuch as they are compelled to deal with problems which are not involved in the work of universities located in smaller cities. . . . Just as the great cities of the country represent the national life in its fullness and variety, so the urban universities are in the truest sense . . . national universities. (pp. 158–160)

To conclude his address, he proclaimed that of all the great institutions in New York City, Columbia University was the greatest. In Chicago, Harper certainly believed, his university held that preeminent position.

The new type of university Harper described would, in turn, be an institution dedicated to realizing America's democratic promise. Earlier, in an 1899 speech at the University of California, Harper heralded the preeminent democratic mission of the university. Although he and other "captains of erudition" at the turn of the 20th century did not work (indeed could not have worked) to create genuinely democratic, egalitarian partnerships,[3] Harper (1905) did, with extraordinary foresight, *conceptualize* the engaged urban university that is now *beginning* to emerge at the turn of the 21st century:

> The university, I contend, is this prophet of democracy— *the agency established by heaven itself to proclaim the principles of democracy.* . . . It is the university that fights the battles of democracy, its war-cry being: "Come, let us reason together." It is the university that, in these latter days, goes forth with buoyant spirit to comfort and give help to those who are downcast, *taking up its dwelling in the very midst of squalor and distress.* . . . The university, I maintain, is the prophetic interpreter of democracy; the prophet of her past, in all its vicissitudes; the prophet of her present, in all its complexity; *the prophet of her future, in all its possibilities.* (italics added, pp. 19–20)

It does not seem like too much of a stretch to argue that UWM has adopted something like a "Harper-Dewey strategy" of working to solve the highly complex real-world problems of its community and city to realize the university's democratic, civic purpose and achieve institutional eminence. From more than 20 years' experience working with colleagues to create democratic, mutually beneficial, mutually respectful partnerships involving the University of Pennsylvania and its ecological community of West Philadelphia, I can attest to the value of the Harper-Dewey strategy of community, real-world problem solving. I cite a recent example from Penn's work with the West Philadelphia community to illustrate the benefits produced by such an approach.

In recent years, it has been increasingly recognized that lack of accessible, effective healthcare is one of the most serious problems affecting poor urban communities. In the spring and summer of 2002, a group of undergraduates in an academically-based community service seminar I directed focused their research and service on helping to solve the healthcare crisis in West Philadelphia. The students' research and work with the community led them to propose establishment of a community health promotion and disease prevention center at a public school in West Philadelphia, the Sayre Middle School.[4]

From their research, the students were well aware that community-oriented primary-care projects frequently flounder because of an inability to sustain adequate external funding. They concluded that for a school-based community healthcare project to be sustained and successful, it had to be built into the curriculum of both the university and the public school. Only then would it gain a degree of permanence and stability. They proposed, therefore, the creation of a health promotion/disease prevention center at a local school that would serve as a teaching and learning focus for medical, dental, nursing, arts and sciences, social work, education, design, and business students. Their proposal proved to be so compelling that it led to the development of the school-based Community Health Promotion and Disease Prevention Center at Sayre Middle School.

The school-based center at the school was formally launched in January of 2003. It functions as the central component of a university-assisted community school designed both to advance student learning and democratic development and to help strengthen families and institutions within the community. A community school is an ideal location for healthcare programs; it is not only where children learn but also where community members gather and participate in a variety of activities. Moreover, the multidisciplinary character of the Sayre Health Promotion and Disease Prevention Center enables it to be integrated into the curriculum and cocurriculum of both the public school and the university, assuring an educational focus as well as sustainability for the Sayre Center. In fact, the core of the program is to integrate the activities of the Sayre Center with the educational programs and curricula of both Sayre Middle School and Penn. To that end, Penn faculty and students in medicine, nursing, dentistry, design, social work, and arts and sciences, as well as other schools to a lesser extent, now work at Sayre through new and existing courses, internships, and research projects. Health promotion and service activities are also integrated into the Sayre students' curriculum. In effect, Sayre students serve as knowledgeable, caring, and active *agents* of healthcare improvement in the Sayre neighborhood.

It should be noted that a considerable number and variety of Penn academically-based community service courses provide the resources and support that make it possible to operate, sustain, and develop the Sayre Health Promotion and Disease Prevention Center. Literally hundreds of Penn students (professional, graduate, and undergraduate) and dozens of faculty members, from a wide range of Penn schools and departments, work at Sayre. Since they are performing community service while engaged in academic research, teaching, and learning, they are simultaneously practicing their specialized skills and developing, to some extent at least, their moral and civic consciousness and democratic character. And since they are engaged in a highly integrated common project, they are also learning how to communicate, interact, and collaborate with each other in wholly unprecedented ways that have measurably broadened their academic horizons.

The dean of Penn Medicine, Arthur Rubenstein, recognized the extraordinary potential of the Sayre Health Promotion and Disease Prevention Project when he appointed Bernett L. Johnson, Jr., M.D. to the newly created position of senior associate dean for diversity and community outreach in the School of Medicine. Dr. Johnson, a distinguished professor of dermatology and the senior medical officer of the Hospital of the University of Pennsylvania, had played the key role in engaging the Medical School with the Sayre project, recruiting students, residents, house staff, and faculty to contribute to various health education and health promotion activities.

In the announcement appointing Dr. Johnson, Dean Rubenstein wrote: "He will build upon our successful community efforts, many of which Dr. Johnson initiated, and work closely with colleagues at the University level to coordinate interactions with community groups and organizations" (A. H. Rubenstein & R. W. Muller, personal communication, December 22, 2004). Though I had been advocating such a position for nearly 13 years, I am convinced that the Sayre Health Promotion and Disease Prevention Project provided the real-world demonstration necessary to convince the dean and other administrative leaders of the benefits that would accrue to both Penn Medicine and West Philadelphia from creating an office designed to substantially increase and enhance the medical center's work with the community.

It is worth noting, indeed emphasizing, that in April 2005, the U.S. Department of Health and Human Services informed the Sayre Community Health Advisory Council, a nonprofit corporation founded for the purpose of opening a primary care health center, that its application for approximately $1.5 million over three years to support the Sayre School-Based Community Health Center (SBCHC) had been approved. The Sayre SBCHC will serve the socioeconomically distressed inner-city area surrounding the school, which has been designated both as a Medically Underserved and a Primary Care Health Professions Shortage Area. The target population is the low-income Sayre students and their families.

(More than 85% of Sayre students come from low-income families.) The goal is to integrate health promotion activities with the school's educational programs and curricula as part of providing accessible, culturally sensitive services.

The center is still in its early days, of course, but I think that the successful creation and operation of the Sayre Health Promotion and Disease Prevention Center strongly supports the validity of the Harper-Dewey approach to university and community improvement through democratically identifying and trying to solve a highly complex, highly significant, real-world, local community problem which, by its very nature, requires sustained interschool and interdisciplinary collaboration. Indeed, the UWM democratic, university-community partnership implementation strategy has predictably resulted in increased institutional alignment and effectiveness.

The changes described above are neither unique to UWM nor to Penn. Examples of similar activities are occurring at colleges and universities across the country. But as promising as this development is at present, *the rhetoric of engagement far exceeds the reality of university engagement.* We still have a long way to go before Harper's vision of "a new type of university" is realized in practice. *Creating a New Kind of University* concludes on that very note, by quoting from the final report from a spring 2004 meeting at the Wingspread Conference Center cosponsored by UWM and the University of Cincinnati, which I had the good fortune to attend.

Titled "Calling the Question: Is Higher Education Ready to Commit to Community Engagement?" the report, while acknowledging the significant progress that has been made in recent years, emphasizes that the progress has been neither rapid nor thorough enough. In bold and unequivocal language, the report, signed by all 41 conference participants, called for "the transformation of our nation's colleges and universities" (Brukardt, Holland, Percy, & Zimpher, 2004, p. ii) through serious, sustained democratic university-community partnerships.

The UWM story, told so well in this volume, illustrates the many significant benefits that result for a university and its community when democratic, community-university, problem-solving partnerships function as the primary means to realize a university's democratic civic mission. As its editors observe, *Creating a New Kind of University* does not provide "a blueprint." It does, however, help us better understand what a truly engaged university looks like. And, more importantly, it provides us with ideas and a strategy for *how* we might get from here (somewhat engaged) to there (truly engaged, truly democratic universities). For that, we owe the editors and authors our admiration and our gratitude.

Ira Harkavy
Center for Community Partnerships
University of Pennsylvania

Endnotes

1) The discussion of institutional alignment is significantly derived from a paper coauthored by Ira Harkavy and Lee Benson (2002).

2) The members of the faculty and researcher working group were Tony Chambers, Arthur Dunning, Edwin Fogelman, Ira Harkavy, Leonard Ortolano, and Jane Rosser.

3) For an excellent discussion of the concept of captains of erudition, see Diner, 1980.

4) For a more detailed discussion of the Community Health Promotion and Disease Prevention Center at the Sayre Middle School, see Benson, Harkavy, and Hartley, 2005.

References

Benson, L., & Harkavy, I. (2002, October). *Truly engaged and truly democratic cosmopolitan civic universities, community schools, and development of the democratic good society in the 21st century.* Paper presented at the Research University as Local Citizen conference, San Diego, CA.

Benson, L., Harkavy, I., & Hartley, M. (2005). Integrating a commitment to the public good into the institutional fabric. In A. J. Kezar, T. C. Chambers, & J. C. Burkhardt (Eds.), *Higher education for the public good: Emerging voices from a national movement* (pp. 185–216). San Francisco, CA: Jossey-Bass.

Brukardt, M. J., Holland, B., Percy, S., & Zimpher, N. (2004). *Calling the question: Is higher education ready to commit to community engagement?* Milwaukee, WI: The Milwaukee Idea.

Dewey, J. (1927). *The public and its problems.* Athens, OH: Swallow Press.

Diner, S. J. (1980). *A city and its universities: Public policy in Chicago, 1892–1919.* Chapel Hill, NC: University of North Carolina Press.

Harper, W. R. (1905). *The trend in higher education.* Chicago, IL: University of Chicago Press.

Preface

This book came to be as a result of two important gatherings on the shores of Lake Michigan. Whatever the contributions of that Great Lake, it served as an inspiring backdrop for meetings that, while held almost eight years apart, continue to create ripple effects in the lives of the participants and the institutions they serve.

The first gathering was convened by the University of Wisconsin–Milwaukee (UWM) in October of 1998. A group of 100 university and community members assembled in the Italian Community Center on Milwaukee's waterfront. Invited by the university's new chancellor, Nancy Zimpher, they were, foremost, curious to see the new leader and, secondarily, intrigued by her invitation to help create a new vision of the university as a vital community partner and regional collaborator. Within two years, that group of 100 had launched what became "The Milwaukee Idea," more than a dozen initiatives in partnership with civic, educational, non-profit, and business leaders that crossed disciplines and colleges, created new research and learning opportunities, and literally transformed the way in which UWM defined itself. The "engaged university," a term made popular by the Kellogg Commission on the Future of State and Land-Grant Universities in the late 1990s, became a new way for universities like UWM to describe a distinctive approach to their mission and practice. That meeting by the lake in 1998 galvanized UWM to rediscover the power of connecting its vision for a modern, urban research institution to a shared future with the communities and world its faculty, staff, and students served.

The second meeting took place in the spring of 2004 just a few miles south at the Johnson Foundation's Wingspread Conference Center in Racine, Wisconsin. With a mild April wind blowing off the lake and through the windows of Frank Lloyd Wright's Wingspread, 41 leaders and practitioners from engaged institutions across the country—including faculty and staff from UWM—gathered to answer the question of how to sustain and institutionalize university engagement. In the years since the Kellogg Commission and Ernest Boyer's call for new scholarship, colleges and universities across the United States and abroad in Canada, Great Britain, and Australia had blazed new trails, demonstrating the benefits of engagement to the academy, to students, and to community partners. Case studies of institutions large and small, public and private, two-year and four-year, have provided guidance to institutions that sought to expand and support the efforts of faculty and administrators to integrate engagement, assess its progress, and to nurture the difficult work of partnering.

This book is the product of both these gatherings and a lot of what has transpired between them. It is a clear-eyed look at university engagement through the lens of UWM and its ongoing efforts to create an institution suited to its urban setting and the students it serves. And it is also a look at the state of engagement nationally—how far it has come, what is required to assure its health, and how it can best prepare for a challenging future. The specific examples and lessons learned at a single institution resonate with what we are learning on the larger stage as we pause, briefly, to look at where we are and where we want to be.

Like a leaf dropped into Lake Michigan, this book is arranged in ripples that radiate outward from the first UWM meeting in 1998. The first two chapters describe The Milwaukee Idea and its institution-wide commitment to university engagement. Its usefulness as an engagement model is assessed by those who experienced its creation from within, and by Jon Wergin, an external evaluator who documented its development and provides a comparison to another engaged institution near Lake Michigan, the University of Illinois–Chicago. Both chapters identify critical markers essential to nurturing engaged practice and also significant barriers that can impede its progress.

The second "ripple" in the book provides three different perspectives on UWM's experience—perspectives from groups outside the administrative mainstream, yet critical partners for universities seeking to make their engagement efforts sustainable. Deborah Fagan held a series of conversations with UWM's community partners—often the forgotten voices when academics gather to assess institutional engagement. Their insights, while focused on the UWM experience, are useful reminders of the challenges and rewards of collaboration. Ellen Murphy explores ways in which shared governance can be a powerful tool, rather than an impenetrable barrier, for institutional change. And Susan Kelly reminds us of the valuable role that continuing education faculty and staff, who are frequently old hands at community partnerships and engaged teaching and research, can provide to colleagues across all disciplines.

One of the important ripples that university engagement has created across all of higher education is its impact on our understanding of the nature and role of scholarship. Led by a growing acceptance of service- and experiential-learning, faculty and administrators often find the "way in" to community-university engagement through changes to student learning and pedagogy. Elizabeth Hollander and Jennifer Meeropol explore the history and impact of engaged learning, providing an important context for how we think about university engagement and its importance to preparing our students for a diverse democracy. Greg Jay and Sandra Jones from UWM describe the real world of engaged learning and how one university is seeking to transform general education by connecting its students to the multicultural world outside campus classrooms. David Cox expands on the importance of defining the meaning of engaged scholarship and finding ways to assess it. In the concluding chapter of the section, Anthony Ciccone looks more closely at the scholarship of teaching and learning, the questions it raises for the future, and the important role its proponents can play in supporting engaged faculty and staff.

The Milwaukee Idea at UWM has been an all-university focus for more than five years, ample time to begin to assess what it takes to create sustainable engagement. Two very different initiatives are described in Chapters 10 and 11, providing a detailed look at the nature of community partnerships and what it takes to sustain them. Marlene Pugach, Linda Post, and Alfonzo Thurman have been part of a far-reaching university-community partnership that seeks nothing less than the transformation of Milwaukee's public schools. The chapter provides practical and detailed guidance on how such partnerships can be structured for long-term success. Rita Cheng describes a partnership that was led, not by the university, but by the philanthropic community. Institutions of higher education are frequently more comfortable leading than following. In this chapter, Cheng provides a template for shared collaboration.

While university engagement is becoming more broadly accepted, practiced, and even supported at institutions across the country, finding ways to institutionalize it and sustain momentum beyond the first wave of enthusiastic adopters is a significant challenge. In the final section, titled "Engagement: Implications for Sustainability," the authors identify the questions the academy must ask and specific actions it can take to better integrate engagement across our institutions.

Armand Carriere provides an important look at funding engagement, with a focus on the contributions by the U.S. Department of Housing and Urban Development and its Office of University Partnerships. John Wanat explores the ways in which university administrators can and cannot support engagement. And Nancy Zimpher reflects on the role of leadership, particularly that of the president, chancellor, and provost, in nurturing and institutionalizing university engagement.

Together, these chapters provide a candid and informative snapshot of the state of the engaged college and university today. But like the waves crashing into the Lake Michigan shoreline, neither our institutions nor our understanding of engagement remains still or fixed. The final ripple we examine is a look to the future. "What's next?" we asked the 41 leaders at Wingspread. The answer we received was unexpected. We do not need another call for institutions to join the movement. We do not need another plea for faculty and staff to explore the benefits of engaged discovery and teaching. As UWM illustrates, much good work is already going on across the country, in institutions large and small. Instead, said the Wingspread group, we must call the question. It is time to ask America's colleges and universities: "Are you ready to commit to engagement?"

If so, the challenges to create an individual institutional vision that can be sustained amid the vagaries of changing funding, technological innovation, and shifting public expectations will be great. Just as large, however, will be the benefits, as colleges and universities find in a mission to serve the common good a renewed vigor for a new century. It is time to take a stand and answer the call.

And so, in a way, the final chapter returns us to the beginning—a decision point to create a "new kind of university" through the transformative power of community engagement. When we make that decision—whether as individuals, as an institution, or as contributors to higher education—the ripples extend outward, again.

Acknowledgements

Our thanks begin with the countless dedicated faculty, staff, students, and administrators who have led the way in renewing higher education through a commitment to the power of community-university partnerships. At UWM, our colleagues in The Milwaukee Idea, as well as those who quietly and behind the scenes have worked for years as engaged scholars and practitioners, have provided both the example and the encouragement for our belief that change is possible.

Our contributing authors have been generous with their time, ideas, and patience, and it has been a privilege to work with each of them. We thank especially our two editorial reviewers, Ira Harkavy at the University of Pennsylvania and Lorilee Sandmann at the University of Georgia, who provided expert counsel to our authors and have been invaluable in helping to shape the book. We also thank those members of the Milwaukee community who shared their perspectives and continue to support UWM.

The 41 members of the 2004 Wingspread conference on university engagement comprised a group of great wisdom, insight, and energy. We echo their challenge to higher education to commit to the transformative future that community-university engagement promises.

As editors, it was our privilege to work together at UWM on The Milwaukee Idea. It has been a continuing pleasure to extend that relationship over the years through several publishing endeavors and the personal friendship we share.

Stephen L. Percy
Nancy L. Zimpher
Mary Jane Brukardt

PART I
Engagement in Context:
The Milwaukee Idea

1

Moving Forward Along New Lines

Mary Jane Brukardt, Stephen L. Percy, and Nancy L. Zimpher

In 1963 just a few years after the University of Wisconsin–Milwaukee (UWM) was officially incorporated, Fred Harvey Harrington, president of the University of Wisconsin, outlined for the regents the mission of the state's newest urban university. Drawing on its 19th-century roots as a normal school and state college, UWM was to "move forward along new lines—to experiment, to generate and try out original ideas and approaches in instruction, research, and public service" (Klotsche, 1966).

It is doubtful that Harrington could have imagined the modern public urban research university that UWM has become—serving a diverse student body of 26,000 students, on campus and online—but his advice was prescient. His vision for UWM, one relevant for all universities, especially America's urban institutions, rings as clearly today in this time of rapid change as it did four decades ago. Pressing social problems, both at home and abroad, increasing student calls for relevant learning, and demands from state legislatures and corporate funders for academic returns on investment demand of higher education new ways of learning, new applications for discovery, and new avenues for service.

For increasing numbers of universities, the answers to Harrington's challenge have been found in the forging of new and expanded community-university partnerships. The movement to engagement—"the mutually beneficial exchange, exploration and application of knowledge, expertise, resources and information," as Holland defines it (2001, p. 24)—has been

3

gaining ground as institutions find in it a pathway to reinvigorate their mission to serve the common good.

Since Boyer's (1994) call for a "new American college" that defines professional service as a "central mission" and the Kellogg Commission's 2000 report on engagement, more and more colleges and universities are adopting service-learning, moral and civic education, research derived from and applied to community issues, and scholarship that links students, faculty, staff, and community in the real work of changing the world. The 2003 Annual Membership Survey conducted by Campus Compact—a leader in encouraging colleges and universities to support civic engagement—indicated that four out of five of its 900 member institutions have an office that supports community service and/or service-learning. The Department of Housing and Urban Development has provided seed money for community-university partnerships for more than a decade (see Chapter 12). And educational associations, such as the National Association of State Universities and Land-Grant Colleges and the American Association of Colleges and Universities, have led major initiatives to encourage and assess community-university collaboration.

The results have been a wide array of engagement efforts that range from individual, faculty-led service-learning courses to research efforts that span colleges and extend beyond campus walls to diverse communities. A 2002 Urban Institute report on 25 universities involved in the Community Outreach Partnership Center program identified 11 different categories of community engagement, ranging from community development, technical assistance, and life-skills training to graduate students providing professional services in healthcare, social work, law, and even engineering (Vidal, Nye, Walker, Manjarrez, & Romanik). These efforts are also being mirrored abroad—in Canada, England, South Africa, and Australia. A 2001 report from the Association of Commonwealth Universities (ACU), for example, challenged its members to respond to expectations of society by letting engagement define the "whole orientation and tone of a university's policy and practice" (p. i).

Looking at the higher education landscape today, it would seem that Harrington's call to move forward along new lines—especially new lines of engagement—is being answered, both broadly and creatively. The larger question, however, is whether the experimentation and creativity he called for are being matched by like measures of sustainability. Calling for more university engagement, even creating programs and initiatives that implement it, are only the first steps in the continuing effort to integrate engagement fully into the fabric of higher education.

Making engagement sustainable is no small goal: Shifting institutional leadership and grant-based funding, for example, often relegate community partnerships to boutique initiatives that wither away after the dollars dry up. Many community engagement offices are tucked away in outreach centers or isolated in a single school or college. Judith Ramaley (2000) estimates that even at "engaged universities," only 10–15 percent of faculty may be committed to engagement, while almost two-thirds remain skeptical of engagement becoming a long-term university priority.

Creating a "new kind of university"—an engaged university—will require that colleges and universities move beyond experimentation to institutionalization. There is no blueprint for this formidable task, but like engagement itself, only lessons to be shared with partners of like mind. Such is the task of this chapter and of this book.

In its consultation document on engagement, ACU (2001) discusses the importance of the "dialogue of practice with theory" (p. i). That dialogue is the goal of this volume: to juxtapose the experiences of UWM in its efforts to center its mission more clearly on its community collaborations with the scholarship of national leaders able to identify hallmarks of successful efforts to make engagement sustainable. Taken together, it is hoped, this dialogue will encourage and advance the understanding and practice of engagement for other colleges and universities also looking to shape new kinds of institutions.

UWM: Milwaukee's University

Born in 1956 with the merger of the University of Wisconsin Extension Center and Wisconsin State College–Milwaukee, UWM was to serve students from the metropolitan region and state. Created to be "Milwaukee's university" (Cassell, Klotsche, & Olson, 1992), the new university's programs and research were, from the start, geared to the industrial heartland and to the urban center it called home. UWM faculty have a long history of partnering with community arts, healthcare, and corporate organizations. As Susan Kelly discusses in Chapter 5, faculty in UWM's School of Continuing Education are "old hands" at the practice and scholarship of engagement. When the dean of the School of Architecture and Urban

Planning, for example, was named to direct planning and design for the city of Milwaukee in 2004, it was a logical culmination of decades of community collaboration by the university's faculty, staff, and students.

As one of the University of Wisconsin System's 26 state colleges and universities (including the flagship research institution, the University of Wisconsin–Madison), UWM was also heir to a century-long, statewide tradition of engagement known to citizens and academics alike as the "Wisconsin Idea." Championed by University of Wisconsin President Charles Van Hise and the progressive Governor Robert La Follette at the turn of the 20th century, The Wisconsin Idea proclaimed that "the boundaries of the university are the boundaries of the state" (Stark, 1995, p. 101). From its earliest years, the university's professors and students were called on to provide policy advice and research to the legislature; in turn its pioneering extension service found willing partners in the state's farmers and industrialists. The resulting university-community collaborations produced the creation of a milk test that revolutionized the dairy industry and the nation's first workers' compensation program (Stark), among countless other benefits.

The Journey to Engagement

By the late 1990s, however, a decade of financial pressures and many decades in the research shadow of its sister institution in Madison found UWM struggling to find its place as an urban-focused research institution in its own right. Certainly there were no shortages of opportunities for engaged leadership. Milwaukee's public schools graduated only four out of 10 of its African American students, the city's infant mortality rate was higher than New York City's, and the unemployment rate for blacks was the highest in the Midwest (Battle, 2000).

Holland (2001) has identified four paths to university engagement, each of which affects the organizational directions colleges and universities take in focusing their engagement practice. They are essentially pathways that address either external pressures or internal calls for change. These include the need to respond to a pressing external regional or national social, economic, cultural, or political challenge, or the immediate concerns of the often decaying neighborhoods that surround their campus. They may also come to engagement as a result of an internal crisis such as enrollment shifts or budgetary problems, or as they seek to transform their teaching or research performance.

Ostrander (2004), on the other hand, sees the journey to engagement as a result of three different visions for institutional change. Engagement is the answer for colleges and universities seeking to clarify their purpose in the new century. The first vision for higher education is based on personal transformation and individual change, most often rooted in student learning that educates for civic and political engagement and leadership. The efforts of Campus Compact and its 900 member institutions to institutionalize service-learning and civic education exemplify this approach.

The second vision is rooted in the belief that higher education must support democracy through community building and civic work, which creates the spaces and opportunities for citizenship. Boyte and Kari at the University of Minnesota's Center for Democracy and Citizenship argue for collaboratively engaging students as well as the community and university in "collective labors" that create lasting civic value—the public work that "solves common problems" with an "eye to general, other-regarding consequences" that build agency and democracy (Boyte & Kari, 1996, p. 4).

The third vision begins with the belief that engaged pedagogy and university-community collaboration can create institutional and social change that will lead to a more just society. Harkavy (1996) of the University of Pennsylvania has argued that higher education must move beyond "symbolic actions" to "strategic, academically-based community service" to solve what he calls the central problem of our time, namely "the problem of creating democratic, local, cosmopolitan communities" (p. 58). This kind of strategic service must, of necessity, engage the entire university across its learning, discovery, and service missions.

In the case of UWM, the university's change process was motivated by a range of factors, including pressing external challenges in its surrounding urban communities (especially in education, healthcare, and economic development), by a strong desire to create its own research identity, and by the recognition that resource growth would only be possible by transforming its mission to better meet the needs of the state. At the same time, university leaders and change participants believed that transformation at the individual and institutional levels, through renewal of student learning and institutional culture, was critical to the future of UWM and to the society it serves. Certainly, the university's history of engagement and its tradition of service under The Wisconsin Idea positioned it well for a renewed focus on engagement.

It was at this juncture that UWM's efforts were galvanized by the arrival of a new chancellor, Nancy L. Zimpher. In her inaugural faculty senate plenary address, she announced her support for UWM's engagement mission: "Our goal is nothing less than to change forever the quality of our life together by joining the urban renaissance of Milwaukee and transforming ourselves as Milwaukee's and someday the nation's premier urban university" (Zimpher, Percy, & Brukardt, 2002, p. 11). Calling on the university to model civic engagement and to prepare its students for active lives of citizenship, she launched a multi-year process that ultimately involved hundreds of faculty, staff, students, and community members in identifying new collaborative opportunities, setting a renewed institutional mission and institutionalizing engagement. She called her efforts "The Milwaukee Idea," echoing the state's historic Wisconsin Idea, and challenged the university to find opportunities, institution-wide, to connect to the region's communities.

The Change Process

Becoming an "engaged institution" is an "extraordinary quest that requires taking extraordinary measures" (Rosaen, Foster-Fisherman, & Fear, 2001, p. 24). At UWM, this involved a change process that first enabled faculty, staff, and students to engage with one another, across disciplines, departments, and colleges, and that also made possible new engagement between the university and its community. (The story of this change process has been documented in a companion volume, *A Time for Boldness* [2002, Anker], by Nancy L. Zimpher, Stephen L. Percy, and Mary Jane Brukardt.) In the next chapter, Jon Wergin assesses this process and draws implications for other institutions that seek to tackle engagement at the institutional level.

UWM had always had initiatives scattered across the institution that brought together faculty and community members around service-learning, joint research opportunities, or civic service. What the change process sought to do was to extend those collaborations more broadly by actively involving community and corporate leaders in helping the university define and implement its engaged mission.

The UWM change process was both top-down and bottom-up. It was top-down in the sense that it was championed and led by the chancellor and her leadership team. As Bringle and Hatcher (2000) note, "deliberate institutional planning" (p. 283) is important to institutionalizing the practices of engagement, and the leadership of UWM's chancellor was a major factor in its ongoing success, as the community comments compiled by Deborah Fagan in Chapter 3 attest. Critical also was Chancellor Zimpher's ability to articulate the rationale for engagement in terms that resonated with both campus and community. For UWM, this rationale embraced the opportunities for applied and collaborative research, the potential for enhanced student learning and community connections, university transformation and prestige, and fulfillment of civic responsibility. These goals mirror the priorities that others have identified as core to the engagement movement (ACU, 2001; Holland, 1999).

UWM's change process was bottom-up in that the identification of engagement opportunities and their implementation were very much the product of a community/campus conversation, created in the chaos and trial-and-error of the real world of collaboration. The "Cultures and Communities" initiative around student learning, about which Greg Jay and Sandra Jones write in Chapter 7, came out of months of lively discussion that brought together faculty, staff, and community leaders unused to working together but surprised at the possibilities their shared concerns offered them. The creation of UWM's nonprofit education program actually developed from community-led impetus, as Rita Cheng describes in Chapter 11. And the university-school partnerships that led to the Milwaukee Partnership Academy resulted in innovative and jointly-created institutional infrastructure that crosses university and school district, as Marlene Pugach, Linda Post, and Alfonzo Thurman outline in Chapter 10.

The Milwaukee Idea (which ultimately came to identify the institution-wide engagement efforts of the university) coalesced around three university priorities: education, the economy, and the environment. Within these "3Es," a collaborative planning process identified specific initiatives around which the university's schools and colleges were invited to focus their energies. As of this writing, Milwaukee Idea efforts include 14 major initiatives that span every school and college and encompass: a Consortium for Economic Opportunity that in one year partnered on 42 economic development projects; a Center on Age and the Community providing graduate programs in gerontology in collaboration with a range of community partners; a Healthy Choices initiative that spearheads nationally recognized research on substance use problems; and an Institute for Urban Health Partnerships that oversees one of only two nonphysician, practice-based research networks in the nation (The Milwaukee Idea, 2004).

But is The Milwaukee Idea bigger than the sum of its parts? Despite a great range and depth of community collaborations, has engagement become a sustained and integrated part of the life and practice of the university? With the departure of Chancellor Zimpher for the presidency of the University of Cincinnati, can The Milwaukee Idea survive a leadership change?

Implications for Sustainability

The answers to these questions are not yet in; however, a closer look at UWM in light of recent scholarship on institutionalizing engagement provides some potentially useful insights. While Cavendish (2001) acknowledges that institutionalization "will look very different" (p. 4) across universities large and small, public and private, it usually entails a redefinition of the university culture, includes curricular change, involves and empowers faculty and staff, and necessitates new institutional infrastructure and accountability mechanisms. Holland (1999) goes further and notes that institutionalization requires universities to link engagement to every dimension of campus life, most particularly to mission and strategic planning, a point underscored by Bringle and Hatcher. Indicators that colleges and universities are moving to sustainable engagement include increasing levels of interdisciplinary work—because, as Holland (2001) notes, "community issues do not arrive in departmental packages" (p. 26) —as well as development opportunities and new reward structures for faculty and staff at all levels, to expand engagement beyond the "first adopters" (Campus Compact, 2004).

Calibrating the indicators for engagement is only now beginning to receive national attention, notably at Michigan State University and its Outreach Measurement Instrument, the Indiana University–Purdue University Indianapolis's (IUPUI) Civic Engagement Indicators, and by the Carnegie Corporation–funded Indicators of Engagement Project (IOEP), coordinated by Campus Compact. A review of the literature and IOEP advance results suggest that the engaged university will be characterized by a range of activities that necessitates a re-examination of faculty roles and rewards, campus culture, curriculum and pedagogy, distribution of resources, and community relationships. These indicators for institutionalization of engagement validate and find echoes in the UWM experience. We will focus in particular on four features of UWM's journey to sustainable engagement. We believe that engaged colleges and universities will be:

- Mission driven

- Partnership focused

- Grounded in scholarship

- Institutionally supported

Mission Driven

UWM's historic mission has always been connected to serving the region and state through the students it prepares for citizenship and productive work, its scholarship and research, and the service of its faculty and staff. That mission, however, like that of so many other colleges and universities, has been muddied by the scramble for national research prestige, the competition for *U.S. News & World Report* rankings, and the recruitment battle for the best and brightest students and faculty.

The Milwaukee Idea refocused UWM on the strength of its central mission of service to its community. As Chancellor Zimpher noted, paraphrasing the late Peter Drucker, the process of collaboratively creating The Milwaukee Idea initiatives helped the university to "discover the theory of its life as an institution," (p. 28) and to understand its history in terms that could be relevant for a new century (Zimpher et al., 2002). In this sense, engagement can be seen not just as an isolated or even university-wide initiative, but rather as a means to orient higher education toward the future (ACU, 2001). Engagement is future-looking because it encompasses such a broad range of purposes ideally matched to the demands of our new century. Engagement fits well with the mission of higher education because it serves the needs of the market for skilled professionals and knowledge that can address global as well as local problems; engagement promotes learning that will preserve and expand the individual attributes of independent thought, clear communication, and reasoned analysis that are necessary to a healthy democracy; and engagement challenges the status quo with knowledge constructed with community partners to promote greater social justice and civic change (Ostrander, 2004). Engagement fits educational mission because it enables colleges and universities to create a vision that matters for society at large (Rosaen et al., 2001).

By beginning its journey to engagement by focusing on mission, UWM was able to coalesce both its history of experience and its many divergent collaborations more clearly into a vision that resonated with many faculty and staff. This was possible, not because its new chancellor announced that engagement would be a good fit, but because the campus and community were invited to refocus the mission together. They became willing champions, because the vision made historical sense and fit with the needs of both faculty and community leaders. The process of refining UWM's historical mission for a new century did not happen overnight, of course. It is, in many ways, ongoing. The change process in particular encompassed more than two years and countless meetings, reports, and discussions. It was a process, however, critical to forming the personal and emotional connections that tie institutional mission to individuals and to the real world of everyday practice.

Institutionalization begins by making sure that the individuals who are part of the organization understand the meaning of engagement and the changes it will bring, *in light of university mission* (Cavendish, 2001). Connecting engagement to mission at the level of individual students, faculty, staff, and community members is critical, because mission will determine institutional priorities and guide decision-making. "Simply stated," writes Holland (1999), "I believe mission matters" (p. 25). Her study of 23 four-year institutions indicated that organizational change was not possible unless there was a clear consensus on mission.

At UWM, creating that consensus is an ongoing, not a one-time process. Forging *alignment* is perhaps a more accurate term, as faculty and staff find ways in which to shape their own priorities and interests to the engagement mission. Such alignment is incremental as colleagues share the benefits of engagement in their classrooms, involve each other in cross-disciplinary research, or become a more pervasive presence in university classrooms and activities as community partners. In essence, the university "learns" engagement through its practice, refining the vision for what is possible by what it can do.

Critical to connecting engagement to mission is faculty governance—the "coin of the realm" as Zimpher notes (Brukardt, Holland, Percy, & Zimpher, 2004, p. 17). Ellen Murphy describes UWM's efforts in Chapter 4. If, indeed, colleges and universities seek to strengthen democracy and the social fabric through their community partnerships, their own practice must also mirror habits of collaboration and democratic governance. Collaborative inquiry, a hallmark of engagement, requires that the campus and community—broadly engaged—design, conduct, and assess their collective endeavors (Rosaen et al., 2001). At UWM, this meant that new mechanisms needed to be created to hear more voices. Advisory councils, leadership teams that cross colleges, and forums open to campus and community were and continue to be part of the way the work of the university is done. Most important, initiatives are channeled through faculty governance, and faculty are involved as leaders. By anchoring engagement in both mission and governance process, engagement is immediately an all-university concern, less likely to be isolated or ignored.

Partnership Focused

Early in The Milwaukee Idea planning process, a community leader accurately described the perception that many university faculty and staff had of their community partners: too many voices, too many variables, and demands that often seemed irrational or even bizarre. Too often, university engagement is just too much work for harried faculty and busy students. And yet, university and community members understood that the stakes were too high to let differences overwhelm them. The reality of university-community collaboration is that there are many voices because there is no such thing as a universal "community" (Ramaley, 2000). Community partners will have vastly different capabilities, agendas, resources, and connections to their constituents. Engaged faculty and students must learn to listen closely to this diversity of perspectives and to work with a range of partners. There are no shortcuts to creating the trust and understanding that are essential to complex relationships (Zimpher et al., 2002). It takes time, and it takes hard work.

Community collaboration is at the heart of the engagement movement and yet it is the most difficult part to get right, as UWM continues to learn. Community partnerships are not the university seeking a community collaborator to complete a project but rather a *reciprocal* relationship where university and community together decide what is important and how it is to be accomplished. Cavendish (2001) calls this the "community-oriented model of academic professionalism" (p. 9), a model that, unfortunately, many faculty, staff, and administrators are ill-prepared to follow. Partnering—sharing power, decision-making, even dollars—does not come naturally to the academy. It must be learned and mentored, supported by institutional culture and rewarded. As Deborah Fagan outlines in Chapter 3, the Milwaukee community's scorecard on UWM's collaborative progress is still mixed.

One of the most critical components of community partnerships is the idea of *parity*. Leiderman and her colleagues at the Council of Independent Colleges interviewed 19 community leaders involved in partnerships with 13 colleges and universities (Leiderman, Furco, Zapf, & Goss, 2003). What they heard is that communities expect from their university partners:

- *A commitment to outcomes.* This often means sustained involvement beyond an academic semester or school year to reach project completion in whatever time it takes. One way in which universities can help to provide continuity for partnerships is by creating structures (such as a center for service-learning) that can support long-term relationships even while individual faculty may be oriented to semesters or course timetables. Such infrastructure is important because it provides the framework within which partnership experiences can be retained by the institution even as individual faculty move or shift responsibilities.

- *Shared authority and financing.* Engaged institutions may lead, follow, or step together, depending on the shared goals of the partnership, as Rita Cheng describes in Chapter 11. This kind of reciprocal relationship extends from shared ideas and project leadership to shared financial responsibility. UWM's School of Nursing, for example, operates several community nursing centers at which research projects and grant management may be handled by either a partner or a university team, whichever makes the most sense for the success of the project. That kind of partnership has taken years to develop, but serves as a model for more recent collaborations.

- *A willingness to support the partnership in the community.* This may require stepping up to advocate for the partnership in other civic forums, not just within the partnership. It may also involve partnering with groups that the university does not have relationships with. In Milwaukee, for example, the Milwaukee Partnership Academy brought together a range of educational institutions, some of which could be seen as competitors to UWM. And it also involves a mutual sharing of success and learning to celebrate together for hard-won victories. Another vital support skill required of the university is patience, which involves taking the time to get to know partners, to create a common language, and to work out often complex relationships to mutual satisfaction.

• *Welcoming community partners onto campus in roles normally reserved for faculty or staff.* Holland's (1999) definition of engagement, with its idea of "a trusting and mutually beneficial relationship between campus and community" (p. 70) requires the academy to recognize the assets that the community can bring to the table. At UWM, this meant that teachers-in-residence worked along with faculty and staff as clinical faculty to create a multicultural education curriculum that benefited from the real-world experiences the community team members brought with them.

The implications of this parity, of course, reverberate in the systems of recognition and reward in place for faculty and staff. Engagement demands more time and energy from faculty and staff, its rewards are not as tangible as publishing a peer-reviewed journal article, and its outcomes are frequently difficult to measure in terms that fit tenure-review processes. Engagement is prodding universities, as David Cox describes in Chapter 8, to re-examine such systems anew—a process that is ongoing and that must be connected to faculty governance, as Ellen Murphy reminds us in Chapter 4. As more faculty experience the value of engagement to their scholarship and pedagogy, they will be the source for new solutions that address questions of recognition and reward.

These are rigorous benchmarks, but well worth assessing. And that is another critical indicator of engaged institutions: They evaluate their progress, especially in relation to the success of their community relationships. As ACU notes, engaged institutions must learn to judge themselves, not by institutional rankings or the size of endowment, but by the variety and vitality of their partnerships. UWM, for example, publishes an annual *Report to the Community* that describes its partnerships and their outcomes (see http://www.uwm.edu/MilwaukeeIdea/). IUPUI has created performance indicators for its civic engagement that seek to measure faculty and institutional capacity. Michigan State University evaluates faculty outreach through an institutional survey that covers instruction, research, clinical service, service-learning, and public events and information (Church, Zimmerman, Bargerstock, & Kenney, 2003). What is often missing, as Fagan notes in Chapter 3, is the voice of the community in the university's assessment of its results. Engagement that is institutionalized will partner with the community in its evaluation as well as implementation of partnership efforts.

Grounded in Scholarship

When planning for The Milwaukee Idea began, the visioning teams had grand plans for applied research projects and scholarship around critical social problems. Zimpher and her leadership team were adamant, however, that team members also create space for student learning. The movement to university engagement is so powerful precisely because it is much more than community service. It has the added dimensions of engaged learning as well as engaged discovery. It serves faculty and students by connecting them to the power of community partnerships.

When we say that sustainable engagement is "grounded in scholarship," we are referring to the dual need to institutionalize engagement into *both* student learning *and* into the scholarship and discovery of faculty and staff. This requires different strategies, of course, but springs from higher education's primary task of preserving, generating, and transmitting knowledge. That is why, as Ramaley (1996) notes, change—especially the change involved in creating engaged institutions—is not administrative work. An engaged university cannot be created by appointing a vice president or amending institutional policy. It requires a "scholarly approach that draws on the core strength of the faculty" (Ramaley, p. 150).

This is why each institution's engagement will, of necessity, look different. If it is to be sustainable, it will be the product of its faculty's reflection, analysis, and rigorous evaluation. It will facilitate engaged and applied research that is not only community-based, but answers to the highest scholarly standards. This kind of scholarly dialogue between theory and practice is vital if engagement is to be broadly supported across the campus, because that is how the academy works. As David Cox writes in Chapter 8, "If something is 'new' in universities, that newness has to include changes in the understanding of scholarship." Ostrander (2004) observes that institutionalization will require universities to connect engagement to the creation of new knowledge because that is what faculty value most. The value-added that engagement brings is that the new knowledge it generates can also be in service to the greater good.

Embedding engagement into faculty research and scholarship requires a range of strategies. Communication is of primary importance, and at

UWM, this has taken the form of annual conferences on engagement and learning communities in which faculty examine the implications of engagement to their discipline. Engaged faculty mentors provide role models for junior faculty. There is a growing recognition, however, that engagement must become part of graduate training across disciplines if it is to be truly institutionalized and more broadly adopted (see the Wingspread recommendations in Chapter 15).

Engaged student learning forms the flip side of engaged faculty discovery. Without it, engagement is academic service in fancy dress. For UWM, as for many universities, it takes the form of service-learning and experiential learning, both of which have gained momentum from the proven results they produce in enhanced student learning. Many colleges and universities have come to engagement through the strength of their campus service-learning programs.

Elizabeth Hollander and Jennifer Meeropol look more closely at the impact of service-learning in Chapter 6, and discuss in particular the importance of multicultural education to engaged student learning. Community partnerships will of necessity bring students, faculty, and community members together around shared concerns. Successful collaborations result when the campus partners have a deep understanding of the community and its interests, assets, cultures, and needs (Leiderman, et al., 2003). Too often, however, especially in urban centers, students and faculty do not have the opportunity for real conversations with the diverse communities outside their doors. Higher education can help students examine their own perceptions, explore the rich tapestry of urban communities and grapple with the real challenges they will face with their partners in the civic work they undertake.

This kind of learning requires new curricula as well as support for faculty as they seek to help students and themselves navigate complex issues. UWM's Center for Instructional and Professional Development, about which Anthony Ciccone writes in Chapter 9, has begun to tackle the issues of pedagogy and curriculum in support of engaged learning in a multicultural world.

Institutionally Supported

"Smart people," writes Holland (2001), "*want* to put knowledge to work. Our task is to remove the obstacles" (p. 27). And feed their passion, she might have added. Sustainable engagement requires leadership, institutional infrastructure, and financial support that smoothes the path for faculty and students and continually attracts more individuals to participate and contribute.

Leadership. Institutionalizing engagement requires the leadership of the president or chancellor, provost, and academic leadership team, as John Wanat and Nancy Zimpher note in Chapters 13 and 14. It is not sufficient, of course, but it is essential because these administrative leaders are the voice for the campus and can use their positions to rally support, connect to the community, and identify engagement as an institutional priority. They also, by virtue of being outside the schools and colleges, can provide bridges to interdisciplinary perspectives, bringing together new partnerships across the campus.

Their leadership ideally begins a cascade of leadership across all levels of the university. UWM's dean of nursing made a point to discuss engagement efforts at every faculty event. Now she hears her department chairs and others on her staff taking up the message and continuing the process of integrating engagement.

One of the most important roles for leadership in the process of institutionalization is communication. Engaged leaders will seek to create the dialogues that the university needs—whether they are about integrating with mission or setting clear goals. Leaders will also be the communication points with the community and, as such, form critical bridge roles between campus and community (Ostrander, 2004). At UWM, our goal was "redundant bridges"—many individuals spreading the message and acting as the conduits through whom the community could connect to the university. We communicated through countless presentations to diverse constituent groups, through campus newsletters, and through media interviews and community meetings.

Institutional infrastructure. Trostle and Hersh (2003) remind us that engagement takes place along three pathways: the corporate, curricular, and co-curricular. The corporate and co-curricular require attention to infrastructure that removes barriers and creates new supports. At UWM, Chancellor Zimpher created The Milwaukee Idea office early on as the central focal point for university engagement. Staffed by a newly appointed deputy to the chancellor, reporting directly to her, the office helped to facilitate and communicate while also serving as a connecting point for both campus and community. Bringle and Hatcher (2000) identify a central office as critical to institutionalizing service-learning in higher education—and equally important for engagement. A central office and coordinating function (one that ideally reports directly to president or provost) also offers the institution important continuity, as university leadership changes or initiatives evolve from one center or college to another.

UWM's commitment to redundant bridges is also reflected in its institutional infrastructure in support of engagement. In addition to a central office, the chancellor also appointed a vice chancellor for partnerships and innovation, an individual selected from the community to play an important liaison role with the university's external partners.

Administrative infrastructure is one area in which removing barriers can be as important as providing supports. Crossing disciplines, creating new accountability patterns that include faculty and community, and administering shared resources requires creativity and flexibility. At UWM, two new councils helped to facilitate new ways of working. Deans Councils were formed for each major initiative, including the deans from the colleges involved in the projects. By working directly together, under the aegis of a lead dean, they are able to create cross-disciplinary solutions quickly. A Trustee Council composed of deans, faculty, staff, and The Milwaukee Idea director provides counsel to engagement efforts overall. By involving key constituents in governance structures, the decision-making can be more easily integrated into the ongoing work of the university.

Cocurricular support integrates community engagement outside the classroom—in residence life, student clubs, and activities. At UWM, for example, the Center for Volunteerism and Student Leadership complements the Center for Service-learning and extends community connections more deeply into student life.

Financial Support. In Chapter 12, Armand Carriere recounts the invaluable history of support that Housing and Urban Development's Office of University Partnerships has provided to the engagement movement during the past decade. Such external funding has helped to seed initiatives at universities across the country, UWM included, that have flowered into institution-wide engagement. Major foundations, such as the Pew Partnership for Civic Change and the Kellogg Foundation, have been critical to the gathering momentum.

Institutionalized engagement, however, requires more than external grants or seed dollars. The commitment of institutional resources, especially financial resources, is essential. This can take many forms, from support of a central office to "venture capital" seed money for faculty developing curriculum. While it is primarily invested in university functions and personnel, institutional support should also be available to partnerships. If the university is to be a credible community partner, it must be prepared to step up to the table with dollars and/or fundraising efforts, as appropriate.

At UWM, we discovered the power of leveraged dollars. A startup fund of university dollars provided matching funds for Milwaukee Idea projects. Each initiative was required to match the institutional investment through outside grants or internal reallocation. The result was more diversified funding for engagement that was integrated into existing funding streams.

A New University

The promise that engagement offers higher education in this new century is matched by the challenges for implementation and institutionalization it offers. While UWM has made great strides in integrating engagement into our historic mission, creating reciprocal partnerships, embedding it into learning and scholarship, and creating the structures needed to support it, they are only the first steps to the kind of transformation that engagement can create. The new kind of university we hope to be is still very much a goal.

If the analyses of both reflection and practice in the chapters that follow are to have broader meaning for other institutions, it is in the potential they hold to inspire others to dare to explore the possibilities that engagement can offer—the possibilities for mutual transformation of our colleges and universities and of the communities we serve.

If higher education is to continue to fulfill its calling to serve our students and our world and lead change in the new century, we must return to Harrington's challenge. Let us endeavor to move forward along new lines, finding in engagement the spark for transformation.

References

Association of Commonwealth Universities. (2001). *Engagement as a core value for the university: A consultation document.* Retrieved July 22, 2005, from http://www.acu.ac.uk/policyandresearch/research/engagement.pdf

Battle, S. (Ed.). (2000). *The state of black Milwaukee.* Milwaukee, WI: The Milwaukee Urban League.

Boyer, E. (1994, March). Creating the new American college. *The Chronicle of Higher Education, A48.*

Boyte, H. C., & Kari, N. N. (1996). Young people and public work. *The Wingspread Journal, 18*(4), 4–5.

Bringle, R. G., & Hatcher, J. A. (2000). Institutionalization of service-learning in higher education. *Journal of Higher Education, 71*(3), 273–290.

Brukardt, M. J., Holland, B., Percy, S., & Zimpher, N. (2004). *Calling the question: Is higher education ready to commit to community engagement?* Milwaukee, WI: The Milwaukee Idea.

Campus Compact. (2004) *Indicators for engagement.* Retrieved November 25, 2004, from http://www.compact.org/community-colleges/indicators/indicators.html

Campus Compact. (2003). *Annual membership survey.* Retrieved July 15, 2005, from http://www.compact.org/newscc/stats2003/

Cassell, F., Klotsche, J. M., & Olson, F. (1992). *The University of Wisconsin–Milwaukee: A historical profile, 1885–1992.* Milwaukee, WI: UWM Foundation.

Cavendish, J. (2001). Institutionalizing campus-community engagement: Reflections on the University as Citizen conference. *Metropolitan Universities: An International Forum, 12*(3), 4–12.

Church, R. L., Zimmerman, D. L., Bargerstock, B. A., & Kenney, P. A. (2003). Measuring scholarly outreach at Michigan State University: Definition, challenges, tools. *Journal of Higher Education Outreach and Engagement.* Retrieved July 15, 2005, from http://schoe.coe.uga.edu/benchmarking/msu.pdf

Harkavy, I. (1996). Back to the future: From service-learning to strategic academically-based community service. *Metropolitan Universities: An International Forum, 7*(1), 57–70.

Holland, B. (1999). From murky to meaningful: The role of mission in institutional change. In R. G. Bringle, R. Games, & E. A. Malloy (Eds.), *Colleges and universities as citizens* (pp. 48–73). Needham Heights, MA: Allyn & Bacon.

Holland, B. A. (2001). Toward a definition and characterization of the engaged campus: Six cases. *Metropolitan Universities: An International Forum, 12*(3), 20–29.

Kellogg Commission on the Future of State and Land-Grant Universities. (2000). *Renewing the covenant: Learning, discovery, and engagement in a new age and different world.* Washington, DC: National Association of State Universities and Land-Grant Colleges.

Klotsche, J. M. (1966). *The urban university and the future of our cities.* New York, NY: Harper & Row.

Leiderman, S., Furco, A., Zapf, J., & Goss, M. (2003). *Building partnerships with college campuses: Community perspectives.* Washington, DC: Council of Independent Colleges.

The Milwaukee Idea. (2004). Report to the community 2004 [Special edition]. *The Milwaukee Idea Bulletin, 4*(2).

Ostrander, S. A. (2004). Democracy, civic participation, and the university: A comparative study of civic engagement on five campuses. *Nonprofit and Voluntary Sector Quarterly, 33*(1), 74–93.

Ramaley, J. (1996). Large-scale institutional change to implement an urban university mission: Portland State University. *Journal of Urban Affairs, 18*(2), 139–151.

Ramaley, J. A. (2000). Embracing civic responsibility. *AAHE Bulletin, 52*(7), 9–13.

Rosaen, C. L., Foster-Fishman, P. G., & Fear, F. A. (2001). The citizen scholar: Joining voices and values in the engagement interface. *Metropolitan Universities: An International Forum, 12*(4), 10–29.

Stark, J. (1995). The Wisconsin Idea: The university's service to the state. *1995–1996 Wisconsin Blue Book* (pp. 101–179). Madison, WI: Legislative Reference Bureau.

Trostle, J., & Hersh, R. H. (2003). Lessons from a college promoting civic engagement. *Peer Review, 5*(3), 16–19.

Vidal, A., Nye, N., Walker, C., Manjarrez, C., & Romanik, C. (2002). *Lessons from the Community Outreach Partnerships Center program.* Washington, DC: The Urban Institute.

Zimpher, N. L., Percy, S. L., & Brukardt, M. J. (2002). *A time for boldness: A story of institutional change.* Bolton, MA: Anker.

2 Elements of Effective Community Engagement

Jon F. Wergin

Higher education has played many roles in the life and progress of our society. In the early days of our country American higher education contributed by preparing civic and religious leaders (Boyer, 1996). In the 19th century, thanks to the Morrill Act, higher education added fuel to the Industrial Revolution by inviting agrarian youth to study at newly created land-grant colleges. Access to higher education expanded after the Second World War with the passage of the GI Bill and, later, the Civil Rights Act.

Growth in access has also been accompanied, however, by a growth in scientific specialization. The end of World War II and the start of the Cold War initiated huge investments by the federal government in scientific research, most of it undertaken by faculty members in universities. This investment escalated in the late 1950s with the launch of *Sputnik* and the ensuing national call to better prepare our students in science to meet the challenges of the Soviet Union. Ironically, the very force that propelled universities to such a prominent role has, in the past few years, served to make the university increasingly insolated from its social responsibilities. American college campuses are no longer seen as sources of social wisdom and intellectual leadership but rather as an odd mix of scientific specialists, hopelessly out-of-touch humanities professors, and students who are there mostly to gain a competitive advantage in the marketplace. As Boyer (1996) observed, "Increasingly, the campus is being viewed as a place where students get credentialed and faculty get tenured, while the overall work of the academy does not seem particularly relevant to the nation's most pressing civic, social, economic, and moral problems" (p. 14). The ivory tower seems often to be above the pain and problems of the ordinary American workforce and its daily hassles. Many educational institutions have gates, well-manicured lawns, shrubs and flowers, and walls and trees to buffer the campus from the outside world. The academy does not often believe and act as though the campus is the world and the world is the campus.

As Larry Braskamp and I pointed out several years ago, some welcome counterforces are at work (Braskamp & Wergin, 1998). Constituencies at all levels are asking higher education to open these borders. Educational policymakers want higher education to be more responsive to the continuing crises in our public schools. Parents and employers want universities to pay more attention to undergraduate education. And urban communities plagued with seemingly intractable problems are looking to the campuses for help in their own backyards. Urban leaders have become considerably more sophisticated in their view of what the academy can offer them: not just specialized expertise in the form of in-and-out consultation, but also more intense partnerships calling for creativity and analytical problem-solving skills.

And so American higher education seems poised to evolve into yet another social role, this one led by the urban universities in our major cities, universities like the University of Wisconsin–Milwaukee (UWM). Some have claimed that urban universities will become the land-grant universities of the 21st century (Holland & Gelmon, 1998; Ramaley, 2000; Knight Higher Education Collaborative, 2000). If true, their potential has been slow to be realized. Many urban institutions have attempted to emulate their larger and more traditionally prestigious cousins rather than to create their own niche. The forces of tradition are strong, and change is slow. Faster progress will require that colleges and universities reorient themselves as active partners with parents, teachers, principals, community advocates, business leaders, community agencies, and the general citizenry. Higher education "will enhance its usefulness to society by becoming a forum for critical community dialogues, by advancing practice-based knowledge and policies as well as upholding the creation of theory-based knowledge, and by utilizing faculty expertise in new ways—in short, by forming new social partnerships" (Braskamp & Wergin, 1998, p. 64).

The Challenge of Engagement

These are roles, however, for which higher education is, as yet, not well prepared. The experience of another urban university, the University of Illinois–Chicago (UIC), is illustrative: In the mid-1990s, Chancellor James Stukel introduced a "Great Cities Initiative" (UIC, 1993), designed to be the signature of UIC and to showcase the university's research and outreach activities. Our study of the successes and failures of some 40-odd university/community partnerships emerging from the Great Cities Initiative led my colleague Larry Braskamp and me to make the following observations (Braskamp & Wergin, 1998):

Faculty members are not accustomed to the messiness of direct engagement in societal problems. Faculty typically are uncomfortable with power struggles and partisan conflicts. While they value seeing all sides of an issue and promoting ongoing study and debate, community participants press for closure, decision-making, and implementation.

Faculty members often lack experiential knowledge of the issues being addressed. To community reformers, the form of knowledge which academics bring to the table can seem naïve and unrealistic. Academic references and arcane statistical analyses are no match for the colorful anecdote.

Faculty engagement in social partnerships creates major personal and professional challenges. Many faculty personally developed a renewed commitment to social change as they had to face the realities of Chicago public schools. Others struggled to reframe their notions of what constitutes "scholarship" as they discovered how little control is possible in "action research." As one faculty participant said:

> If the university only relies on a traditional definition of research, then projects like [Great Cities] will not exist. Even the questions have to emerge from the community. The academic person has to go with it in a very committed, long-term way, and to report in such a way that doesn't violate the process that's happened. . . . And then there has to be some outlet for that research to allow the faculty member to be successful as an academic. It's an odd marriage. (Braskamp & Wergin, p. 71)

Collaboration does not occur without the partners spending time together to foster mutual trust. Social capital—that is, networks and trust among members which can lead to achievement of a common good—will not exist initially. Partners may view each other as having not only separate but conflicting agendas: For example, reformers may look to the university as contributing intellectual clout to a predetermined political position, while faculty members may look to the community as a "laboratory." In these circumstances it is easy for both sides to feel exploited. All partners need to make a long-term commitment to the partnership and stick with it.

Collaboration is not always beneficial. The time spent on making the collaboration work takes time away from those whom the partners are there to serve (such as students or clients). Sometimes it is better for one partner to trust the other and simply get out of the way. This in turn suggests that assessing the value of social partnerships is more complicated than just seeing whether the partnership is "working": It also means that one has to address the consequences of the partnership, both expected and unforeseen, and whether results could have been obtained more effectively or efficiently in some other way.

An Appraisal of The Milwaukee Idea

If the Great Cities Initiative was one of the largest and most ambitious projects ever undertaken with the aim of realizing the potential of urban universities, The Milwaukee Idea begun by Chancellor Nancy Zimpher was certainly in the same league. In 2000 I was asked to undertake an extensive case study of The Milwaukee Idea, assessing the extent to which this ambitious project served as a catalyzing force for institutional transformation in ways that would make its behavior more consistent with its urban mission. The study method unfolded as follows. I first made a one-day visit to the campus in August of 2000 to meet the key participants, including Chancellor Zimpher and Chancellor's Deputy Stephen Percy, to undertake a preliminary review of documents and to negotiate a protocol for collection of data. I then returned to campus with my assistant, Jane Grassadonia, for two, two-day visits, the first in October 2000, the second in February 2001. On the first visit we met with most of the leaders of various Milwaukee Idea initiatives, learning of their personal histories with the institution, how they became involved in the work of the Idea, their assessment of that work so far and that of the Idea as a whole, and their prognosis for long-term change. We asked for evidentiary bases for their comments where possible. Using a so-called "snowball" strategy, we also asked who else might help inform the study and used this list as the basis for our second round of data collection. The February visit thus included a wider range of informants: opinion leaders from both faculty and staff (including those opposed to many if not all of the The Milwaukee Idea initiatives), administrative officers, and community representatives.

Before discussing the results of our inquiry I should define the end-point criterion of the study, "transformative change." The American Council on Education, in its widely-read series *On Change*, defines transformation this way: "Transformation (1) alters the culture of the institution by changing select underlying assumptions and institutional behaviors, processes, and products; (2) is deep and pervasive, affecting the whole institution; (3) is intentional; and (4) occurs over time (Eckel, Hill, & Green, 1998, p. 3).

Given this working definition it is not difficult to see how transformative change requires a long-term commitment. Transformative change extends beyond changes in structure and function; it reflects changes in *perspective* as well. People and units not only work differently, they are aware of *why* they're working differently, and view what they do, including their roles and priorities, as natural and reasonable. It is clear that many of those with whom we spoke at UWM had already experienced transformative change at the institution: They had successfully integrated their academic selves with the needs and the opportunities available to them in an urban university, and redefined their academic selves accordingly, which some had done before the official announcement of The Milwaukee Idea in 1998.

Most had done so in virtual anonymity, however. Both faculty and students at UWM see the university as a no-nonsense, non-pretentious sort of institution where people are goal-directed and work hard. It is not an institution to seek, or gain, much publicity. UWM is surrounded by larger, more traditionally prestigious institutions with larger endowments, richer traditions, and more selective entrance requirements. And while its original mission was to "find strength in its urban setting," (Klotsche, 1966, p. 30), many at the institution envied these other places, choosing not to draw attention to initiatives which engaged the community, because these things were not what prestigious *research* universities did. Furthermore, while the university had more than 100 projects in collaboration with the community by 1998, these were typically viewed as efforts of individuals rather than as part of a coordinated university strategy. And so Chancellor Zimpher was faced with several competing tensions upon her arrival that summer:

- A campus culture that was self-effacing yet wanted to compete head-to-head with the flagship campus at Madison

- The desire both to be a first-rate research university and to develop an identity separate from the Madison campus

- A (sometimes) grudging acceptance of the "urban mission" as long as it didn't stand in the way of institutional prominence

- A growing recognition of the unique opportunities available at an urban campus but without a galvanizing concept to give them credibility

- From the community side, a desire for greater institutional engagement, but not at the expense of strong academic programs

Several other observations quickly emerged as we reviewed the data. First, like other institutions, change at UWM, while remarkable in many ways, had been broad rather than deep. Lasting change in the academy rarely comes quickly, and The Milwaukee Idea had only existed as a university vision since mid-1998. True transformative change usually consists of a series

Figure 2.1

Forces Supporting Transformative Change	Barriers to Transformative Change
<ul><li>A charismatic leader</li><li>Administrative support from above and below</li><li>A galvanizing idea which challenges the status quo but also fits the institutional tradition and culture</li><li>An open and inclusive process</li><li>Cultivation of "partners" rather than "markets"</li><li>Resources for long-term commitment</li></ul>	<ul><li>Lack of shared, common definitions of partnership and engagement</li><li>Traditional institutional values</li><li>Territoriality</li><li>Conflict over funding priorities</li><li>Cosmetics vs. infrastructure</li><li>People left behind</li><li>Demands of and for diversity</li><li>Lack of community, especially as experienced by students</li><li>Dependence on the personality of the leader</li></ul>

of incremental moves from the status quo. Second, The Milwaukee Idea was the beneficiary of an enormous amount of energy, stemming primarily from the chancellor's office. Chancellor Zimpher stated clearly that she believes in the power of the "big idea," and she put that belief to work. At the time of the case study, The Milwaukee Idea was still a new idea to many, however, and some doubted its staying power. It thus seemed clear to us that a useful way to proceed would be to identify both the forces for and barriers to change and then to suggest how those barriers might best be addressed. (See Figure 2.1 on the preceding page.)

Forces Supporting Transformative Change

A charismatic leader. The view of Chancellor Zimpher's leadership on campus ranged from an almost breathless loyalty expressed by her supporters, to a grudging respect by even her harshest critics. All, without exception, agreed that she was the most critical force for change at UWM. As a faculty opinion leader noted, "[The chancellor] was a breath of fresh air. She wasn't interested in old fights; her message was, 'let's see what we can build collaboratively.'" Or: "Until Nancy [Zimpher], no one had quite been able to push the magic button linking 'urban' and 'high quality' in the same university . . . she's been able to capture the elusive 'urban' thing and get positive community responses." Further, she was quite public about empowerment: "Before Nancy, UWM was a functional place; there was little sense of its role in the UW system and in Milwaukee . . . [it] related to students in a bureaucratic manner and its mission was rote; now there's a clearer sense of mission, a sense of self, [and] a sense that it's going in the right direction, through coalition building, working with the community, and realizing that [the university] needs to be relevant. Nancy has been key for her passion and energy; she has created new expectations for the position that will carry on."

Administrative support from above and below. A lone voice for change is rarely effective, no matter how charismatic or well-positioned the champion. Zimpher's vision was joined by an impressive supporting cast, ranging from the University of Wisconsin System president to a UWM team of administrative deputies who were intensely loyal both to The Milwaukee Idea and to Zimpher personally. As a leader of one of the "Action Teams" noted, "Several action teams almost failed—some several times—but persistence of the administrative [team] paid off." Administrative staff understood the importance of paying attention to details: making meetings happen, keeping people happy, getting the day-to-day things right.

A galvanizing idea which challenged the status quo but also fit institu-tional tradition and culture. Just as a charismatic leader like Zimpher is not likely to get far without a strong supporting cast, neither is she likely to make much headway without a compelling vision for others to rally around. Our informants made it clear that Zimpher was able to give voice to a spirit of UWM that captured how many already felt about the place and established an identity that they could be proud of and committed to. Any university is a highly complex organization, with multiple and often conflicting missions, and so it would be unrealistic and unfair to attempt to characterize UWM with blanket generalizations. Every university also has a signature culture, a way of thinking about itself and what it aspires to become.

Our informants gave us a clear picture of some of the major threads of this cultural fabric. First, UWM was presented as an institution which, due in part to its complexity and lack of tradition, offered considerable flexibil-ity to those who wish to innovate. There was a sense of openness to experi-mentation, creativity, and manageable risk, by faculty and administration alike. As one of our informants pointed out, "a UWM can innovate faster than a Madison." Second, UWM was seen as an institution of great poten-tial which needed only to be awakened: Two informants called it a "sleep-ing giant." Third, there was a general sense that The Milwaukee Idea pushed the institution in ways that needed pushing. As one faculty mem-ber noted, "The Milwaukee Idea challenges encrusted institutional bound-aries." There was a general consensus among respondents that The Mil-waukee Idea has provided a "signature" for the campus that is both more robust and more extensive than simple sloganeering, which is why, as is de-scribed later in this report, it has also become threatening to many at the university.

An open and inclusive process. The Milwaukee Idea "brought together multiple constituencies, [stimulated an] exciting quality of dialogue, and heightened the quality of conversation," as one respondent put it. Many were highly skeptical of the process at first but were eventually won over: "The whole thing seemed so inchoate, like a bowl of spaghetti . . . [and yet] through some kind of alchemy [it] moved to real plans and outcomes." The process "opened the door for anyone to walk in," said one administra-tor. No one wanted any backroom deals put together by campus adminis-trators. "Open forums were the key to resolving territory disputes," said a faculty leader.

Cultivation of "partners" rather than "markets." The term "market" has become ubiquitous in colleges and universities, much to the chagrin of traditionalists who resent the intrusion of business jargon into the academy. Targets of university outreach do not like to be called "markets," either. From the beginning, Chancellor Zimpher emphasized how UWM would strive to be a partner to the Milwaukee community. We saw converging evidence that both community and campus attitudes were changing: from community engagement as a sort of noblesse oblige attitude by the university, to a beginning appreciation of the community as a true partner, where each party had something to gain and learn. As a faculty member and researcher said, "Before the Idea there was only lip service to the community; now the community is also into the research."

Resources for long-term commitment. Most at UWM would agree that having The Milwaukee Idea depend on funds reallocated from other sources would have sunk it right away. Instead, seed funds for the Idea were scraped together from both external sources and internal discretionary funds. Even critics of the Idea admitted that it was a way to garner resources for the university.

Barriers to Transformative Change

Lack of shared, common definitions of partnership and engagement. The lack of common definitions was apparent. Chancellor Zimpher defined partnership as "not the university seeking a community collaborator to help complete a project [but rather] a reciprocal relationship where university and community together decide what's important and how it is to be accomplished." Barbara Holland (2001), then director of the Office of University Partnerships at the U.S. Department of Housing and Urban Development, defined partnerships as a joint exploration of separate and common goals and interests through a mutual agenda, with success measured in both university and community terms.

Traditional institutional values. Sometimes anything that runs against the organizational grain is resisted simply because of institutional inertia. One faculty member, for example, told of how he couldn't teach a certain class because his chair wouldn't change course times to accommodate community wishes. More serious are policy obstacles. One significant obstacle is the set of institutional policies surrounding research, teaching, and service. We heard from faculty, especially junior faculty, that community engagement is risky for those facing the tenure process, because they must meet traditional objectives for scholarship, service, and teaching. The research model in place does not adequately address the scholarly merit of applied research and "engagement." We were told by the leader of a major partnership initiative, "Young faculty would die to work with us, but would die if they did." For a true shift to occur among faculty and for real transformation to occur at the most core academic levels, promotion and tenure must be aligned with the goals of The Milwaukee Idea.

This issue is directly linked to the question of academic excellence. For some, "interdisciplinary" equals "mediocrity." As one faculty member said, "Where's the discipline in interdisciplinary?" For these faculty members, the sine qua non of excellence is research productivity, preferably in basic research, and these people are concerned about the place of pure research within the Idea agenda. We heard several accounts of faculty who felt they were "better than UWM and belonged in an Ivy." Traditional academic values would dictate that strong academic programs should be supported, whether or not they fall in line with "institutional mission."

Issues of "policy" and "academic excellence" don't tell the whole story, however. A third element to this barrier is a difference in discourse. Academics and those in the community, whether they be educators, organizers, or business leaders, have different perspectives on how to approach problems. The academic value is to take one's time in studying an issue, to analyze it critically from all sides, and to couch any recommendations in careful, probabilistic language. As was found in the Great Cities Initiative, those outside the academy were typically more interested in rough-and-ready solutions to identified problems, with less concern over such nuances as methodology and critical analysis. Their message to academics was, "Tell us what you think. You're supposed to be the experts." We heard this refrain from most, if not all, of the community representatives with whom we spoke. One said, "It's like the community is on one side of a chasm and the UWM faculty are on the other. [The faculty] will come right up to the edge of the cliff but then not do what it takes to clear the divide. . . . If things don't go their way, they'll just retreat to their offices." Several noted significant skepticism about working with the university, based on previous encounters which they had found unsatisfactory. One community leader, one of The Milwaukee Idea's most ardent supporters, said, "The community is waiting to see if this time UWM will deliver the goods."

Territoriality. Time and again we heard about faculty being entrenched in their silos. We were surprised during our group interviews at how many

Idea participants still didn't know one another. This does not negate the movement across disciplinary lines we saw and heard about; but we did discover that some faculty who ventured out of the silos were branded as expatriates. As one senior faculty member said, "There are no firewalls out there. I was told to think out of the box, and so I did. And for that my department treated me as a 'betrayer'!"

Conflict over funding priorities. This barrier is closely linked to the previous two: Traditional academic values and territoriality make any significant change from the status quo highly threatening to those who see themselves as disadvantaged by the change. Faculty in the traditional liberal arts had particular difficulty seeing where they fit within The Milwaukee Idea. In some ways the problem was about perceptions of priorities as well as the priorities themselves.

Cosmetics vs. infrastructure. Conflicts over funding lead to another point. Chancellor Zimpher set out to get UWM noticed, and there is no doubt by anyone that she succeeded. The question then becomes, can the university handle all these changes without the infrastructure collapsing? As a student leader told us: "We can't say we're going to build a new university and change the way things are done, and then not change the way things are done!" Strategic initiatives seldom take into account all of the impacts on infrastructure. These needs usually become identified after the plan has been set in motion and existing systems become overburdened.

People left behind. We heard from several "dissidents" who felt, from the beginning of The Milwaukee Idea process, a subtle influence to be a "company person." For some, the speed at which conversations became public knowledge through the communication campaign meant ideas were treated as finished projects rather than works in progress. These people felt that honest discussion was missing, that dissent was not encouraged because Idea initiatives had already been sold publicly. Some of those who did feel heard also felt co-opted. A common concern at many institutions, but perhaps more critical at UWM given the scope of The Milwaukee Idea, was that the chancellor would simply use it to catapult herself to a more prominent presidency. The average tenure for university presidents is no more than five years nationally. If faculty thought the chancellor would not "see it through," those who opposed the Idea could decide to simply ride it out until she left.

Demands of and for diversity. Milwaukee has a long history of neighborhoods segregated by race and ethnicity, and many still exist. A true partnership with the community must recognize this—and, in fact, UWM identified diversity and multiculturalism as a priority. However, it was difficult to specifically focus on diversity in the course of planning and implementing the Idea initiatives. The chancellor and other participants in The Milwaukee Idea have generally acknowledged this. All of the students with whom we spoke expressed concern about UWM's real commitment to diversity and multiculturalism. There was a sense that the institution was chasing numbers for the state, rather than attending to its own internal "family."

It was clear that diversity concerns were a serious but unarticulated issue on campus. Students remarked on the lack of minority faculty, especially African American faculty. African Americans were 4.9% of the faculty in 2001 as compared to 8% of the students. The new assistant chancellor for partnerships and innovation, herself a long-time member of the African-American community in Milwaukee, told us that there needs to be a widespread understanding that "diversity is more than a word—it must also involve campus sharing of decision-making, policy, and dollars." In a campus publication, *Myriad* (Fall 1999), a faculty member took the university to task for ducking hard questions of racism, suggesting that The Milwaukee Idea needed to revisit issues of marginalization, isolation, and exclusion of minorities if it were truly to succeed as a full partner in the community, otherwise, the university could not create and sustain honest partnerships.

Lack of community, especially as experienced by students. Focus groups conducted at UWM suggested that students had little to no sense of identification with the university. This is certainly not unusual for an urban university, where many students commute to class, see a college education in largely instrumental terms, and juggle the demands of college with other family and work responsibilities. While some level of community exists in the residence halls, this is a distinct culture from the rest of campus. Students are more likely to connect with those in their classes or major; we were told several times that students could take all their classes in one section of the campus and never interact with anyone outside of their discipline. As long as students continue to consider UWM a place to obtain credentials, rather than as a place that exists to enrich the lives of those in the community, an important element of The Milwaukee Idea agenda will be missing.

Dependence on the personality of the leader. A leader's charisma can be both a strength and a barrier. Chancellor Zimpher was such a visible presence and associated so completely with The Milwaukee Idea, that she fostered a certain dependence on herself as leader and spokesperson. As one campus leader noted, "It's a problem trying to convince the community to listen to others than the 'Z lady!'" Internally, we heard some concerns about how the "point people" appointed by the chancellor were not on the same page as she. The chancellor was widely respected for the extent to which she delegated authority and championed inclusion; and ironically this can pose a conflict for someone who is so outward-directed.

The ability to sort out the positive and negative forces, maintaining strengths while shoring up weaknesses, is the principal challenge of leading transformative change. One informant to the case study said that the success of The Milwaukee Idea equaled "tradition plus relevance in the proper proportions": that campus leaders must respect tradition and work within current policies and systems, but must also identify respected champions of change and support them in their engagement efforts. This is largely what UWM did. The ingredients for transformative change were clearly in place in 2001: a readiness for change, presented by a leader who has been able to capture it in a compelling vision; a capable supporting cast; an inclusive process; and new resources. This combination, *especially* the readiness factor, made it likely that The Milwaukee Idea would become much more than simply the latest administrative initiative foisted upon an unwilling or indifferent campus. The Idea caused some faculty members at UWM to work differently and approach their work differently. They grew to understand what it meant to be, for instance, an English professor at UWM in a way that is different from being an English professor at the University of Wisconsin–Madison. Hence the Idea has substance well beyond the charisma of the chancellor.

Implications for Other Institutions: Necessary Conditions for Effective Engagement

The vision of both the Great Cities Initiative and The Milwaukee Idea was that metropolitan universities have a unique mission to engage their urban communities, not to parrot their land-grant cousins. In both cases, care was taken to ensure that becoming an "engaged university" did not leave anyone out, including the traditionalists. All universities, including urban universities, have multiple missions, with plenty of room for multiple goals and epistemologies. If the Great Cities Initiative taught us the importance of preparing both sides of the academy/community partnership for radically different roles, and The Milwaukee Idea taught us the importance of galvanizing leadership and structural change in the academic organization, what then do the experiences of both universities teach us about undertaking transformative change of this sort? I would suggest the following commonalities.

Renegotiate the Social Covenant

In 1940 the American Association of University Professors (AAUP) and the Association of American Colleges (AAC) issued a joint "Statement of Principles on Academic Freedom and Tenure," a document that is still in force today. Its first paragraph included this admonition: "Institutions of higher education are conducted for the *common good* and not to further the interest either of the individual teacher or the institution as a whole. The common good depends upon the free search for truth and its free exposition" (AAUP, 1940, p. 3). What is the "common good"? The AAUP statement does not say explicitly, but it implies that as long as faculty work is driven by a search for truth and not by more venal motives, the common good will be served. More is asked of the academy these days, however. As I noted earlier in this chapter, the general public is seeking greater engagement with social issues from the academy, demanding that higher education better prepare the young for work, frame the research agendas in ways that address social ills, and do away with the traditional attitude of noblesse oblige toward community service. Thus, the AAUP/AAC statement, while still largely valid today, needs a codicil: Academic freedom characterized by the "free search for truth and its free exposition" will serve the common good as long as communities beyond the academy are involved in defining the goals of the search and are active participants in it.

Part of the difficulty in attempting to inject more social relevance into faculty scholarship is the perception that as relevance increases, academic rigor necessarily decreases. When faculty members venture into collaborative efforts to understand and solve societal ills, they often have discovered that their claims on "truth" are rather fragile and incomplete. When they are asked, for example, "What works in school reform?" (as UIC faculty were asked by the Chicago school authority), faculty are reluctant to give answers unqualified by a host of moderating factors. Community leaders quickly become impatient with such fence-sitting: Political judgments must be made. Educators must thus stand ready to help make these judgments more informed by taking the extra step of working with those affected by the results to determine the meaning of research results and the implications for future policy.

Those in the academy must also rid themselves of the distinction between "academic truth" and "political truth" (Corry, 1998). For years the university has assumed and communicated to the citizenry that universities possess a higher order of truth. Bender (1993) argues that universities can serve society better by following John Dewey's argument that they are participants in a community of truth seekers, always searching for, but never finding, ultimate truths.

If so, much work needs to be done within the academic community itself. The notion of what constitutes *scholarship* varied considerably within UWM. Those who were active in Milwaukee Idea initiatives were mostly comfortable with a broadened definition of scholarship, one which includes the scholarship of practice (engagement), the scholarship of teaching, and the scholarship of discovery (basic research). While most academics would agree that the principles of *Scholarship Assessed* (Glassick, Huber, & Maeroff, 1997) define true scholarly activity, some have a hard time accepting faculty work that is not published in mainstream academic journals as genuine scholarship, whether it is peer reviewed or not. Their argument is that scholarly work must be reviewed by disinterested peers prior to entering the academic database, and if these controls are not in place then the work is not real scholarship. They fail to see how scholarly work that is community-based contributes to generalizable knowledge; they see it as little more than traditional community service, dressed up to look like scholarship.

Some positive trends are evident. Boyer's (1990) proposal to expand "scholarship" to include teaching, integration, and application, in addition to discovery, has become the most widely read and widely quoted book in recent years. Wolshok (1995) elaborates on what universities can do for the economy, the workplace, and the community in *Knowledge Without Boundaries*. Her message, in short, is that we can benefit from our analysis of the work of faculty if we accept the premise that faculty can be teachers as well as scholars and professional service providers as well as researchers.

The university can also redefine its commitment to the common good by becoming a setting for an expanded social discourse. While the academy can rarely solve important social problems, it can promote learning about how problems might be solved. While the academy cannot presume to have sole access to higher truths, it can play a major role in the search for them. While faculty members do not hold the secrets to the common good, they can be active participants in defining and shaping it. Seeking and holding truths need not be divorced from personal experiences and knowledge.

Engage the Institution and its Constituencies in Conversations About Important but Widely Misunderstood Terms, Especially "Engagement" and "Scholarship"

In writing about universities and the city, Bender (1996) argues that

> The metropolitan academic ought not work so hard at keeping the city at bay: it is a source of energy, of wonderfully complex intellectual problems, and of nonacademic intellectuals who have much to offer. What is needed is not the old university expert model, but a newer approach that facilitates continuing two-way conversations between the various academic groupings on the campus and the appropriate constituencies in the metropolis. (p. 13)

One of the barriers at UWM that I identified earlier was the problem with discourse: how people often seemed to talk *across* one another rather than to communicate in ways designed to help them learn *from* one another. Influential people both within and outside UWM developed particular and unique mental models of what an "engaged" university does and what true "scholarship" is. Engagement for some in the academy means "giving our agenda to the community" or, as one UWM faculty member wrote, "dumbing down" the university (Moore, 2000, ¶ 16). For these people engagement is a way to mollify an institution's publics and assure them that faculty are in fact accomplishing something worthwhile. They worried that engagement poses a threat to independence and academic freedom, that it will invite "interference that will hamstring universities" from taking risks and exploring controversial topics. Thus, any sort of community partnership compromises the academy's independence and risks converting the university into a group of consultants working for the professional gain of outsiders. From the community's perspective, engagement sometimes is interpreted as a sort of euphemism for finding new ways to enable the university to carry out its research agenda, and so the fear of exploitation exists here, too.

It is critically important, therefore, for the urban campus to engage in conversations about the nature of its campus community and what kind of community it wants to be. As I have already noted, problems of community are typical in an urban university where both faculty and students have multiple responsibilities. Healthy communities, whether inside the academy or out, are characterized by "constructive contention," where their members are free to disagree, and where disagreements are handled in ways that allow all to learn from one another and grow. Issues of race and ethnicity were especially sensitive in Milwaukee, as they are in most urban communities. But if UWM and other urban universities truly see themselves as "communities of learners," then what better place than this to address them?

Work to Balance Public Relations With Infrastructure

I do not mean to present "public relations" in a pejorative context. Rhetoric and symbolism count for a lot, as the Chicago and Milwaukee experiences demonstrate. Still, fairly or not, many at UWM—and in the community as well—regarded The Milwaukee Idea as stronger in style than in substance. Time after time, and not just at urban universities like UIC and UWM, campus-wide initiatives foundered when leaders assumed that everyone had the same understanding of what had to be done and the same commitment to making it successful.

The key for academic leaders, it seems to me, is to be patient and remain focused. Any organization, but most especially an academic one, changes slowly, and true transformation is even slower. The amount of time, energy, and money that has been poured into community partnerships via The Milwaukee Idea represented an enormous investment. After three years, evidence of change was tangible: The campus looked different, it portrayed itself differently, and it surely was seen differently by the Milwaukee community. Internally, the depth of change was less apparent. Some on campus worked—and thought about their work—differently. But most of those closely associated with The Milwaukee Idea at UWM were already active in community engagement of one form or other prior to 1998; and most community interests remained cautious about the *real* commitment of the university.

From the outset The Milwaukee Idea has been guided by theories of organizational change. The story of The Milwaukee Idea, while still unfolding, highlights and reinforces many of the principles found in these other sources. For example, Birnbaum's (1992) classic book on successful college presidents, *How Academic Leadership Works,* describes how important it is for university leaders to capture and articulate the campus's unique culture, rather than to attempt to transform what is there already. The American Council on Education series *On Change* (Eckel et al., 1998), which presents the results of institutional change efforts in selected colleges and universities, suggests the following criteria for effective strategies for transformative change:

- Change begins with an exploration of why a particular change is necessary or important.

- The change is anchored in the institution's mission and values.

- Stakeholders participate in developing and implementing the agenda for change.

- The agenda for change is supported by a critical mass of campus stakeholders.

- Leaders lead by persuasion, through other leaders, and by building trust.

Chancellor Zimpher did these things. In fact, she consciously followed a number of familiar change principles, and did so successfully: She came up with a big idea; she went public with it and stayed on message; she paid attention to the importance of process, but sought alignment rather than consensus; she cultivated key constituencies; she attacked vertical organizational structures; and she held herself accountable.

When universities take on community partnerships, they can become socially transformed themselves. This transformation challenges faculty values and knowledge, such as the uncomfortable insight that an accumulated wisdom exists beyond the campus which faculty may not even be aware of, much less privy to (Harkavy & Wiewel, 1995). Among the issues highlighted by both the UIC and UWM cases, the issue of the value of cultural diversity emerges as a challenge that cannot be pushed aside or dealt with in abstract, postmodern terms. Intellectual elitism and a retreat to comfortable campus confines are not viable solutions. As many writers have observed, higher education is not a sanctuary anymore. It is losing its insularity, having more claimants and partners now. The challenge for

UWM, urban universities generally, and all of higher education, is to become a truly responsive partner as the university reshapes its social relationship with society while retaining its core purposes and standards.

REFERENCES

American Association of University Professors. (1940). *Statement of principles on academic freedom and tenure.* Retrieved January 15, 2005 from http://www.aaup.org/statements/Redbook/1940stat.htm

Bender, T. (1993). *Intellect and public life: Essays on the social history of academic intellectuals in the United States.* Baltimore, MD: The Johns Hopkins University Press.

Bender, T. (1996). *Universities and the city: Scholarship, local life, and the necessity of worldliness.* Keynote address presented at the Urban Universities and Their Cities International Conference, Amsterdam, The Netherlands.

Birnbaum, R. (1992). *How academic leadership works: Understanding success and failure in the college presidency.* San Francisco, CA: Jossey-Bass.

Boyer, E. L. (1990). *Scholarship reconsidered: Priorities of the professoriate.* Princeton, NJ: The Carnegie Foundation for the Advancement of Teaching.

Boyer, E. L. (1996). The scholarship of engagement. *Journal of Public Service and Outreach, 1*(1), 11–20.

Braskamp, L. A., & Wergin, J. F. (1998). Forming new social partnerships. In W. G. Tierney (Ed.), *The responsive university: Restructuring for high performance* (pp. 62–91). Baltimore, MD: The Johns Hopkins University Press.

Corry, J. J. (1998). Sifting and winnowing: Accountability/assessment and academic freedom. In W. L. Hansen (Ed.), *Academic freedom on trial: 100 years of sifting and winnowing at the University of Wisconsin–Madison* (pp. 264–274). Madison, WI: University of Wisconsin Press.

Eckel, P., Hill, B., & Green, M. (1998). *On change: En route to transformation: Vol. I.* Washington, DC: American Council on Education.

Glassick, C. E., Huber, M. T., & Maeroff, G. I. (1997). *Scholarship assessed: Evaluation of the professoriate.* San Francisco, CA: Jossey-Bass.

Harkavy, I., & Wiewel, W. (1995). University-community partnerships: Current state and future issues. *Metropolitan Universities: An International Forum, 6*(3), 7–14.

Holland, B. A. (2001). *Characteristics of engaged institutions and sustainable partnerships, and effective strategies for change.* Unpublished manuscript, Office of Community Partnerships, U.S. Department of Housing and Urban Development.

Holland, B. A., & Gelmon, S. B. (1998). The state of the "engaged campus": What have we learned about building and sustaining university-community partnerships? *AAHE Bulletin, 51*(2), 3–6.

Klotsche, J. M. (1966). *The urban university and the future of our cities.* New York, NY: Harper & Row.

Knight Higher Education Collaborative. (2000). Strategic community partnerships. *Exemplars,* 1–12.

Moore, J. (2000). *UWM, faculty workload, and the "engaged university."* Retrieved October 31, 2005, from the University of Wisconsin–Milwaukee web site: http://www.uwm.edu/~jcm/governance/workload.txt

Ramaley, J. A. (2000). Embracing civic responsibility. *AAHE Bulletin, 52*(7), 9–13.

University of Illinois–Chicago. (1993). *Summary Report of the Great Cities Advisory Committee.* Chicago, IL: Author.

Wergin, J. F., & Grassadonia, J. M. (2002). *The Milwaukee Idea: A study of transformative change.* Washington, DC: U.S. Department of Housing and Urban Development, University Partnerships Clearinghouse.

Wolshok, M. L. (1995). *Knowledge without boundaries: What America's research universities can do for the economy, the workplace, and the community.* San Francisco, CA: Jossey-Bass.

PART II

Inside and Outside The Milwaukee Idea: Thoughts on Change From Three Perspectives

3 UWM Community Conversations

Deborah Fagan

When it comes to institutionalizing university-community engagement, it may be the journey rather than the destination that is important. Determining whether a university or college can be termed "engaged," how such engagement can be measured, and whether or not it is sustainable has been the subject of much debate. Certainly the metrics for measuring successful engagement must be determined and evaluated by each university and its community partners. And yet even within those institutions and their partner groups there is often disagreement over expectations, delivery, and definitions of success.

The University of Wisconsin–Milwaukee (UWM), as described in Chapter 1, is no exception. While it has found in engagement a powerful new paradigm to invigorate its learning, discovery, and outreach, it cannot, by any measure, lay claim to having arrived as an engaged institution. It is, however, well on its way to becoming one, and in this light, it can be useful to explore how its progress is being assessed—especially by those outside the university.

What follows are the voices of UWM's community partners. They candidly reveal both the strengths and weaknesses of UWM's efforts to partner. They highlight the vital importance of leadership in creating new community-university collaboration, the need for changes to institutional infrastructure, and a reminder that university engagement is not just the latest institutional growth strategy, but a commitment for the long haul.

With the launch of The Milwaukee Idea in 1998, UWM set out to become a more relevant, vital, and engaged institution. Taking a giant step off the beaten path, UWM mounted a planning effort that embraced an unprecedented number of community participants and asserted a public commitment to building broad and enduring partnerships well beyond the confines of campus. These partnerships would enrich teaching and learning at UWM, bring university and community representatives to the table as equals, and drawing on their respective resources and expertise, enhance the common good, together.

The Milwaukee Idea is still a work in progress; its aspirations for creating a wholly engaged university are still being realized. But just how well is it doing in forging ties to the community? Have perceptions of UWM's role in the community changed? Has the university been as accessible as it set out to be? What could it do better?

Informal interviews with a cross-section of 12 community leaders yielded rich conversations on these and other issues—from UWM's leadership, to its evolving identity, to the accomplishments and pitfalls of community engagement. Interviewees represent the nonprofit, philanthropic, education, and corporate sectors, and all have worked with UWM.

Reflections on Leadership

It's obvious that UWM has become more engaged, more active, and more participatory in all kinds of different activities... also more assertive when it comes to working with the business community. And when it comes to fundraising, its profile is higher. [Chancellor] Nancy Zimpher seems to be the person who spearheaded the change.

—Jeff Browne, Executive Director
Public Policy Forum of Milwaukee

Nearly all of those interviewed cited the leadership of UWM's former chancellor, Nancy Zimpher, architect of The Milwaukee Idea and its charismatic champion, for putting UWM solidly on the metropolitan Milwaukee map and community engagement in the community's consciousness. Jean Tyler, a consultant who was actively involved in planning for The Milwaukee Idea, believes Zimpher authored and developed it to create a significant dialogue with the community. "She was a spectacular leader," Tyler said. "People listened to her and were excited about what she had to say. By the time the 'First Ideas' [UWM initiatives for community engagement] were presented, and the first action teams had completed their work, The Milwaukee Idea had permeated all different layers of the community. They knew what it was and they knew who Nancy Zimpher was."

Jeanette Mitchell, who directs the leadership program at Cardinal Stritch University in Milwaukee, also said Zimpher's leadership influenced community perceptions about UWM: "My view of how UWM approaches the community has changed, and very honestly, I have to say it goes back to Nancy Zimpher. I think Nancy raised the level of visibility of the university and her Milwaukee Idea caught on. It was a good PR point. It was an umbrella for creating a conversation; a way to talk about UWM."

Freelance writer Fran Bauer noted that with Zimpher at the helm, "I began to see the potential for working with the university in ways that I had never envisioned before." Bauer served on a planning committee for The Milwaukee Idea's Age and Community initiative and is now a member of its leadership council. She also comments, "I was impressed that Nancy Zimpher was trying to reach out to the community and set up communication that I don't think existed before that. She was a unique person in her ability to get the political and business leadership not just from the Milwaukee area, but also from Southeastern Wisconsin, to begin talking to one another. I hope this continues. I hope we don't sink back into being little islands that don't speak to one another."

Changing Perceptions:
Before and After The Milwaukee Idea

The Milwaukee Idea provided a front porch for the university where people from the community could come for information and assistance and have conversations about mutual issues. I think many of us thought that UWM was a sleepy giant on the East Side, that if we could just rouse it, big things could happen, and I think when Nancy Zimpher came she gave that sleepy giant a swift kick and got it moving.

—Robin Mayrl, Vice President
Program Development, Helen Bader Foundation

Like Mayrl, many of those interviewed said that with the advent of The Milwaukee Idea, perceptions about UWM began to change, and at the same time, the university became more accessible to the community and more collaborative in its approach. Others were less certain about the impact of The Milwaukee Idea on university-community relationships, suggesting that outreach efforts that predated The Milwaukee Idea continued much as they had before.

Cathy Washabaugh, a teacher at Milwaukee's Riverside University High School, just blocks from UWM, and the wife of a UWM faculty member, believes the university looks like a far different institution today than it did several years ago: "My perception of UWM has changed dramatically. When my husband and I got here, I was less than impressed with the lack of outreach. We had many heated arguments about the role of the university because it was so research-based and academic. I was constantly asking, 'What good is it doing this community, and why can't it be more community oriented?' I couldn't wait to hear about The Milwaukee Idea, and I followed it from the first time it was covered in the paper because I was so excited about the idea and the possibilities." Those possibilities have led to a growing number of partnerships which are bringing UWM students and faculty into Riverside classrooms to help on a variety of skill-building projects.

Rob Meiksins, executive director of the leadership development program Future Milwaukee, believes UWM's efforts to collaborate with the community through The Milwaukee Idea have positively changed attitudes on what it has to offer academically. "UWM was once perceived as very much a second-tier organization within the community," he said. "Very recently, that has changed 100%, and it is now seen as a peer of any of the other academic institutions in town."

Juila Taylor, executive director of the Greater Milwaukee Committee (GMC), which represents metropolitan Milwaukee's business community, has built both strong professional and personal ties to UWM since the launch of The Milwaukee Idea: "The Milwaukee Idea has dramatically changed my involvement at UWM and my perception of UWM. I am on campus more frequently, I know many more of the faculty, and I know the deans," she said. "There is a more significant connection than there ever has been before." In her work with the GMC, that connection makes it easier for her to facilitate major partnerships between the university and the business community, such as UWM's Center for Workplace Diversity. The center works with businesses and other organizations to recruit and retain a diverse workforce and build organizations that value diversity.

Ricardo Diaz, executive director of Milwaukee's United Community Center, said he sees UWM trying to develop a larger community presence, but contends there is a gap between the rhetoric and the reality of The Milwaukee Idea: "I think The Milwaukee Idea embraces a concept of community engagement, but in many cases the execution has fallen short of the publicity it received. There were many people who were doing outreach before The Milwaukee Idea. What The Milwaukee Idea did do, I think, was give much more credence to what those people were already involved in."

Howard Snyder, executive director of the Northwest Side Community Development Corporation in Milwaukee, agreed that UWM is working to expand its role in the community, but professed some confusion about whether or not certain engagement efforts were considered part of The Milwaukee Idea, and which ones had predated it. "There are a lot of things that have happened in the past few years that have been positive, but I don't necessarily know if they come from The Milwaukee Idea or somewhere else," he said, citing the new Helen Bader Institute for Nonprofit Management and ENTECH, a program which provides technology support to nonprofit organizations. Both are housed at UWM and both are operated as university-community partnerships. "I realize there has been a change," Snyder continued. "I do think that the criticism that the university is disengaged from the community is not relevant anymore."

Getting Engaged: Plaudits and Problems

The Milwaukee Idea has raised the visibility and profile of UWM and also raised the issue and importance of an urban research university like UWM making greater connections with the community. It has put that issue up front. Now we have to execute and capitalize on it.

—Tim Sheehy, President
Metropolitan Milwaukee Association of Commerce

Sheehy's call for expanding connections was echoed by many of those who shared their thoughts on community engagement and The Milwaukee Idea at UWM. But how well the university made those connections in the past and what it might do differently in the future was also on their minds.

Several respondents acknowledged that a strong foundation for partnership was already in place and observed that The Milwaukee Idea had helped the university build bridges to businesses, nonprofit organizations, funders, and local government. In fact, nearly all interviewees mentioned one or more major university-community initiatives or partnerships in which UWM played a significant role. Among them were:

- *The Helen Bader Institute for Nonprofit Management.* The Institute grew from a joint planning and development effort undertaken by several local foundations, Milwaukee area nonprofits, and UWM. Today, the Institute offers degree and nondegree programs in nonprofit management and a variety of activities to help strengthen nonprofits (see Chapter 11).

- *The Milwaukee Partnership Academy.* This very broad collaboration, created with substantial impetus from UWM, aims to significantly improve the quality of teaching and learning in Milwaukee's schools (see Chapter 10). Partners include Milwaukee public school leaders, the teachers' association, UWM, the business community, and the Milwaukee Area Technical College.

- *Center on Age and Community.* This multidisciplinary academic center connects university expertise with the experience of those who work in the field of aging in an effort to improve the lives of seniors. It offers degree and nondegree programs in gerontology, is expanding research in the field, and training practitioners in the latest techniques for working with older adults.

- *TechStar.* TechStar is a management services and investment organization formed to stimulate entrepreneurship, facilitate technology transfer, and invigorate the economy. It was born from a collaborative effort led by UWM that brought several metropolitan Milwaukee academic institutions together.

Despite these successes, however, respondents said there was room for improvement in how UWM relates to and organizes its work with the community. Among their concerns were the need for a broader and deeper institutional commitment to engagement spearheaded by UWM leadership, a strong university infrastructure to bolster the growth of new initiatives, a system that rewards faculty for community engagement activities, and a clear process that ensures the community access to the university and brings members of both groups together as equals. In addition, several noted the importance of solid fundraising capability—which some felt had been lacking—to sustain engagement efforts.

Robin Mayrl, of Milwaukee's Helen Bader Foundation and a leader in two major UWM community partnerships, believes the university needs to create sustained institutional support for community engagement. "The infrastructure for The Milwaukee Idea was never adequately built within UWM," she said. "There were wonderful initiatives that took flight [when The Milwaukee Idea was launched], but there has never been a really firm infrastructure for those ideas to grow. . . . This business of getting rid of the silos within the university and actually transforming it into a multidisciplinary, engaged university—we are not there yet. The university has to be clearer on how this [Milwaukee Idea] will fit in long-term and how it will make sure these ideas will continue to be nurtured and will continue to grow."

Howard Snyder, of Milwaukee's Northwest Side Community Development Corporation, said not only was such an infrastructure lacking, but that a commitment to community engagement had yet to penetrate the university very deeply: "What I found was that some institutional things don't change. Even though people are coming out and marketing things to you that are different than before, and even though there is new thinking and the set-up is different, when you get past that first layer you still hit a lot of institutional walls that have always been there.

"If it takes 5 or 10 years for that to change, then I am not unhappy, because there are people who are marketing the university—its resources and its human capital—to change stuff in Milwaukee, because Milwaukee has to change. That doesn't mean that when you get down beneath sales and marketing or center directors, that your idea as a community person is going to get very far."

Creating structural change within the university itself also concerned educator Cathy Washabaugh. "We need more opportunities and coordinators at UWM whose job it is to do that kind of outreach [partnership building], to lay the groundwork and help bring different groups of faculty and community together. It just doesn't happen on its own. I would put that as number one."

Running a close second, in her view, was the need for a transformation in how UWM recognizes and rewards faculty. "Many people feel pressure to publish and do research and teach," she said. "Now, many are struggling with the notion that they should also do community outreach, and I think some see it as a 'this or that' rather than an 'and.' Faculty need more incentives. I don't really think it is fair to suddenly talk in a way that many people were never schooled in and expect that suddenly they are going to understand it and understand their role and not feel resentful. I think there needs to be a culture change and that doesn't happen overnight."

Getting Engaged: Living Up to the Promise

Concerns about how equitably UWM partners with the community were voiced by interviewees who suggested that the university needed to make significant strides in this area.

Ricardo Diaz of the United Community Center expressed frustration with the way UWM sometimes approaches community organizations, particularly those that are well-established. "When you look at an organization like ours that has been around for 33 years and has an $11 million budget, you can't come with an attitude of 'What can we do for you?'" Diaz said a true joint-venture approach was needed, through which the university and the community sort out problems and seek funding together. "I think what often tends to happen is a grant is already in hand by the time the university comes to the community and says, 'We've already applied for this, we got it, now we need to do something with you to make this grant active.'"

Rob Meiksins of Future Milwaukee concurred: "The university is beginning to be perceived as something of a magnet, drawing stuff in and taking advantage of the expertise of the community to draw things in, but then not truly looking to reach out and partner. If the university saw a need for something, they wouldn't necessarily look around and see who has the potential to implement it—to work and invest with them. Instead, they would just create it internally, and then say they have a great idea and to come work with them.

"I think the whole idea of The Milwaukee Idea when it first came out was this wonderful sense of 'Oh my gosh, the place is opening up!' There were all of these wonderful resources, and then gradually, exactly the impact it was going to have and where partnerships were going to happen really kind of dwindled."

Looking Ahead

Staying the course to engagement was seen by many as critical for UWM's growth as a major urban research university.

Jane Moore, director of research and development at the Greater Milwaukee Foundation, is encouraged by the progress UWM has made: "I would hope that once the university has moved along these lines of being an urban institution actively involved in the community, it doesn't retreat and go back into its own ivory tower. Once you're involved in the community, it opens so many doors. It becomes very exciting and it engages faculty. If you want to attract new, young, dynamic faculty, this is the way to do it. It's active, it's real world . . . putting your research into practice."

Tim Sheehy of the Greater Milwaukee Committee said UWM has the potential to become "a necessary and viable partner in improving the economic prosperity of the region. If one of the university's goals is to grow from $38 million in funded research to $100 million, the implications to the region's economy are that there would be much deeper and greater connections to the business community in terms of new ideas, startups, and entrepreneurial activity as well as connections to established industry.

"There has to be a constant movement by UWM to make sure that the community in which it is located is aware of the assets and contributions it can make. I think this goes far deeper than just technology transfer. It goes to the role of educating the kids in the city of Milwaukee. UWM is the largest producer of teachers in the 10th largest school system in the country—it is central to our ability to grow as a city and a region. We need to understand that as a community and get it right and support it.

"I am interested in seeing UWM grow by leaps in its research stature and the capabilities of the faculty and the students it is attracting. Having a vibrant research university in your backyard is something that is of value across the board."

4 The Role of Shared Governance

Ellen Murphy

Shared governance is a revered, statutorily protected tradition in the University of Wisconsin System. The Wisconsin State Legislature (2005) has even written it into law: "The faculty shall have the primary responsibility for academic and educational activities and faculty personnel matters. The faculty of each institution shall have the right to determine their own faculty organizational structure and to select representatives to participate in institutional governance" (p. 3).

Academic staff have similar statutory rights to be "active participants" in policy development for the institution and have "primary responsibility . . . for all policies and procedures concerning academic staff members" (Wisconsin State Legislature, 2005, p. 3). Academic staff members also have the right to "arrange themselves in a manner they determine" (p. 3).

These faculty rights are so inculcated at the University of Wisconsin–Milwaukee (UWM) that most faculty members refer to this Wisconsin Statute as codifying "faculty governance" rather than "shared governance" (Wisconsin State Legislature, 2005). They sometimes overlook the introductory provisions in the statutes which provide that faculty are subject to the responsibilities and powers of the board, the president, and the chancellor for each of the Wisconsin System's 26 two- and four-year colleges and universities. Academic staff rights are subject to these same entities plus the rights of the faculty.

The faculty's primary authority regarding educational programming and personnel issues could be viewed as an obstacle to transformational change agents or administrators seeking to institutionalize engagement across the university. But to do so would be a mistake. Active support and buy-in by faculty and staff are the sine qua non of transformational change implementation and stabilization. Astute use of and respect for the existing governance systems are strategies to facilitate change.

Nature of Change

The literature is replete with change theory under a variety of rubrics. Advocates of transformational change are well advised to consult them, not as tactical recipes, but for explanatory insights amid the process.

Lewin's (1948) elegant explanations about human behavior, for example, describe the necessity of "unfreezing" the status quo before movement or change can occur. Schein (1996) observed that human change, in individuals or groups, is a "profound psychological dynamic process that involve(s) painful unlearning *without loss of ego identity* and difficult relearning as one cognitively attempt(s) to restructure . . . one's thoughts, perceptions, feelings and attitudes" (italics added, p. 28). Most useful to this author, especially when considering how to institutionalize transformational change at universities, has been Schein's discussion of the need to move from "planned change" to thinking about such processes as "managed learning."

Successfully managing learning to create a sustainable, engaged university will require that change leaders keep the ego identity of faculty, staff, and administrators intact, as those individuals who have been successful in traditional university roles attempt to relearn different attitudes and perceptions. Shared/faculty governance structures and traditions can provide credible, faculty-designed mechanisms to manage the relearning that can keep faculty ego and values intact during the change process.

Governance Structures at University of Wisconsin–Milwaukee

Faculty at UWM, like those on many campuses, have organized themselves for academic program and personnel purposes into departments, housed in schools and colleges, and in divisions, independent of schools and colleges, in related areas of research and teaching. Increasing numbers of interdisciplinary centers and institutes foster more focused research and teaching interests among faculty and academic staff from various departments, but each faculty member retains one tenure-home department.

Cross-campus senate and faculty committee memberships are structured to ensure representation by departments, schools and colleges, and/or divisions, depending on the substantive charge of the committee. The faculty senate and some committees are composed solely of elected faculty members (such as Faculty Appeals and Grievances and the divisional executive committees). The membership of others (such as the Athletic Board and Academic Program and Curriculum) include appointed faculty as well as elected or appointed students and academic staff members. Relevant administrators typically serve as nonvoting, ex-officio members. All faculty committees are chaired by and contain a majority of faculty members. No faculty member can be hired, granted tenure, or promoted without an affirmative recommendation of a faculty-exclusive department executive committee; no educational program can be initiated or substantially restructured without an affirmative recommendation of the relevant faculty-controlled committee; no change to tenure and promotion criteria can be made without the affirmative recommendation of faculty-exclusive divisional executive committees; and no change to faculty policies and procedures can be made without the approval of the faculty senate.

Such structures could be seen as barriers, precluding any hope of change. More usefully, however, they can be viewed as pre-existing communication and discussion venues to develop and refine proposals, refute skeptics, reassure the uncertain, clarify both intended and unintended consequences, and ultimately to accrue buy-in from the very people who can make or break implementation. Governance structures also provide a reassurance to those apprehensive of administrative overreaching.

Additionally, some of the leaders of any movement toward enhanced engagement will be faculty members able to directly influence the process by their membership and service as chairs on influential committees. They can also recruit like-thinking faculty colleagues to do the same. While administrators should make no similar attempts to influence the contours of faculty elections, they can and should strategically use the appointments available to them to populate influential committees with faculty who realize the benefits of engagement.

Respect for governance structures requires resisting the temptation to establish administrative committees populated solely by persons already amenable to engagement. Doing so could negatively entrench faculty members who could otherwise have been brought on board and unnecessarily alienate others committed to a shared governance process.

Working within the parameters of shared governance to strengthen the institutionalization of university engagement requires that administrators, faculty, and staff pay attention to three key aspects of governance:

- The "extra-governance" structure

- Reassurance and resources

- The old and the new

The "Extra-Governance" Structure

While existing governance structures can and should be leveraged to the full extent of their functions, new initiatives will also require new structures. This does not mean that existing governance structures need be changed but that new or additional "extra-governance" structures can expand opportunities for involving faculty and staff in integrating engagement. These extra-governance structures may include ad hoc groups formed around engagement-related issues, task forces, steering committees, faculty and staff affinity groups, action teams, or evaluation teams. Whatever the moniker, the functions of the extra-governance unit must include the creation of interlocking relationships with relevant codified governance units. These relationships are especially beneficial when governance representatives are involved, from the beginning, in campus initiatives and at all steps along the way, because input from elected faculty makes acceptance of engagement and change initiatives more likely.

Those elected faculty representatives who are antagonistic to the concept of engagement also have a role to play, because "every team needs a skeptic" (Engelkemeyer & Landry, 2001, p. 8). It is more likely that skeptical faculty or staff members will be persuaded by the energy and enthusiasm of committee colleagues than they will be by being isolated or kept outside the change process.

Representation from elected governance units on extra-governance groups also serves as a bridge into the governance units and a direct dissemination pathway for information on change efforts. Both faculty and administrative champions of engagement should seek every opportunity to use the agenda of all relevant committees to provide information and seek input well before formal action by the governance group is needed.

Engagement discussions led by top leaders should appear on every senate agenda, because senate meetings, in particular, provide access to a broad representation from every school, college, and division. It is a venue well suited to giving and getting information, cajoling skeptics, reassuring the hesitant, and empowering supporters.

Reassurance and Resources

Faculty who have done well in traditional academic institutional roles typically include those with successful research programs and those who have substantial federal funding or other sources that pay large indirect costs. These faculty members may need reassurance that their contributions will not be devalued by engagement initiatives or that engaged teaching and research is less rigorous or professionally fulfilling than more traditional approaches. One way to counter these perceptions is to attract and assign new dollars for engagement efforts rather than only reallocating existing resources. By backing engagement initiatives with new funding, existing research efforts are not jeopardized while institutional priorities are clearly demonstrated.

An infusion of new resources can also encourage more support from faculty and staff who may be reluctant to participate until they can benefit from being a part of an engaged university. A rising tide is less feared when the faculty boat is being lifted and not swamped.

The Old and the New

In addition to creating extra-governance structures that can connect engagement initiatives to the ongoing governance of the university, successful institutionalization also requires that existing governance structures are acknowledged and used—and also that brand new structures are created. UWM's engagement initiatives involved both of these change avenues.

Using the Old: Alternative General Education. Like many universities, UWM's criteria for completion of the baccalaureate degree includes meeting a general education requirement, which consists of completion of a predetermined number of credits in each of several designated areas that include science, arts, and ethnic diversity. As part of The Milwaukee Idea, the Cultures and Communities group (see Chapter 7) desired to give students another option of completing a more integrated program of coursework that emphasized interdisciplinary, multicultural, and engaged learning. While faculty response to the new ideas ranged from welcoming to dismissive, Cultures and Communities needed to travel through the elected Academic Program and Curriculum Committee (APCC) if it was to gain acceptance. Proponents for the new Cultures and Communities alternative courses recognized the importance of working within the existing governance structures, reassuring skeptics that legitimate protocols were followed. And so a pilot program was launched. Working within existing governance protocols also helped the engagement advocates to pay closer attention to creating a program that met APCC criteria.

Creating the New: Tenure and Promotion Criteria. While change experts and most faculty agree that incentives must align with outcomes, changing tenure and promotion criteria to more clearly value engagement activities has been difficult. Research has traditionally been viewed as "more equal" in the tenure equation than its partners, teaching and service. Disciplinary or division-based chauvinism may also play a role, as each discipline considers its research paradigms more rigorous (hence more acceptable) than those of others. And the natural sciences and the humanities may have more difficulty, or perhaps less desire, to define how engagement "fits" with their research than will some of the professions and arts for whom engaged discovery and learning has long been accepted practice.

Two activities of the engaged university, however, present opportunities to transform even the most entrenched operational definitions of research. Interdisciplinary centers bring scholars from a variety of research models together around subjects of mutual interest. Increased exposure to and understanding of the contributions of other research paradigms usually means increased acceptance that scholarship can be manifested in different ways. Similarly, centers for instructional and professional development can help articulate and promote the scholarship of learning. At UWM, for example, the Center for Instructional and Professional Development (described in Chapter 7), led by a respected faculty member from a "traditional" discipline, has brought the scholarship of learning into everyday dialogue at UWM. While still lacking total acceptance, the scholarship of learning is not the outlier it once was.

Creating the New: Milwaukee Idea Trustees' Council. As UWM's Milwaukee Idea was set to launch with new engaged research and learning initiatives vying for space and personnel allocations, governance groups and the Deans' Council became anxious that needed resources were being usurped and traditional means of assigning faculty workload (through deans and executive committees) were being circumvented.

While extra-governance (i.e., nonelected) structures, such as affinity groups and evaluation teams, had been embraced or at least tolerated during the planning and administrative development phase of The Milwaukee Idea, both the traditional structures of the faculty senate and Deans' Council wanted and needed more input on such pragmatic decisions as "who would be doing what with which resources from where." The solution was to establish a Trustees' Council for The Milwaukee Idea. The trustees were representatives of the Deans' Council and the faculty and academic staff senates. All were appointed by the bodies they represented. Besides their obvious role of providing confidence to their constituencies and providing counsel to Milwaukee Idea officials, they served as another valuable communications path to keep the campus aware and involved in ongoing engagement activities.

In Summary

Existing governance structures can be used strategically and effectively, rather than marginalized or disregarded, in the process of transforming the engaged university. The democratic process may be slower than desired, but it provides the ultimate avenue for transformational change. Most important, by using shared governance to facilitate engagement, the university learns to model the values on which its engagement is based.

References

Engelkemeyer, S. W., & Landry, E. (2001). Negotiating change on campus: Lessons from five years of AAHE's Summer Academy. *AAHE Bulletin, 53*(6), 7–10.

Lewin, K. (1999). Group decision and social change. In Gold, M. (Ed.) *The complete social scientist: A Kurt Lewin reader* (pp. 265–284). Washington, DC: American Psychological Association. (Reprinted from *Readings in social psychology,* by E. Maccoby, E. Newcomb, & E. Hartley, Eds., 1948, New York, NY: Holt)

Schein, E. H. (1996). Kurt Lewin's change theory in the field and in the classroom: Notes toward a model of managed learning. *Systems Practice, 9*(1), 27–47.

Wisconsin State Legislature. (2005). *University of Wisconsin System, Chapter 36.* Retrieved July 22, 2005, from http://folio.legis.state.wi.us/cgi-bin/om_isapi.dll?clientID=54862274&infobase=stats.nfo&jump=ch.%2036

5 When the Work on the Margins Becomes the Main Game

Susan Kelly

Those universities that choose the engagement path typically do not do so because it is a soft option. Given that successful engagement involves large investments of time and money by many people with diverse interests and constituencies, and that it requires long-term relationships to work on some of the most difficult human problems, it is hardly a clear path to stardom. Universities most often adopt the engagement agenda because it makes sense in their setting (often urban) and usually because they already have a toehold in the area. Frequently, there is a hardy (but often small) group of faculty and staff who are actively involved in community, civic, or business partnerships, working on projects with the goal of building a better society. Typically, universities adopting the engagement agenda are also surrounded by a "problem-rich environment" with community and corporate interests who are eager for a university partner that is willing to bring its intellectual and human resources to the table.

The University of Wisconsin–Milwaukee (UWM) and metropolitan Milwaukee fit this description. The university graduates most of the area's teachers, many of its nurses, all of the state's architects and urban planners, and has a broad program array, particularly in its professional schools, yet it has a subterranean profile. At the same time, metropolitan Milwaukee provides a problem-rich environment, with a struggling public school system, systemic racism, major crises in urban health, and significant rates of unemployment and underemployment in some locales. The opportunities and the capacity for the creation of a more engaged institution were in place.

Engaging in a long-term, mutually beneficial way with community and nonprofit organizations, industry, local government, and schools was not a new way of operating for UWM, nor was it a new mission for some units and individual faculty and staff within UWM. Many units, such as the College of Nursing, the School of Architecture and Urban Planning, the Center for Urban Initiatives and Research, and the Helen Bader School of Social Welfare had been solid community partners for a decade or more. And the School of Continuing Education (formerly known as the Division of Outreach and Continuing Education Extension) had been committed to, and productive in, broad scale and deep community engagement for more than 40 years.

The School of Continuing Education (SCE) and its various predecessor organizations has worked with community partners to secure grant and contract funds to undertake capacity building projects, action research, technical assistance, and continuing and professional education since it grew out of the University of Wisconsin Extension in the 1960s. Its more than 100 full-time and 600 part-time faculty, professional, and support staff have become national models of the practice and scholarship of engagement. They work with community and industry partners to set the agenda, articulate the problem and the intervention, design the project and the evaluation, secure the necessary grants and funds, write the reports and recommendations for other similar ventures around the country and around the world, and aid in the empowerment of individuals and groups to take charge of their own futures. Faculty and staff in SCE, as at many outreach and extension centers in universities across the country, are old hands at engagement, as they are at the research associated with the philosophy, methodology, and efficacy of engagement. This chapter explores several phenomena: the role such old hands can play in the new university and some pointers for a traditional university considering going down the engagement path.

As noted earlier, SCE has been visible in many quarters of the southeastern Wisconsin community—and in some fields nationally—for decades. But paradoxically, until recently its achievements have been largely invisible and its modus operandi mostly misunderstood by departments and individuals on the main UWM campus. Because SCE does not grant degrees (although it does develop and teach undergraduate and graduate courses), the work of SCE is not known in many departments.

SCE serves more than 30,000 people every year through its on-campus and online courses, and its programs, grants, research, and contracts. In the last 10-year period, more than 340,000 individuals have participated in SCE programs, most of them in southeastern Wisconsin, but others located in 35 states and 11 countries. A 2002 survey by Versant revealed that 91% of respondents found the quality and value of SCE programs to be good, very good, or excellent. More important for understanding the relationship between SCE (the engaged school) and UWM (seeking-to-be-more-engaged university), 70% of our students said they had no links with UWM other than through SCE. They came to UWM because they were deeply connected to various capacity-building initiatives that SCE had developed, or because they wanted access to selected credit or noncredit professional development and personal enrichment programs.

Because SCE faculty and staff work predominantly with individuals not already connected to the university, they have learned important engagement skills and values over the years. In community engagement the values that dominate are deep respect for cultural and ethnic diversity; working together for the greatest good; creating resources to improve people's quality of life and their capacity to make better choices; providing access to resources and mutual support; promoting social justice, empowerment, and mutually respectful—not exploitative—relationships; equity in partnerships; and fostering/modeling shared decision-making. In this context, research is typically a tool for action, evaluation, and improved practice, rather than an end in itself.

These values may, at times, be at odds with those of the traditional academy where the generation of knowledge regardless of its uses is paramount; the reward structure is based on the publish-or-perish imperative; there is often little or no focus on outcomes or value-added results from research or student learning; research participants are seen as subjects; and researchers operating autonomously, with no continuing obligation after the report is written and the money is spent. For some regular faculty, it is still an affront to suggest that usefulness or application might be criteria for determining the value of research and scholarly activity.

It is true that engagement values are not held solely by SCE faculty and staff—many across the UWM campus share them—but more traditional values are also in evidence. It can still be said that, for the most part, faculty agendas, systems for allocating resources, administrative procedures and policies, the program array, tenure and promotion criteria, and general reward and recognition systems are unchanged by UWM's new, bold, and totally worthy plan. In this regard, faculty and staff at university outreach centers can be important models for the kinds of values and skills that will be needed more broadly by engaged individuals across the entire university.

While SCE has helped to affect The Milwaukee Idea through the participation of our faculty and staff and our continuing practice of community engagement, it has also, in turn, been affected by The Milwaukee Idea. What effects has the "engaged university" had on the "old hands," especially those at the School of Continuing Education? All said, they have been mixed.

- Some SCE faculty and staff, because they had developed long-standing and strong relationships with campus colleagues and the community, are integral to several of the new Milwaukee Idea engagement initiatives. However, they are not usually in leadership roles, and their successful approach to integrating theory and practice is not widely emulated across campus.

- The additional new revenue generated by The Milwaukee Idea and assigned to initiatives in which SCE faculty and staff have roles has improved both the fiscal position and effectiveness of SCE.

- SCE faculty's proven, published model of the scholarship of engagement has not been adopted by many faculty colleagues who are implementing other aspects of The Milwaukee Idea. This may be because their work is not as widely known or that colleagues new to engagement, while respecting the individual members of SCE faculty, feel the need to reinvent the wheel.

- There has been increased competition among UWM faculty and staff for outreach and engagement funds that come from the state, foundations, federal and local governments, and donors. While this competition often centers around "nice-to-have" initiatives for schools and colleges on UWM's main campus, it has been competition for core business funds for SCE. SCE has learned, however, to rise to the new competitive challenge.

- There are structural issues associated with a university adopting an engagement mission. At UWM, this involves a central office on the main campus that has had several implications for SCE. There is currently duplication in some roles, such as marketing functions, grant writing, and fiscal management. The establishment of the new office has also served to marginalize some SCE faculty and staff.

Lessons Learned

The success of adopting an engagement mission must be judged in a number of ways: the impact on the quality of life in the community; the energy and commitment to the idea by faculty and staff; their output as engagement scholars; changes to the curriculum; the cost of the whole endeavor; and the commitment to, and acceptance of, the initiative by community people, alumni, potential donors, regents, legislators, and the press. In almost every regard, The Milwaukee Idea has been successful to one extent or another, even though it is still in its infancy. In my view, in no area is the university less effective or less prominent than it was before 1999. But in some areas, progress is slow and detractors abound.

What follows is a view of some of the lessons learned from UWM's first five years of implementing an engaged university agenda, from the perspective of those experienced in SCE engagement.

- Engagement requires a tireless inspirational champion, a risk-taker, and a cheerleader-in-chief. Institutionalizing engagement requires the efforts of the university's top leaders, not only the heads of its divisions, colleges, or schools.

- Value—and build on—what is already there. Publicly and frequently recognize those faculty and staff who have already made a success of outreach and engagement, especially value those who have a track record of bringing equitable partnerships and extramural dollars to the university. Actively encourage them to share their insights and game plans with others across the institution.

- Establish the university's engagement office as either completely separate from all other research and outreach units or establish clear lines of communication, accountability, and personnel and budget management authority such that there is role clarity and decisions can be made quickly.

- Early on in the process, in a deliberate but participatory way, take up the thorny question of faculty rewards for engagement activity.

- Build into the selection criteria for new tenure-track faculty the need to provide evidence of commitment to an engagement agenda.

- Push through changes to tenure and promotion criteria, such that there are explicit requirements for evidence of adherence to the engagement mission that go beyond membership on advisory boards, clinical practice, private consulting efforts, and public speaking.

- Establish systems by which administration and governance structures will overtly reward interdisciplinary efforts by faculty and staff. Ensure that funds follow such efforts. When real money is on the table, traditional rivals can be encouraged to work together to generate new, worthwhile interdisciplinary projects.

- Establish clear guidelines for the distribution of overhead in multi-school initiatives that recognize the contributions of the engagement office but also those of college and school deans who also incur long-term personnel and match obligations.

With 20/20 hindsight there are some aspects of the implementation of the engagement agenda at UWM that have made the task harder, less inclusive, and less efficient than it might have been. And yet the journey to engagement has been critical to the university and its mission. The social, economic, and cultural futures of this urban research university and greater Milwaukee are inextricably entwined.

Reference

Versant. (2002). *Brand research survey.* Milwaukee, WI: School of Continuing Education, University of Wisconsin–Milwaukee.

PART III
Exploring the Scholarship of Engagement

6 Engagement in Teaching and Learning

Elizabeth Hollander and Jennifer Meeropol

Introduction

This chapter traces the 20-year history of the national movement to promote campus-based service, service-learning, and civic engagement, from its initial focus in the mid-1980s on student cocurricular service to the recent idea of the engaged campus—a campus that educates its students for active civic participation and is itself engaged in its local community. Along the way the chapter pauses at key milestone moments to reflect on important ideas, initiatives, new works, and organizations that have influenced the movement, as well as the challenges and successes of each stage of development. These milestones are the mid to late 1980s, the era of student volunteerism; the early 1990s, which saw the rise of service-learning; the late 1990s, with the birth of the "engaged campus" amid concerns about the disengaged student; and the early 2000s, which have seen a rapid expansion of the idea of the engaged campus. We end with a discussion of the challenges ahead to bring the civic mission of higher education into clearer profile, including concerns about the evidence of impact and the need for diversity.

This chapter is not meant to be a full history of higher education's civic mission, but instead is designed to give the reader a sense of the sweep of the last 20 years, one remarkable for the growth and expansion of interest in educating students not just for the workplace, but also for their role in fostering American democracy. Because the authors are both employees of Campus Compact, the only higher education association devoted entirely to fostering the civic mission of higher education, we see the growth and development of the field through this lens.

The Era of Student Volunteerism

The mid-1980s are generally seen as marking the rebirth of higher education's focus on its civic mission. Within higher education, general unrest had been building about the dominance of the German research university model, which focused on pure research and disciplinary specialization. In addition, many educators were concerned that in trying to attract students after the recession of the 1970s, higher education was increasingly catering to students as consumers and overemphasizing the workplace benefits of a college education. There was widespread concern about creating a self-centered "me" generation of college students who were motivated by their own self-interest, with little regard for the larger public good. Students were expressing more interest in making money than in developing a philosophy of life (Astin, Vogelgesang, Ikeda, & Yee, 2000). Boyer and Hechinger's (1981) *Higher Learning in the Nation's Service*, written during the height of the "me" generation, highlights the general trend of a lack of a larger civic, national purpose in colleges and universities at the time.

These concerns drove the birth of new structures to reclaim the purposes of higher education to educate students for citizenship as well as for the workforce. Students organized in 1984 to demonstrate their own civic concerns and, under the guidance of a recent Harvard University graduate, Wayne Meisel, created the Campus Outreach Opportunity League (COOL) as a vehicle for student volunteerism. The following year, a group of higher education presidents—Frank Newman of the Education Commission of the States, Don Kennedy of Stanford University, Tim Healy of Georgetown University, and Howard Swearer of Brown University—followed suit in founding Campus Compact. In each case, the organization, which grew rapidly, was founded by visionary leaders who sensed that students were merely waiting to be asked to serve their communities. By 1988, COOL had worked with students at more than 450 universities across the country and had hosted several national student summits while Campus Compact had 225 member campuses and three state offices in California, Michigan, and Pennsylvania (See http://www.idealist.org/ioc).

These early engagement efforts emphasized public and community service as the most common form of civic action and focused on cocurricular activity that was supported by student life, urban ministry, or student activities staff—or driven entirely by students themselves. There was little discussion of connecting service to teaching and learning in the curricular sense, although there were scattered faculty efforts. The 1988–1989 Campus Compact *Annual Report* spoke to the importance of the faculty role in promoting service and cited a Campus Compact study on the faculty role in contributing to "students' understanding of the importance of service and citizenship and . . . helping . . . them achieve the full learning potential from their service experiences" (Campus Compact, 1989, p. 16). The few examples the report could cite at that time included public service leaves for faculty at the University of Utah, a lecture series at Ohio Wesleyan on the responsibilities of citizenship, and an academic intern program at Michigan State University that allowed students to work directly with community groups under faculty supervision. While all of these were worthwhile programs, they were far from the sophisticated service-learning courses that were developed in the next decade.

During this era there was a belief on the part of college presidents that "participation in service engages students in active learning experiences and teaches them the importance of active citizenship" (Campus Compact, 1989, p. 4). Presidential leadership included not only encouraging such activities on their campuses, but also starting state Campus Compact offices and promoting national service legislation.

The senior President Bush had called for service to be a regular part of all students' lives, and there was a gathering political consensus about the importance of public service, expressed by the Points of Light Foundation and Democratic congressional leaders such as Edward Kennedy of Massachusetts in the U.S. Senate and Matthew Martinez of California in the U.S. House of Representatives. Another key congressional development was the Committee on Education and the Workforce, led by Representative Augustus F. Hawkins. This committee was responsible for passing the Volunteers and the Importance of Volunteerism resolution, which stated that volunteer work should be listed on employment application forms and considered by employers in hiring (Committee on Education and the Workforce, 2004). These legislative efforts culminated in the passage of the National and Community Service Act of 1990, which created the bipartisan Commission on National and Community Service to encourage more volunteer hours. This commission called on college students to serve their nation, "removing barriers to service that have been created by high education costs, loan indebtedness, and the cost of housing" (Commission on National and Community Service, 1993, p. ix).

The Rise of Faculty Involvement and Service-Learning

The next five years of the movement were characterized by increasing frustration with the quality of undergraduate education and rising interest in youth service. These two hallmarks came together to spark interest in the idea of service-learning. An attempt to connect service with academic course content, service-learning sought to increase student and campus involvement in communities and to enhance learning.

The Academy Under Fire

In the early 1990s, there was a pervasive sense that "the quality of undergraduate teaching in the United States is in decline—or—if it is not getting any worse, it is already bad enough to justify public concern" (Winston, 1994, p. 8). Many people seemed willing to place the blame for this situation squarely on the faculty. As Winston notes (without agreeing), "There is a near consensus . . . that the root cause is a moral failure of American professors; they simply have too much power and they pay too much attention to their research and consulting and graduate students and too little attention to their undergraduates and lectures and advising and caring" (p. 8).

DeZure (2000) concurs with the following characterization of the negative public perception of higher education in the 1990s and notes that part of the impetus for publishing the collection was the increase in attacks against higher education during this period:

> Higher education has been under attack for failing to produce graduates with skills in the workplace and for active participation in a democratic society. . . . The charges have been harsh and inclusive, attacking the leadership, the faculty, and the students; the curriculum; the organizational structure and infrastructure; the models for evaluation of faculty, students, and institutions; the methods of instruction; and the speed and slowness of integrating technology. (p. xxii)

Clearly, concern about the quality of higher education was widespread. But, at the same time, important cultural and societal forces were converging to support increasing engagement in teaching and learning. As noted earlier, political interest in the ideal of individual responsibility for self and community led to new structures to support volunteerism. While some argued that this was an individualistic, rather than a collaborative, view of civic and community engagement, it did create space in the national dialogue for discussions about volunteerism and service. In addition, the interest in experiential education was growing (including service-learning) and major research universities, such as the University of Pennsylvania, were reexamining the quality of their undergraduate education.

This public dialogue expanded in September 1993 when President Clinton signed the National and Community Service Trust Act, creating AmeriCorps and the Corporation for National and Community Service (CNCS) to expand opportunities for Americans to serve their communities. CNCS brought increased visibility to service and would be an important funding source for the growing efforts to incorporate service into the heart of the academy, that is, the curriculum. Derek Bok (1990), then president of Harvard University, contributed to the conversation with his book, *Universities and the Future of America,* in which he recommended that colleges advocate social responsibility, mainly through collegiate programs and the curriculum.

One program that provided community service opportunities was the Summer of Service (SOS). Summer of Service started in 2002, when 300 young people, ranging in age from 14 to 20, volunteered 40,000 hours of service in Washington, DC (Service for Peace, 2005). One year later, the program grew to include more than 1,000 young people in 16 cities, working in conjunction with more than 100 community partners, such as the Boys and Girls Clubs, the YMCA, the American Red Cross, and the Police Athletic League.

Faculty Enter the Picture

One key outcome of the rise of service-learning was a new focus on the importance of faculty involvement in efforts to engage students. Evidence of this increased interest in the role of faculty can be found in a spate of influential publications on the topic, as well as in survey data and in association initiatives, notably Campus Compact's creation of the Integrating Service with Academic Study (ISAS) project, as outlined in the pages that follow.

Two key publications of the 1990s were Boyer's *Scholarship Reconsidered: Priorities of the Professoriate,* published in 1990, and his article "The Scholarship of Engagement," published in 1996. Both publications discussed a new concept of scholarship that included discovery, integration, application, and teaching. They also highlighted the central role of faculty in transforming teaching and applying the knowledge of higher education to the problems of the world. Along with the National Society for Experiential Education's three-volume collection *Combining Service and Learning,* (Kendall & Associates, 1990), and the Association of American Colleges and Universities' (AAC&U's) *Learning for the Common Good: Liberal Education, Civic Education, and Teaching About Philanthropy,* (Jeavons, 1991), these books explored questions of faculty tenure and promotion, experiential teaching and service-learning, the meaning and public nature of scholarship and engagement, and the public purposes of higher education. They also provided powerful examples of how to carry out this work, with sample syllabi, model programs, and recommended resources for deepening faculty engagement.

Campus Compact was moving in a similar direction. The ISAS project, which began in 1989, marked an important shift in the work of Campus Compact from promoting only community service on college and university campuses (service outside the curriculum) to including an emphasis on service that is integrally connected to course content in a wide variety of disciplines. With its curricular focus, ISAS was primarily concerned with the needs of faculty who adopt service-learning as a teaching methodology and who sought to deepen its practice in their courses, in their departments, and at their institutions. ISAS brought former faculty members to Campus Compact as full-time staff members who understood the challenges of faculty workloads and the realities of tenure and promotion policies.

Soon after Campus Compact launched the ISAS project, it published *Integrating Public Service with Academic Study: The Faculty Role* (Stanton, 1990), which summarized the findings and recommendations gleaned from a series of focus group discussions held at Compact-member campuses across the country concerning the role of faculty involvement in community service. The same year, Campus Compact held the first in a series of annual Introductory Service-Learning Institutes that had a "dramatic impact" (I. Harkavy, personal communication, July 12, 2004). The institutes brought together campus teams that included both faculty and community service directors to develop specific strategies for implementing and expanding service-learning on their campuses.

The success of these institutes indicated that a significant percentage of Campus Compact members was interested in expanding community service programs to include service-learning. Data from Campus Compact's

1992 annual member survey also illustrate the growth of service-learning courses and programs. Indeed, the first trend highlighted in the 1992 survey report was the rise of service-learning:

> Within any institution, the faculty play central roles in shaping students' undergraduate education. In an attempt to expand the definition of "education" to include service linked with academic study, Campus Compact and its member institutions have made these linkages a priority. (Campus Compact, 1993, p. 105)

The report also noted that 52% of member campuses provided academic credit for service related to a course and 23% had policies or incentives to encourage faculty involvement or foster links between service and academic study.

As Campus Compact shifted its focus to include faculty engagement and service-learning, other organizations took similar steps to support this new pedagogy. Together, these organizations helped created an infrastructure of researchers, national associations, and funders that would support the rapid expansion of service-learning over the next decade. In addition to the federal role mentioned earlier, higher education associations also initiated projects supporting faculty and student engagement. In 1993 AAC&U began American Commitments: Diversity, Democracy, and Liberal Learning, a multiprogram initiative focused on preparing and encouraging students to contribute to the success of a just and diverse democracy. The same year, the Council of Independent Colleges (CIC) created a grant-making unit entitled the Consortium for the Advancement of Private Higher Education in order to strengthen the ability of private colleges to make significant contributions to society. One year later, the U.S. Department of Housing and Urban Development (HUD) founded the Office of University Partnerships to encourage colleges and universities to partner with their communities to address pressing needs.

During the early 1990s, conferences cosponsored by The Johnson Foundation at its Wingspread facility in Racine, Wisconsin, had significant impact on the early period of collegiate civic engagement and service-learning. These meetings helped shape standards for the pedagogy and a research agenda (Stanton, Giles, Jr., & Cruz, 1999). The increased focus on service-learning and interest in connecting faculty to efforts to engage college students took place during a time of rapid growth for Campus

Compact. By 1992 Campus Compact had 305 members, an increase of 210% from 1987. By the end of 1992 new state Compacts existed in Florida, Washington, Colorado, Illinois, Ohio, and West Virginia. As it approached its 10th anniversary, Campus Compact's growth mirrored the expansion of the national service and service-learning movement.

The Engaged Campus and the Disengaged Student

By the late1990s, even as service-learning was gaining considerable traction as a pedagogy in higher education, the first murmurings of concern about the lack of political engagement by students was being heard. As early as 1993, Arthur Levine, president of Teachers College in New York, had documented college students' cynicism about government and the American political system. At that time, it was thought that service activities would help connect students to their democracy.

Surveys conducted by the Peter D. Hart Research Association (1998) for Public Allies and by the National Association of Secretaries of State (1999) about youth engagement made it clear that students were actively engaged in service activities and felt they could make life better for people on a one-on-one basis, but students felt little agency in the larger democracy. Research also indicated that the quality of the service-learning experience had a huge impact on whether it deepened students' understanding of larger public-policy questions and their subsequent engagement. For instance, Benjamin Barber found that students who had a sustained service experience, such as with Public Allies (a full-time, full-year program with regular training), deepened their understanding of public policy and the role of government in addressing social ills. Other researchers also documented the correlation between the duration and intensity of a service or service-learning experience and its impact on students (Barber, Higgens, Smith, & Ballou, 1997; Eyler, Giles, Stenson, & Gray, 2001).

In the late 1990s the concern about youth disengagement from the democracy precipitated major efforts to get out the youth vote in the 1996 election. The National Association of Independent Colleges and Universities tried to make voter registration a requirement of the Higher Education Act, enacted in 1998, and then to promote the practice on campus. Rock the Vote, a nonprofit organization founded by members of the recording industry in 1990, joined with MTV and other organizations in 1996 to register more than 500,000 new voters for the presidential election and to publish 200,000 free pamphlets providing youth with nonpartisan information about the major issues and the candidates (Rock the Vote, 2005).

Growing concern about college students dropping out of the democracy precipitated a meeting of university and college presidents in 1999, cosponsored by Campus Compact and the American Council on Education. The *Presidents' Declaration on the Civic Responsibility of Higher Education* (Campus Compact, 1999), issued at that meeting, acknowledged that service and service-learning were important but that more conscious involvement of students in the "real, hard work of citizenship" was needed. The declaration also acknowledged that institutions of higher education had to model this involvement by addressing the needs of their own communities (Campus Compact).

The idea that the campus, as an institution, has a responsibility to its own community and could lend a hand in community development was also a major development in the thinking of this era. This idea of the "engaged campus" has been defined as having "an integrated approach to fostering students' citizenship skills through both educational and co-curricular programs and activities, and conscious modeling of good institutional citizenship through external partnerships and activities" (Thomas, 2000, p. 66). An engaged campus reflects full acceptance of the larger sense of institutional alignment that Boyer (1996) identified as "the scholarship of engagement"—namely, scholarship that "connect[s] the rich resources of the university to our most pressing social, civic and ethical problems" (p. 11). HUD's Community Outreach Partnership Grants supported this ideal by creating new models of reciprocal campus/community partnerships. For the most part, however, these grants were not connected to the service and service-learning activities on campus; the truly integrated model of the engaged campus, such as that undertaken at the University of Wisconsin–Milwaukee, was still to be devised.

A more sophisticated conceptualization appeared in a report of the Kellogg Commission on the Future of State and Land-Grant Universities, formed by the National Association of State Universities and Land-Grant Colleges. Entitled *Returning to Our Roots: The Engaged Institution,* the report was issued in 1999 as part of a series on renewing the role of the land grant colleges for the 21st century. This report was heavily influenced by the thinking of Judith Ramaley, then-president of Portland State University, who reconceptualized the traditional triumvirate of university functions—

teaching, research, and service—as "learning, discovery, and engagement" (Kellogg Commission, 1999, pp. 23, 41).

This dual emphasis on student political engagement and institutional engagement was taking place within the setting of a major focus on volunteerism and the state of the civil society. In general, however, this focus did not recognize the role of higher education in fostering civic development. For example, in 1997 the larger service movement got a boost from the calling of a nonpartisan service summit, attended by all of the living U.S. presidents (or their spouses). The summit, cosponsored by CNCS, the Points of Light Foundation, and the United Way, resulted in the launch of America's Promise, a high-profile organization headed by Colin Powell. The effect of this summit on higher education was limited, however. Only a few college presidents were invited to the summit (most at the last minute), and those who went found they had no role when they arrived. Student attendees were similarly frustrated that there was no formal way for their voices to be heard. Several years later, America's Promise sought out campuses that had extensive outreach programs and began to recognize them as "Universities of Promise."

This lagging recognition of the role of higher education in civil society is evident in another seminal activity of the era. A major bipartisan report (the Nunn-Bennett Commission) of the National Commission on Civic Renewal (1998) documented the decline of American participation in civic life and called on many institutions to help reassert civic engagement. Although informed by many academics, and drafted by William Galston of the University of Maryland, the report called on virtually all sectors of society *except* higher education to act as vehicles for public engagement.

So, while college presidents were increasingly thinking about their role as agents of a vital democracy in America and of the health of their local communities, their efforts were little recognized in the larger context. The *Presidents' Declaration*, which cited the role of colleges as "architects and agents of a flourishing democracy," (Campus Compact, 1999, p. 3) was designed to address this problem by giving their efforts a greater profile. This succeeded best, perhaps, within the higher education community, which continued to expand its work in this area. Public recognition of the role of higher education in educating citizens was harder to attain.

Educating for Citizenship

During the five years between 1997 and 2002, there was tremendous growth in the spread and depth of the service-learning movement in higher education, including the development of sophisticated models for an engaged campus, assessments of the impact of this approach, and an increasing call for scientific research on the impact of engagement on campuses, communities, and students. At the same time, the call to reengage young people in the democratic process was growing louder across the country and was reflected in public policy at the state and federal levels.

The expansion of the service movement during this period included an increase in both the prevalence of service-learning and the idea of the engaged campus. According to Campus Compact's annual member surveys, an average of 22 faculty on each campus offered service-learning courses in 2002, an increase of 63% over the 1998 figure. The average number of service-learning courses per campus had also grown dramatically, from 16 in 1998 to more than 30 in 2002, an increase of 88%. The proportion of member campuses offering service-learning courses also continued to grow, increasing from 80% in 1997 to 87% in 2002. This commitment to campus engagement is further evidenced in the continued expansion of Campus Compact membership, which had burgeoned to more than 900 campuses by the end of 2002, and in the organization's supporting infrastructure, had reached 28 state offices (nearly all hosted by member campuses).

Just as the early 1990s were characterized by the rise of service-learning, the late 1990s and early 2000s have seen the rise of civic engagement and the notion of "the engaged campus." In both cases, these new conceptualizations of engagement expanded, rather than superceded, the existing movement, allowing curricular and cocurricular service and engaging students with the democracy to reinforce and redefine each other. Thus, the idea of the engaged campus can be seen as the institutionalization of the best practices of curricular and cocurricular service and civic engagement advocated in the publications and initiatives that had driven the movement in the preceding decade.

Assessing Engagement and Impact

As campus-based service-learning and civic engagement programs grew and developed, finding ways to measure, assess, expand, and improve these programs became an increasingly important priority. To meet this need, in the late 1990s Campus Compact developed the Service-Learning Pyramid, a schematic representation of the developmental levels of service-learning on campuses. The pyramid has three levels: Introductory, Intermediate, and Advanced, and each level has a set of characteristics appropriate for the constituency involved. The full picture of each level is quite complex, defined as it is by the roles and needs of multiple constituencies who act as stakeholders and as agents of institutional change: presidents, chief academic officers, faculty, community service directors, community partners, and students. The pyramid reflects the journey of an institution in achieving a richer and deeper commitment to service-learning and allows campuses to assess not only their progress, but also to create strategies for deepening their engagement and progress along the pyramid.

The pyramid was not the only model designed to help document and assess campus engagement. In the late 1990s a group of researchers associated with Campus Compact's Western Regional Consortium's Continuums of Service project created a self-assessment tool for campuses to gauge and deepen their practice of service-learning. This assessment tool was structured around five dimensions or components that experts felt were the key factors for institutionalizing service-learning in higher education—philosophy and mission, faculty support and involvement, student support and involvement, community participation and partnerships, and institutional support. Andrew Furco, the founding director of the University of California–Berkeley Service-Learning Research and Development Center, revised the self-assessment tool as part of his work as an engaged scholar for Campus Compact in the early 2000s. In 2001 Campus Compact published this revised rubric. Another model is Barbara Holland's matrix. Holland, then senior scholar with the Indiana University–Purdue University Indianapolis Center for Service and Learning, developed a system that identifies key organizational factors that promote civic engagement (Gelmon, Holland, Driscoll, Spring, & Kerrigan, 2001).

With the expansion of the service movement to include civic engagement in addition to service and service-learning, Campus Compact recognized the need for a tool to help conceptualize and assess the engaged campus. In 2001, more than 80% of respondents identified Campus Compact's most valuable services as providing resource materials (87%) and identifying model programs (83%). National leaders also called upon Campus Compact to provide more information on campus engagement practices, regarding such information as an essential tool in advancing national policy. To meet this need, Campus Compact launched the Indicators of Engagement Project in 2002, with funding from the Carnegie Corporation of New York. The project expands on the Service-Learning Pyramid to include 13 indicators of campus engagement that address issues of institutional culture, curriculum and pedagogy, faculty roles and rewards, institutional infrastructure, and campus/community partnerships. These indicators were developed by Campus Compact executive director Elizabeth Hollander, ISAS project director John Saltmarsh, and senior faculty fellow Edward Zlotkowski (Hollander & Saltmarsh, 2000; Hollander, Saltmarsh, & Zlotkowski, 2002) to capture the various approaches to engagement they observed at institutions across the country. The indicators recognize that institutions use a range of approaches to engagement, depending on their particular culture and priorities. The indicators are designed to help campuses assess their current levels of engagement and create strategies to deepen their work. It is unlikely that any one campus, however engaged, will exhibit all of the indicators to an equal degree. For this reason, the indicators are not prescriptive; their value lies primarily in the possibilities they suggest.

Other initiatives also recognized the importance of creating models for specific types of institutions as national organizations funded programs to document and deepen engagement at their member institutions. Organizations ranging from the CIC to the American Association of Community Colleges to the United Negro College Fund all created programs to help their members engage with their communities and document best practices to share with the field. The government joined the effort, with HUD's investment in and documentation of three programs aimed at supporting engagement at tribal colleges, Native Hawaiian, and Native Alaskan–serving institutions; Historically Black Colleges and Universities; and Hispanic-Serving Institutions.

In addition to these efforts, a range of national organizations, states, and individual campuses focused on developing best practices for civic engagement across higher education. The National Society for Experiential Education, the National Association for Equal Opportunity in Higher Education, the Alliance for Equity in Higher Education, and the New England Resource Center for Higher Education all created networks of institutions that have partnered with their communities. Minnesota Campus Compact received funding from the state to conduct an exhaustive study of the status of civic engagement at all colleges and universities in the state.

Meanwhile, Grey Davis, then-governor of California, provided funding to institutionalize service-learning on all 23 campuses in the California State University system. Finally, individual campuses such as the University of Wisconsin–Milwaukee, Kapi'olani Community College in Hawaii, Trinity College in Connecticut, and many others created programs based on meaningful, institution-wide engagement with their communities.

While the recent research devoted to assessing engagement and documenting impacts is a promising step in the right direction, clearly there are important questions that still must be addressed about the long-term impact of engagement on students and the correlation between service and participation in the democracy. This correlation is particularly important to politicians and policy leaders.

Public Policy

During the early part of the new century, major focus was put on the expectation that young people and others would "serve" their country. President George W. Bush's inaugural address called for overcoming the problem of a "nation of spectators." The new administration organized the USA Freedom Corps and appointed John Bridgeland, an energetic and visible champion of service, as its first director. The administration also expressed its support for the reauthorization of the Corporation for National and Community Service. Meanwhile, Senators John McCain and Evan Bayh were calling for an increased number of positions for AmeriCorps and a focus on public health and safety, as well as an increase from 7% to 25% in the mandated proportion of federal work-study students doing community work. (The White House subsequently called for 50%.) The events of September 11 further increased the interest in promoting public service.

The new administration expressed deep concern that young people did not know enough about the history of their own democracy to become good citizens. These concerns, coupled with low civic participation rates (mainly expressed in low voter turnout) led to a major bipartisan effort to restore civic education to the elementary and secondary school levels. A state scan conducted by the Education Commission of the States (2004) demonstrates that momentum for promoting civic education is mounting at the state level as well.

In the run-up to the 2004 election, every major candidate included some service platform. As in earlier years, however, there was little public discussion of civic education at the college level, except among private foundations. During this period, foundations, which had been focused on funding service opportunities for young people (and service-learning), began to ask whether service and service-learning opportunities actually encouraged students to engage in politics and public policy making. Some claimed that one-on-one service was, in fact, young people's substitute for such engagement.

Campus Compact set out to gain a better understanding of how the current generation understood their own civic engagement and educational needs. A gathering of 34 college students from across the country resulted in the publication of the student-written book *The New Student Politics: The Wingspread Statement on Student Civic Engagement* (Long, 2002). This group of students concluded that service was not an *alternative to* politics but in fact an *alternative form of* politics. The students took deep exception to the idea that they were not engaged, but rather indicated that they needed to deal with problems hands on, as part of the process of getting involved in public policy or politics. The students also made it clear that they believed that doing the work of diversity was doing the work of democracy and that, in their service work, many were negotiating in communities very different from the ones in which they grew up. They acknowledged that this was difficult and demanded a level of understanding that they did not readily find in their coursework.

Soon after this gathering, Campus Compact was approached by the Pew Charitable Trusts to undertake a large student mobilization effort designed to increase the civic involvement of tens of thousands of college students on hundreds of campuses. Interestingly, in naming this campaign, student focus groups rejected all of the common language of a concerned older generation such as *citizenship, civic engagement,* and *politics,* in favor of the slogan "Raise Your Voice: Student Action for Change." The idea of the campaign is to provide motivation, tools, and space for students to take action on issues of their choosing, whether service, advocacy, politics, dialogue on issues, or initiatives such as arts in action. Raise Your Voice mobilized student organizers in 14 states to work with student leaders on campuses in those states. A web site provides action guides for students, college administrators, and faculty (www.actionforchange.org). Student activities focused on a week of action during February 2003 (Presidents' Week) and a month of action the following year. Preliminary studies of a sample of participating campuses show that service-learning is positively associated with every kind of student engagement from volunteering to voting (Billig, 2003).

During the week of action in 2003, students in five states approached their state legislatures to talk about the importance of colleges fostering student civic development. Civic engagement students from Maine spent a week in Washington, DC, doing service work and lobbying Congress on behalf of the clients they were serving and the programs that helped them to do so. Students in five states met with their governors or lieutenant governors to discuss their service work and its importance in their own civic education. Clearly, students can be mobilized to use the political system to advance their own democratic participation. There is, however, every indication that student leaders, faculty, and administrators must nurture students' sense of agency in the democracy. The relevance of politics, or even public policy, is often not immediately apparent to students. It may be more so during an election year, especially if candidates are purposeful about including students. According to a study by the Center for Information and Research on Civic Learning and Engagement (CIRCLE), for example, there was a significantly higher youth turnout in the 2004 election than in the last presidential election in 2000; the 51.6% youth turnout in 2004 is the highest the nation has seen in more than a decade (CIRCLE, 2004).

What does all this mean for the teaching enterprise? Is service-learning the wrong approach, and is something else required? Can faculty be helpful in increasing student civic engagement? Studies show that the level of student engagement is likely to increase among students engaged in active reflection (most likely to happen in a service-learning class) (Keeter, Zukin, Andolina, & Jenkins, 2002; Vogelgesang, 2001). Service-learning classes can be organized successfully around a civic engagement activity, for example, researching a public policy issue, helping to write legislation and then advocating for its adoption, organizing debates and writing editorials, and organizing others to take action. On some campuses, such as DePaul University and James Madison University, there is an organized, developmental approach to service-learning designed to raise students' consciousness of poverty issues through service, and then to teach the skills of public policy and how to influence it. In sum, active pedagogical approaches that involve students in the "real, hard work" of democracy are a promising way to engage students. One-on-one volunteer work can be an important eye-opener for many students about "how the other half lives," but the practice of service-learning needs to include activities beyond this experience to have a deep and long-lasting impact.

Several new centers and studies started in the early 2000s hoped to uncover the correlation between engagement and participation in the democracy and to recommend best practices for achieving it. The National Survey of Student Engagement (NSSE), piloted in 1999 and conducted in 2000, and its offspring, the Community College Survey of Student Engagement (CCSSE), begun in 2001, both seek to document the prevalence and impact of engaged learning on students. In 2001, The Pew Charitable Trusts and the Carnegie Corporation of New York, both longtime funders of service-learning and civic engagement, supported the establishment of CIRCLE, to conduct, collect, and fund research on the civic and political participation of young Americans. One year later, AAC&U and Campus Compact joined forces to found the Center for Liberal Education and Civic Engagement as a means of deepening understanding of the relationship of liberal arts education to service and civic responsibilities (see www.aacu-edu.org/civic_engagement/index.cfm).

As noted earlier, students are also asking for greater understanding of cultures and races other than their own. Service-learning courses are a natural avenue for these lessons, but again, they must be deliberately pursued. On most campuses today, the multicultural center or office is disconnected from the service-learning center, which means that both miss great opportunities for increased understanding. Too often, the service-learning movement in higher education has a white female face. Female students participate in service-learning activities at a much higher rate than do their male counterparts. White students participate at a higher rate than minority students (at least in white-majority institutions). Civic engagement practices at minority-serving institutions are not showcased at major service-learning conferences to the extent that the practice would merit. One of the major challenges of the next era of the service-learning and civic engagement movement is to integrate both the diversity and democracy efforts. This is important because America is becoming an increasingly diverse nation and maintaining the civil society will require, as students recognize, an ability to work effectively across different cultures and perspectives.

The University of Wisconsin–Milwaukee is in the forefront of this melding of democracy and diversity in its reorganization of the basic curriculum to promote cross-cultural understanding, as Greg Jay and Sandra Jones outline in Chapter 7. "Cultures and Communities, Learning for the New Century" has fostered 60 interdisciplinary courses in 24 departments that integrate community-based learning and cross-cultural learning. Examples range from a course in Hmong life stories to a freshman seminar in global religion. An office and faculty mini-grants help to promote this work. Taking advantage of the rich diversity of the residents of America's metropolitan areas will increasingly be a hallmark of campuses engaged with their communities.

An Era of Challenge and Possibility

As we look to the future of the civic engagement movement, we see both incredible opportunity and daunting challenges. The growth of the movement in the past 20 years has provided a firm foundation to sustain continued expansion. The development of best practices and campus models has increased the quality of service and service-learning programs, while national organizations, researchers, foundations, and the federal government have helped create an infrastructure that has increased the prevalence of multiple forms of engagement.

While we celebrate the important achievements of the civic engagement movement in higher education, we also acknowledge that there are key challenges we must meet if we wish to continue to expand our reach. With the creation of new models of engaged campuses and new tools for assessing campus engagement in the last decade, an important next step is to develop a way of connecting these models and rubrics so that they reinforce and support each other. Campuses that have used Furco's (2001) self-assessment rubric would benefit from recommendations about how to translate that work to the Indicators of Engagement and vice versa. Although the growing abundance of assessment models and best practices allows campuses to choose the tool best suited to their specific needs, both researchers and campus constituents could clearly benefit from the ability to compare and contrast findings generated from these various models.

Such a "meta-tool" for assessing engagement must, at its core, illustrate the correlation between student engagement and participation in the democracy. It must demonstrate that students involved in service, service-learning, and/or civic engagement activities are more likely to participate as full, active members of their communities and the nation. If our goal is not just to engage students while they are in college but instead to prepare them for lifelong participation in the democracy, then this question—

already of fundamental importance to funders, politicians, and educators—must drive the civic engagement movement.

But this is not our only challenge. As we focus on the connection between service and engagement in the democracy, we need to define our terms and measure our success. What is the test or definition of civic literacy for higher education, and how do we develop it? What is true civic literacy, and how do we get there? Is there a developmental spectrum for civic literacy? If so, who designs it and how?

Finally, we must also ask what service-learning and the civic engagement movement is doing to engage the diverse democracy of the 21st century. As the students at the Wingspread gathering clearly understood, the work of diversity is the work of engagement. Unfortunately, this is not sufficiently reflected in either our theory or our practice, both of which have too often relied on white European theories and theorists. We need to expand the theoretical foundations of our movement, draw upon the excellent work of cultural studies, critical race studies, and ethnic studies, and the diversity of the leadership of our field by deliberately connecting our work to these movements and practitioners. The increasingly diverse communities that surround our campuses need to be viewed as an opportunity for teaching, learning, and reciprocal partnerships.

We hope that the next 5, 10, and 20 years will see the same growth, discussion, and commitment to civic engagement that has marked the last 20 years. Perhaps by then, community-based scholars, such as those supported by the University of Wisconsin–Milwaukee, will be institutionalized positions and faculty will talk about the old days when tenure and promotion policies inhibited their interest in community engagement. We look forward to reading the 40-year review of the movement in 2022. We believe it will surprise and challenge us all.

References

Astin, A. W., Vogelgesang, L. J., Ikeda, E. K., & Yee, J. A. (2000). *How service learning affects students.* Los Angeles, CA: University of California, Higher Education Research Institute.

Barber, B. R., Higgens, R. Smith, J., & Ballou, J., with Dedrick, J., & Downing, K. (1997). *Democratic theory and civic measurement: A report on the Measuring Citizenship Project.* Rutgers, NJ: Walt Whitman Center.

Billig, S. (2003). *Initial national civic engagement results* (Unpublished report). Denver, CO: RMC Research Corporation.

Bok, D. (1990). *Universities and the future of America.* Durham, NC: Duke University Press.

Boyer, E. L. (1990). *Scholarship reconsidered: Priorities of the professoriate.* Princeton, NJ: The Carnegie Foundation for the Advancement of Teaching.

Boyer, E. L. (1996). The scholarship of engagement. *Journal of Public Service and Outreach, 1*(1), 11–20.

Boyer, E. L., & Hechinger, F. M. (1981). *Higher learning in the nation's service.* Washington, DC: Carnegie Foundation for the Advancement of Teaching.

Campus Compact. (1989). *1988–1989 Annual report.* Providence, RI: Author.

Campus Compact. (1993). *National members' survey and resource guide.* Providence, RI: Author.

Campus Compact. (1999). *Presidents' declaration on the civic responsibility of higher education.* Retrieved July 15, 2005, from http://www.compact.org/presidential/declaration.html

Center for Information and Research on Civic Learning and Engagement (CIRCLE). (2004, Nov. 29). *Youth Vote Surges in 2004: The Real Numbers: Young Voters Surpass Previous Records and Match Significantly Higher Voter Turnout.* Retrieved July 25, 2005, from http://www.compact.org/newscc/news-detail.php?view story=3548

Commission on National and Community Service. (1993). *What you can do for your country.* Washington, DC: Corporation for National and Community Service.

Committee on Education and the Workforce: U.S. House of Representatives. (2004). *History of the Committee on Education and the Workforce and the members who have served as chairman.* Retrieved July 18, 2005, from http://edworkforce.house.gov/committee/history.htm

DeZure, D. (Ed.). (2000). *Learning from change: Landmarks in teaching and learning in higher education from* Change *Magazine, 1969–1999.* Sterling, VA: Stylus.

Education Commission of the States. (2004). *ECS National Center for Learning and Citizenship's (NCLC) state policies for citizenship education database.* Denver, CO: Author.

Eyler, J. S., Giles, D. E., Jr., Stenson, C. M., & Gray, C. J. (2001). *At a glance: What we know about the effects of service-learning on students, faculty, institutions and communities, 1993–2000* (3rd ed.). Washington, DC: Corporation for National and Community Service.

Furco, A. (2001). *Self-assessment rubric for the institutionalization of service-learning in higher education.* Providence, RI: Campus Compact.

Gelmon, S. B., Holland, B. A., Driscoll, A., Spring, A., & Kerrigan, S. (2001). *Assessing service-learning and civic engagement: Principles and techniques* (Rev., 3rd ed.). Providence, RI: Campus Compact.

Hollander, E. L., & Saltmarsh, J. (2000). The engaged university. *Academe, 86(4),* 29–31.

Hollander, E., Saltmarsh, J., & Zlotkowski, E. (2002). The indicators of engagement. In L. A. Simon, M. Kenny, K. Brabeck, & R. Lerner (Eds.), *Learning to serve: Promoting civil society through service-learning* (pp. 31–49). Norwell, MA: Kluwer.

Jeavons, T. (1991). *Learning for the common good: Liberal education, civic education, and teaching about philanthropy.* Washington, DC: Association of American Colleges and Universities.

Keeter, S., Zukin, C., Andolina, M., & Jenkins, K. (2002). *The civic and political health of the nation: A generational portrait.* College Park, MD: The Center for Information and Research on Civic Learning and Engagement (CIRCLE).

Kellogg Commission on the Future of State and Land-Grant Universities. (1999). *Returning to our roots: The engaged institution.* Washington, DC: National Association of State Universities and Land-Grant Colleges.

Kendall, J. C., & Associates. (1990). *Combining service and learning: A resource book for community and public service* (Vols. 1–3). Alexandria, VA: National Society for Experiential Education.

Long, S. E. (2002). *The new student politics: The Wingspread statement on student civic engagement.* Providence, RI: Campus Compact.

National Association of Secretaries of State. (1999). *New millennium project—Part 1, American youth attitudes on politics, citizenship, government and voting.* Lexington, KY: Author.

National Commission on Civic Renewal. (1998). *A nation of spectators: How civic disengagement weakens America and what we can do about it.* College Park, MD: Author.

Peter D. Hart Research Associates. (1998). *New leadership for a new century: Key findings from a study on youth, leadership, and community service.* Washington, DC: Public Allies.

Rock the Vote. (2005). *Rock the Vote timeline.* Retrieved July 22, 2005, from http://www.rockthevote.com/rtv_timeline.php

Service for Peace. (2005). *Our history.* Retrieved July 22, 2005, from http://www.serviceforpeace.org/aboutus/history.htm

Stanton, T. K. (1990). *Integrating public service with academic study: The faculty role.* Providence, RI: Campus Compact.

Stanton, T. K., Giles, D. E., Jr., & Cruz, N. I. (1999). *Service-learning: A movement's pioneers reflect on its origins, practice, and future.* San Francisco, CA: Jossey-Bass.

Thomas, N. L. (2000). The college and university as citizen. In T. Ehrlich, (Ed.), *Civic responsibility and higher education* (pp. 63–97). Phoenix, AZ: American Council on Education/Oryx Press.

Vogelgesang, L. (2001, July 23). *Service-Learning Discussion Group archives.* Retrieved September 1, 2005, from http://servicelearning.org/resources/lesson_plans/index.php?popup_id=1236

Winston, G. C. (1994). The decline in undergraduate teaching: Moral failure or market pressure? *Change, 26*(5), 8–15.

Recommended Reading

Are we good citizens? Civic engagement and higher education. (2000). [Special issue]. *Academe, 86*(4).

Bowley, E., & Meeropol, J. (2003). Service-learning in higher education: Trends, research, and resources. *Generator, 21*(3), 12–16.

Boyte, H., & Hollander, E. (1999). *Wingspread declaration on renewing the civic mission of the American research university.* Providence, RI: Campus Compact.

Bringle, R. G., Games, R., & Malloy, E. A. (Eds.) (1999). *Colleges and universities as citizens.* Needham Heights, MA: Allyn & Bacon.

Colby, A., Ehrlich, T., Beaumont, E., & Stephens, J. (2003). *Educating citizens: Preparing America's undergraduates for lives of moral and civic responsibility.* San Francisco, CA: Jossey-Bass.

Eyler, J., & Giles, D. E., Jr. (1999). *Where's the learning in service-learning?* San Francisco, CA: Jossey-Bass.

Holland, B. (1997, Fall). Analyzing institutional commitment to service: A model of key organizational factors. *Michigan Journal of Community Service-Learning, 4,* 30–41.

Holland, B. (1999). Factors and strategies that influence faculty involvement in public service. *Journal of Public Service and Outreach, 4*(1), 37–43.

Holland, B. A. (2002). Private and public institutional views of civic engagement and the urban mission. *Metropolitan Universities: An International Forum, 13*(1), 11–21.

Maurasse, D. J. (2001). *Beyond the campus: How colleges and universities form partnerships with their communities.* New York, NY: Routledge.

Sirianni, C., & Friedland, L. (2001). *Civic innovation in America: Community empowerment, public policy, and the movement for civic renewal.* Berkeley, CA: University of California Press.

Walker, T. (2000). The service/politics split: Rethinking service to teach political engagement. *PS: Political Science and Politics, 33*(3), 647–649.

Zimpher, N. L., Percy, S. L., & Brukardt, M. J. (2002). *A time for boldness: A story of institutional change.* Bolton, MA: Anker.

Zlotkowski, E. (Ed.). (1998). *Successful service-learning programs: New models of excellence in higher education.* Bolton: Anker.

Zlotkowski, E. (2001). Mapping new terrain: Service-learning across the disciplines. *Change, 33*(1), 25–33.

7 The Grassroots Approach to Curriculum Reform: The Cultures and Communities Program

Gregory Jay and Sandra E. Jones

Can community engagement really become part of the core curriculum at a large research university in the 21st century? And how should such engagement be conducted given the university's corresponding commitments to diversity and multicultural education? These questions increasingly arise on campuses across the nation as institutions undertake two difficult, related tasks: revising their "general education" or "core" undergraduate requirements to be more diverse and repositioning their programs to more broadly and effectively partner with their communities. Since taking on either one of these challenges has provided more than enough frustration for many campuses, why would an institution tackle both at the same time in a single coordinated effort?

At the University of Wisconsin–Milwaukee (UWM), we came to see these twin concerns as deeply intertwined and were convinced that neither could be adequately addressed separately. Community engagement undertaken as peripheral add-ons to the core curriculum would never have broad impact on the undergraduate student body; core curriculum revisions that failed to engage students in real-world activities that enhance learning through diversity would likewise accomplish little. If a campus is serious about diversity and community engagement, it needs to commit itself structurally to mainstreaming these principles in the everyday practice of its primary task—the education of undergraduate students. The campus's core requirements present a terrific place to begin.

In October 2002, the provost at UWM gave final approval to launch just such a curriculum option. Designed over a three-year period by the new Cultures and Communities (CC) Program Office, this plan allows students to organize their general education distribution requirements in a meaningful way, complete at least one service-learning experience, and earn a certificate upon graduation that documents their training in cross-cultural understanding and community engagement. (In the University of Wisconsin System, a *certificate* is distinguished from a major or minor by its interdisciplinary concentration of related courses from various departments.) Beginning in 2003, enrollment in the certificate program began and by December 2004 hundreds were involved in CC-affiliated classes and more than 150 students had signed up to complete the entire program. Though it is too early for predictions, we believe it safe to surmise that CC will become the largest undergraduate certificate program at UWM and a major force in altering the direction of the undergraduate general education experience. While every campus faces unique obstacles and local challenges, the CC experience offers lessons many will find useful in undertaking a revision of their core curriculum with an eye to increasing student engagement and diversity.

An Action Plan for Culture and Education

How did it all start? In 1998 the then-new-chancellor, Nancy Zimpher, asked more than 100 administrators, faculty, staff, students, and community representatives to meet regularly in order to come up with some "big ideas" for moving the campus in new directions. Eventually, the results became unified under the banner of The Milwaukee Idea, with a promise of supporting funds and the mentorship of a new chancellor's deputy, Stephen Percy. One of the working groups, "Culture and Education," debated at length how we might infuse our commitments to diversity and multiculturalism, community engagement, critical thinking, and recruitment and retention into the campus's new plans. Participants in the working group included more than 20 faculty from the Schools of the Arts, Education, and Social Work and the Colleges of Health Sciences and Letters and Science; 10 or so academic staff from Enrollment Services, the student union, and the library; and community representatives such as Deborah Blanks, executive director of Milwaukee's Social Development Commission, and Anne Kingsbury, director of the Woodland Pattern Book Center. Also represented were the university's Institute for Service-Learning, the UWM Roberto Hernandez Center for U.S. Latino Studies, and the Vice Chancellor's Office for Student Affairs. These participants became an "Action Team" led by two conveners, Gregory Jay, professor of English, and Marcia Parsons, professor of dance. Faculty and staff of color were well represented and expressed their frustration at lack of progress on diversity issues in the past and their excitement at the prospect that a coalition of campus and community participants might at last forge an alliance with real prospects for success (and funding!).

The Cultures and Communities Action Plan

From the fall of 1998 into the following spring the team talked, argued, and planned, surprised at the momentum that seemed to build. All of us were astonished when a meeting called for an afternoon in August (a time when most academics have gone AWOL) drew a standing-room-only crowd exceeding 40 people. Most of these had a hand in writing the final Action Plan submitted that fall, which articulated the team's educational vision and provided a draft outline for the certificate. The plan recommended establishment of the Cultures and Communities Program Office, which UWM chartered in January of 2000 with an initial staff including a half-time faculty director, a full-time academic staff assistant director, and a full-time clerical office manager.[1]

The preamble to the Action Plan read, in part:

> Citizens of the 21st century will live amidst diversity—at school, at work, and at play, from the arenas of art and science to religion, sexuality, and politics. Everyday life will be increasingly a multicultural experience for everyone. Cross-cultural understanding will not be a luxury, or only a survival skill, but a key to human relations, economic prosperity, creative expression, and personal growth.

> For the student of the 21st century, cross-cultural literacy will be an essential aspect of learning, no matter the field or profession.... Just as the original Liberal Arts grew out of the expanding humanistic vision of the Renaissance, so

a renewed Liberal Arts for the 21st century will emerge from a multicultural, global vision that appreciates the true diversity of humankind and recognizes the challenge of living with differences. . . . Situated in one of the most racially and ethnically diverse American cities, UWM is well positioned to meet the challenge of educating citizens for the coming century. Despite good intentions, however, UWM has yet to fulfill its potential in regards to the communities of the greater metropolitan area, especially those with high proportions of Latino, Asian American, American Indian, and African American citizens, or communities that are predominantly working class.

Wisconsin's cultures and communities are rich with resources that can be brought into our classrooms. At the same time, our classrooms need to get out into our communities so that students better understand the world they are studying. As Milwaukee becomes a hub of international commerce, scientific inquiry and socio-cultural exchange, students will need to learn about communities around the globe, as well as around the city and state, and to develop global perspectives in their chosen fields of study. UWM must be an engaged university, combining its research and scholarship with an innovative program of undergraduate education serving students from every background. It must be a place where every student feels welcome, and where students from vastly different backgrounds talk, laugh, argue, analyze, experiment and learn together.

The series of conversations, meetings, and workshops that produced the Action Plan were characterized by a grassroots approach to program building. The Action Team looked at how comparable institutions were responding to the same issues, but realized that the problem of curriculum reform is always stubbornly local. While one can find great ideas at other institutions, developing the right formula for your home campus depends on a grassroots process of soliciting ideas, listening to stakeholders, mapping the terrain, piloting experiments, codifying best practices, and only then institutionalizing what works.

Our grassroots philosophy meant that we were not going to get three people together to draw up a master plan on a cocktail napkin to impose on our colleagues. Instead, the Cultures and Communities initiative set up processes—later on including faculty fellowships and mini-grants—that would allow faculty, staff, students, and community members to bring their best ideas to the CC office. The office, in turn, responded by trying to empower as many of these ideas as it could and then evaluate the results. Only when we had a sense of what people actually wanted to do, and what they were achieving, would we be ready to piece these together into a curricular design ready for formal university consideration.

Engagement, Diversity, and General Education

Why did the Action Team focus on the long-term goal of creating a general education certificate program? As a large comprehensive research university, UWM already had dozens of fine majors, minors, and upper-division degrees and certificates. And there were more than 100 community engagement projects, ranging from one-time collaborations to large, multi-year commitments. Yet people in the community thought of the university as distant and inaccessible, and students did not see any connection between their degree programs and the campus's general education requirements. Clearly the many parts of our institution were not linking up well with one another, nor were they articulating themselves with, or to, the community. We needed to network what we were already doing to give it more transparency and focused direction, and we needed to add central components to achieve coherence as we expanded our efforts. Plus, we needed to focus on who our students were. The vast majority are not from the city of Milwaukee, yet move here and expect to work and flourish in a diverse urban setting. UWM needed a first-year curriculum that addressed this demographic reality and the sociocultural contradictions it contained.

What would be our vehicle? We needed not only an instrument for change, but one that would lead to institutionalization, meaning real stability and real resources. Too many smart college initiatives have been consigned to the dustbin of history, tossed aside after a few bright years of success because they did not have the money, support, or administrative means to endure. The Milwaukee Idea office would fund our start-up efforts; our long-term success, however, would depend on inventing programs that could be woven deeply into the fabric of the university.

Analyzing the university's strengths and weaknesses, we quickly turned our focus to the undergraduate general education distribution requirements. Like most state universities, the University of Wisconsin System had abandoned any notion of a real core curriculum and instead asked students simply to take a sprinkling of self-selected classes in the arts, humanities, and social and natural sciences (including one labeled "cultural diversity.") Targeting the general education requirements had the advantage of affecting all students and involving most of the campus's schools and colleges.

Useful National Models

In the national context, much debate was underway about the fate of "liberal education" in the 21st century, including how to refashion that traditional mission to accommodate concerns about diversity and engagement. Researchers were consolidating data that correlated diversity education and civic participation with numerous positive outcomes:

> There is . . . a significant body of literature which suggests that serious engagement of diversity in the curriculum, along with linking classroom and out-of-class opportunities, positively affect students' attitudes and awareness about diversity, as well as their commitment to education, and their involvement. The research also shows connections between taking such courses and increased satisfaction with college. (Smith & Associates, 1997, p. 36)

That national context would provide both impetus and resources for our effort, as we soon sensed when looking at the web sites for the Association of American Colleges and Universities and the American Council on Education (and others), whose annual conferences proved to be of essential help during our formative years of exploring models and best practices.[2] Across the nation, parents, legislators, and students were clamoring for more accountability in higher education, and more substantive engagement by the "ivory tower" with the communities providing its funding and social setting.

Among the campuses the Action Team initially studied, we found the Arts of Citizenship program at the University of Michigan to be a superb model and inspiration. Arts of Citizenship develops collaborative projects between the university and diverse neighborhood groups and community organizations, helping to create art installations, K–12 curricula, radio broadcasts, youth theater performances, and dozens of other collaborative activities. What struck us about their work was the reciprocity characteristic of its relationships with its partners, the rigorous oversight of projects by Arts of Citizenship staff, the truly interdisciplinary involvement of faculty, and the commitment to engaging students in service to a diverse metropolitan area. Though our own goal of creating a certificate program was not mirrored in Arts of Citizenship's agenda, its way of creating partnerships struck us as exemplary.

Another impressive model is the University Studies core curriculum at Portland State University, which has earned much national praise for its ambitious structure of sequenced courses that take students from their freshman to senior years. We learned a great deal from the sheer scope of their vision, their creativity in course design, and their focus on student-learning outcomes. Portland State University also makes community service a hallmark of its general education strategy and has a number of successful community engagement initiatives serving its metropolitan area. For a few months one summer we actually dreamed of replicating some of the cohort learning and sequencing of classes in the Portland model, but eventually abandoned that effort, because we could not make it work logistically at our particular institution.

In terms of diversity and the curriculum, we also saw the Core program at Occidental College as a wonderful example of an institution committed to a vision of rigorous student learning infused with the values of pluralism. Occidental College's (2005) mission statement makes its aims clear: "The distinctive interdisciplinary and multicultural focus of the College's academic program seeks to foster both the fulfillment of individual aspirations and a deeply rooted commitment to the public good." Such a concise and bold articulation of progressive values made Occidental's program one to emulate. Some progressive campuses are working to highlight diversity issues early in the college program. Brown University, for example, conducts mandatory lectures and seminars on understanding and respecting difference as part of its freshman orientation, and promotes dialogue across differences during its freshman year program, "Building Understanding Across Differences" (Curtis, 2002).

But useful as these models might be, the Cultures and Communities program would need to keep its eye stubbornly on the issues raised by the particular setting and contradictions of UWM. Nestled in a beautiful residential neighborhood near Lake Michigan, this "urban research university" is worlds away from the lives of the people living just a mile or two away in

Milwaukee's inner city, the majority of whom are no longer of European ancestry. The Great Migration of the early 20th century brought a large and vibrant African American community to the city, where its members worked in many of Milwaukee's then-bustling factories. Since the relaxation of immigration quotas in the 1960s, Milwaukee has become home to a new influx of immigrants from Mexico, Latin America, and Asia, including a substantial Hmong community. According to the *Milwaukee Journal Sentinel*, "the number of Latinos in Wisconsin more than doubled from 1990 to 2000 and has grown by at least 8% since then. A similar rate of growth is taking place in Milwaukee County, where the Latino population has jumped from nearly 45,000 in 1990 to more than 89,000 in 2002. Similarly, in Milwaukee County, the number of Asians jumped by 76% from 1990 to 2002" (Pabst, 2004).

The issue of diversity presents a special challenge to UWM because of the historic mismatch between its student population and the population of the surrounding city and county. According to the 2000 census, 54% of the city of Milwaukee residents were listed as minorities, 37% of whom were black (Borsuk & Sykes, 2001); a majority of Milwaukee Public School students are students of color (MPS, 2003). Yet according to the UWM Fact Book for 2002–2003, university minority enrollments were only 8% African American, 2% Asian, 1% Native American, and 4% Hispanic. These data indicate that UWM needs both to increase its nonwhite enrollment through increased community engagement and, at the same time, provide its predominantly white student body with the skills for cross-cultural understanding that they will need to succeed as productive future citizens of the metropolitan area. Students of color also need support for developing their leadership skills as they work on behalf of their communities. And students from all backgrounds need more experience working together in the common cause of fulfilling our nation's democratic promise.

Mainstreaming Diversity in the Core Curriculum: The Cultures and Communities Alternative

Like most American universities and colleges, UWM has a token "diversity" requirement in its core curriculum: Students must take one three-credit course that focuses on the experiences, cultural traditions, and worldviews of African Americans, Native Americans, Hispanic/Latino Americans, and/or Asian Americans (the four "targeted underrepresented" groups according to University of Wisconsin System diversity guidelines). Since most students pursuing a bachelor's degree earn a minimum of 120 credits in approximately 40 different classes, this one-class requirement represents the most minimal of gestures towards multiculturalism and diversity. Currently there is no campus-wide requirement for community engagement or service-learning.

Moving Beyond "Tokenism" to "Critical Multiculturalism"

While some campuses across the country have begun to increase their requirements to two or even three classes (often adding an international component), this pattern of tokenism remains the national norm. According to the Association of American Colleges and Universities' (2000) survey of 543 higher education institutions, 54% of responding institutions have some kind of diversity requirement. Of these positive respondents, 58% require students to take one "diversity" course and 42% require two or more.

The Cultures and Communities general education option aims to address this situation in two related ways. First, it creates a different distribution of course rubrics, within which students may find multiple classes carrying the "cultural diversity" (CD) accreditation. This means effectively that students who complete the certificate are more likely to take three, four, or even five classes with the CD designation. And even classes without the designation are more likely to address issues of multiculturalism and diversity because of the way courses are chosen for the program and how faculty are involved in designing them. Second, the service-learning component of the certificate ensures that students experience the pluralism that *is* Milwaukee. Academic learning about diversity in the classroom gets tested, expanded, and reflected upon through real-world experiences in the community.

Officially, the UWM requirement stipulates one class covering "Minority Cultural Diversity in America," focused on understanding the perspective, traditions, and life ways of one or more of the underrepresented groups. The requirement does not address "diversity" in the larger sense often used today, encompassing differences in sexuality, gender, and class. Nor does it address structures of racism, discrimination, bigotry, bias, and institutional or structural oppression. This kind of diversity education has the potential to degenerate into the cafeteria approach of "celebratory multiculturalism," or a superficial tourism of exoticized "others."

The Cultures and Communities initiatives instead embraced "critical multiculturalism," which includes self-reflective critiques of multiculturalist ideologies and agendas (May, 1999). In implementing the certificate, faculty discussions have often centered on debates over the issue of what kind of multiculturalism we are practicing and how to extend the definition of "diversity" without losing the virtue of the original requirement. Some consensus emerged that our courses should analyze racial and ethnic formation *processes* instead of treating groups as objectified or reified entities. In looking at how race and ethnicity emerge historically and socially, we inevitably had to include the kinds of "other differences" we knew needed inclusion if our studies are to be at all complex. This entailed breaking with the habit of positioning white students as "not raced," and discarding pedagogical norms in which race is only discussed when people of color are the subject. Likewise it led to more systematic articulations of sexism, homophobia, and class exploitation within the context of ethnic and racial formation. In the classroom this approach invites, indeed challenges, every student to reflect critically on his or her ethno-racial formation and cultural identity.

Segregation is still the norm for Wisconsin students, no matter their skin color. Most of UWM's enrollment continues to come from outside the Milwaukee city limits. Our students arrive from suburbs and small towns where they have had little experience of the racially and culturally diverse landscape they find in Milwaukee and at UWM. We regularly hear comments such as, "I never knew a person of color before," and, "There were only two or three minorities at my high school."

Students from Milwaukee and students of color continue to feel that the institution and its curriculum do not adequately address their experiences. They have had to learn much about the dominant culture in order to survive, though people from the dominant culture do not have to know much about them. Moreover, African American students know little about the experiences of Jews or Latinos, and vice versa; the same could be said for any number of combinations. New students at most urban research universities in the United States arrive with a roughly similar load of baggage. Unless faculty and administration recognize how this baggage adversely affects student learning (and recruitment and retention), success in teaching will be limited at best. Serving these quite distinct student groups together requires a careful plan of curricular and cocurricular opportunities that build bridges of understanding rather than reinforce traditional divisions.

Linking Diversity and Community Engagement

Scholars have argued that service-learning and community engagement must be integrated with multicultural education and undertaken with a critical awareness of how social justice issues remain caught up in legacies of racial, ethnic, class, and gender discrimination. Nieto (2000) observes,

> Community service conjures up images of doing good deeds in impoverished, disadvantaged (primarily black and brown) communities by those (mostly white people) who are wealthier and more privileged. The parenthetical terms are seldom expressly mentioned in community service because they make some professors and students uncomfortable, expressing the inequalities around them too explicitly. . . . Those who do community service at colleges and universities. . . . are generally young people who have more advantages than those they are serving. This being the case, concerns about racism and other biases, injustice, oppression and unearned privilege should figure prominently in discussions of community service. (p. ix–x)

By challenging students to question their "assumptions about society and about the people with whom they interact in their community service experiences . . . [we can help them] to move beyond their stereotypical notions of difference" (Nieto, 2000, p. x) as biological, fixed, or innate and towards an historical and structural analysis of how social inequalities originate. In turn this shift of emphasis moves community service "from an individual feel-good experience to a social responsibility," (p. xi) since inequalities are now understood as the result of systemic arrangements that we can change rather than originating in the "natural" characteristics of individuals or social groups or races.[3]

Confronting the Economics

In order to mainstream a community engagement curriculum infused with a critical approach to multiculturalism, we had to introduce new courses and reengineer current offerings. Here we had to confront the politics and financial realities of general education at the large public university. UWM's distribution requirements scheme drives substantial numbers of students into entry-level classes in many departments, often taught in large lecture courses or by inexpensive adjuncts and teaching assistants. These classes bring essential revenues to departments and collegiate divisions that are increasingly dependent on enrollment figures for their budgets; the dollars brought in through these lecture courses then underwrite smaller, faculty-taught classes at the upper division and the graduate level.

The economics of this system inevitably degrades the quality of course offerings in the freshman and sophomore years, and thus in the classes making up the bulk of general education offerings. Given this budgetary structure, the Cultures and Communities team quickly decided against creating a new school, college, or division of undergraduate study that would compete with current departments for enrollment dollars. It was highly unlikely that deans or department heads would approve such a proposal, which might threaten their revenue stream directly. Nor could such a separatist approach achieve our goal of mainstreaming critical multiculturalism and community engagement, since it arguably would have little or no impact on the bulk of current course offerings or faculty.

Instead, we would have to build an alternative program by using some of the courses already offered by the departments themselves, and by inducing faculty to create in their departments new classes that would be in line with our student learning goals and institutional mission. After analyzing the undergraduate catalogue and schedule of classes, we easily determined that there were dozens of general education courses already on the books that might be networked together in a new arrangement, though these would for the most part not include some of the big, moneymaker introductory lecture courses. Since research and anecdotal evidence suggests that such lecture courses often leave new undergraduates feeling disconnected and have high rates of failure for students from underrepresented target groups, it made sense to put our energies into classes with 35 students or less, where discussion and personal faculty-student relationships were more likely to occur. No doubt there would be some financial pressure when we lobbied to have a faculty member teach a smaller course, but we gambled that, at least initially, the impact would be relatively slight, and certainly less costly than a "Freshman Seminar" program (which the university had already begun some years before but found increasingly difficult to fund).

The Cultures and Communities Certificate

Beginning in spring 2000, the Cultures and Communities Program Office began meetings with department chairs and associate deans to discuss an outline of the certificate and which classes from their units might fit. Faculty became involved through annual fellowships that provided released time for research and course development, as well as for interdisciplinary workshop sessions where personal and intellectual alliances across divisional boundaries were initiated. At the same time, our community-university mini-grant program began to fund community engagement partnerships among faculty, students, and community organizations, bridging the gap between the campus and the city and helping to identify best practices for collaboration. In these startup years, the fellowship and grant activities assisted in curriculum development, intellectual exchange, and the enlargement of the roster of community partners. CC also worked more and more with UWM's Institute for Service Learning, which had already created numerous student learning opportunities in sites around the city (this partnership eventually led to the formal incorporation of the Institute for Service Learning into the CC program in Fall 2003).

The CC staff continued to evaluate what was working and what was not, who the committed allies were, and what processes we needed to institutionalize. More than 30 faculty worked with these programs in our first three years, and more than 20 mini-grants solidified our community engagement efforts. By the spring of 2002 we were ready to take a plan for the certificate to UWM's curriculum committee, for by then we had built an extensive network of allies and a track record of success. Still it took two long hearings and some negotiation to win approval, for we were asking to create a unique certificate, limited only to general education classes and without a fixed list of classes. Candor requires emphasizing that we would not have succeeded without support and guidance from the highest levels of campus administration, who championed our work through their public speeches to the faculty and in the everyday commerce of administrative meetings. The chancellor effectively protected our experiment, though of course we were held to high standards when it came to judging the results.

For each of the CC certificate's four general rubrics, we sought to affiliate courses that already carried GER accreditation. We produced a set of "Program Guidelines" written collectively by CC faculty and articulating principles for approaching curriculum priorities, diversity, pedagogy, and community engagement (see http://www.cc.uwm.edu/guidelines.htm).

University of Wisconsin–Milwaukee's Cultures and Communities Certificate Required Areas of Study

Cultures and Communities Core Course (3 credits). "Multicultural America." Currently offered as English 150 or History 150 (satisfies Humanities and Cultural Diversity General Education Requirements [GER]) or Anthropology 150 or Sociology 150 (satisfies Social Sciences and Cultural Diversity GERs).

Cultures and Communities of the United States (at least 3 credits). Issues and methods in the comparative study of cultures and communities of the U.S. May be fulfilled by appropriate accredited GER or Cultural Diversity courses in any discipline, school, or college.

Global Perspectives on Culture and Community (at least 3 credits). Issues and methods in the comparative study of cultures and communities outside North America. May be fulfilled by appropriate accredited GER courses in any discipline, school, or college.

Art, Culture, and Community (at least 3 credits). May be fulfilled by courses that relate the theory and production of art (dance, music, visual arts, film, and theater) to cultural and community contexts. Restricted to courses in the Peck School of the Arts, except through special petition.

Science, Culture, and Society (at least 3 credits). Includes courses that examine how scientific knowledge can be understood in relation to issues in culture and society. May be fulfilled by enrollment in classes with a natural sciences or social sciences accreditation.

Community Engagement and Service-Learning: Within their course distribution, students will take at least one class with a service-learning or community engagement component.

The CC staff use these guidelines to evaluate courses and help faculty who are planning new classes. Department chairs were given these guidelines and asked to nominate appropriate classes for affiliation; faculty were then asked to provide syllabi for assessment. Each semester certificate classes are marked with a "CC" in the schedule of classes, where they also appear as a separate list for easy reference. Students can log on to the certificate web site to see a list of the classes that fulfill each area of the CC distribution areas.

The successful implementation of the certificate depended on the hiring of a full-time student services coordinator. This coordinator advises CC students, markets the program to classes and faculty, and works as a liaison with other advisors and with student organizations. The CC director, assistant director, Institute for Service-Learning (ISL) director, and student services coordinator meet weekly in staff sessions to review all program activities, including course developments and offerings, administrative issues, and event planning.

Designing a Core Course: "Multicultural America"

To give our curriculum a foundation, the certificate needed a core course. Our approach to designing the core was influenced by the American Cultures Program at the University of California–Berkeley, where every student must take at least one American Cultures–accredited class. One of the program's architects, historian Ronald Takaki, coincidentally came to UWM as a visiting lecturer during this time and made a persuasive case for the controversial comparative requirement of University of California–Berkeley courses. For a department's class to qualify for American Cultures, it must address theoretical or analytical issues relevant to understanding race, culture, and ethnicity in American society and *take substantial account of at least three groups* drawn from the following: African Americans, indigenous peoples of the United States, Asian Americans, Chicano/Latino Americans, and European Americans. It must also be *integrative and comparative* in that students study each group in the larger context of American society, history, or culture.

University of California–Berkeley's approach embodies what can be described as today's "progression in intellectual curricular design," from "first, the study of one's particular inherited and self-chosen communities," to "second, an examination of the dynamic interaction among several groups" (McTighe Musil, 1997, p. xii). In a study of recent innovations in diversity requirements, Humphreys (1997) likewise observes that "while frequently beginning from the perspective of a group identity category, courses in these programs tend to teach about identity groups neither in isolation nor ahistorically. Instead, they focus on interconnections and comparisons and on the systematic and structural workings of prejudice and discrimination" (p. 5).

The course at Berkeley was opposed by some who saw its comparative mandate as a threat to enrollments in departments or units focused on only one of the specified groups. These groups (except for the Europeans), after all, had fought for decades to gain representation in the curriculum and thus feared they might again be marginalized. But CC imagined that our own core course could be positioned as a kind of gateway to the more specialized classes in such departments; moreover, since those departments would be invited to list their classes in our certificate program, it seemed unlikely they would find the core course threatening.

Creating a Pilot Core Course

Using the Berkeley model as a starting point, Cultures and Communities' Sandra Jones and Gregory Jay used an English department course, "Introduction to Ethnic and Minority Literatures," as a vehicle for piloting the new core offering. Initial grant funds to assist course development came from our participation in the UWM School of Education's federal Title II project to improve the preparation of future urban teachers. The Title II program mandates revision and improvement of liberal arts training for future urban teachers, outside the course work done within the School of Education. The development of the CC certificate took place with the intention of creating a general education experience that would provide these future teachers, in particular, with knowledge of the communities they would serve when they received their degrees.

Fortunately, our team for designing and piloting the core course included two Milwaukee Public School teachers, Darrell Terrell and Thomas Brown, who worked full time for two years at Cultures and Communities as part of UWM's Teachers in Residence Program. Elsewhere we have written of how the team put the course together and what goals we set for our students and ourselves (Brown, Jay, & Terrell, 2002). Terrell and Brown were invaluable colleagues, in part because their collaboration meant that community engagement constituted the *process* as well as the *outcome* of the course project. By this, we mean that we, as university educators, did not presume in advance to design an engagement component that we would then impose on the community. Rather we began by enlisting community partners in the process of curriculum development itself. We aimed to avoid the common "missionary position" adopted by many institutions of higher education when they set out to engage their communities: The missionary attitude puts the college or university in the position of dictating both the nature of the problem to be solved and the best methods for addressing it. The university uses the community as a laboratory or guinea pig just long enough to get results, then leaves. The core course's development also followed the grassroots principles that had informed CC's philosophy from the start.

In terms of the syllabus for the English department version of the core course, we quickly settled on a structure that combined historical and literary study with analyses of popular culture. To provide the history, we chose Takaki's (1993) *A Different Mirror: A History of Multicultural America*, which begins with Shakespeare's Caliban and the "racialization of savagery" (p. 24) during the Colonial period and then proceeds through chapters focused on the experiences of specific groups—primarily those of African, Mexican, Chinese, Japanese, Irish, Jewish, and Native ancestry. Takaki's schema proceeds chronologically from the 17th to the late 20th centuries, but does so in chapters that focus on the struggles of these groups for identity, land, wealth, and power. While each group gets individual treatment, the analyses are also comparative and integrative, giving students critical thinking tools for connecting the experiences of various groups through such common themes as labor, family, citizenship, and assimilation. The syllabus can follow this schema week by week, aligning short stories and novels with the Takaki chapters to explore the literary work of these groups as a response to their historical experience. For this we have used various literature anthologies, particularly Brown and Ling's (2003) *Imagining America* and Rico and Mano's (2000) *American Mosaic*. From the beginning, student evaluations regularly cited the comparative treatment of multiple ethno-racial groups as among the course's strongest points and expressed the desire for more such classes.

The Service-Learning Component

The first semester, we spread the service-learning placements among a wide network of social service agencies and schools. Though our pilot group of students was mainly from the School of Education, we became dissatisfied with placements that had them doing only youth tutoring or after-school care. These placements put our white students into relationships primarily with younger children of color, over whom they might tend to feel superior or towards whom they might have inappropriate feelings of pity or condescension. In any event, these students would have plenty of opportunity to serve in schools when they did their upper-division placements. In their freshman and sophomore years they needed to learn about Milwaukee communities outside the walls of the schools and to establish relationships with adults from whom they could learn.

A key best practice here was setting up the service-learning placement in a manner that did not always position the community as a "problem" or "deficit," but rather as co-teacher. Working with UWM's Institute for Service Learning, we were able to identify a core list of 10 agencies where students would likely develop skills of crosscultural understanding. These included food pantries, senior centers, and adult tutoring in English as a Second Language programs, places where students could really get to know individuals from many nations. A writing assignment asked students to profile, through conversation and oral history, one of the people they met. This paper encouraged their reflections on diversity and helped position their community partner as a resource for education, not a "problem" to be fixed.

Studying "Whiteness"

Another major change we made as the core course evolved concerned the study of "whiteness." White student attitudes of resistance to antiracist or multicultural education are all too familiar: they think it is not about them; they are being made to feel guilty; racism is something that happened in the past (Jay, 2005). These white students believe that since they are not personally racist, studying multiculturalism has nothing to do with them. Many have been taught that multiculturalism is a "celebration of differences," analogous to a folk fair or food court where you get to taste all the nice things "those people" create. And many believe that America is a place where anyone can make it if they just work hard and play by the rules, and thus people who are poor, illiterate, in jail, or stuck in dead-end jobs got what they deserved.

The first step in a pedagogy of whiteness begins with recognizing "white privilege," for, "you can't deal with a problem if you don't name it" (Johnson, 2001, p. 11).[4] At first, this term surprises our students, for it names a reality that they have been taught not to see. And since many UWM students are working class, they react with skepticism to the notion that they are privileged. Their consciousness of privilege functions mainly along lines of class and wealth, which they rarely racialize. By reading a packet of articles on whiteness studies, including McIntosh's (1997) classic essay, "White Privilege and Male Privilege," white students examine concrete examples of the way they are implicated in racism regardless of whether they themselves are "racist." The privileges and preferences given to whiteness are not dependent on what the individual feels or thinks about race.

Analyzing white privilege can thus be one way to get past white resistance, since it moves the discussion from the personal to the structural, from hazy feelings about guilt to practical, objective recognitions of how society works. For students of color, the McIntosh (1997) essay gives expression to what they see every day, and so validates observations that these students offer and that are sometimes dismissed in other classes. White privilege becomes the first of a number of keywords and concepts—such as cultural identity, oppression, social dominance—that students become competent in using, and that thus create a common language among them, despite the differences in their backgrounds. The whiteness unit also benefits from screening one of Jane Elliott's powerful "blue eyed/brown eyed" workshop videos, which puts critical multiculturalism to work in devastating and disturbing role-playing scenarios that spark much discussion.[5]

This unit on whiteness helps most students write reflectively about their service-learning experience, often because they either suddenly see their own whiteness which had long been invisible to them or they see the whiteness of others in a new light. Crucial to this transformation is building relationships of trust with people in the community: These people become their teachers as well as their friends, and students build bonds of communication with them that establish commonalities as well as differences. Students write analytical reflections on their own cultural identities, conduct family tree investigations, and compose narratives about people that they have met. In presenting these assignments to the class, students regularly express a sense of transformation, of having discovered their place in a social system that had previously been invisible to them, and of having discarded old stereotypes through the intercultural communication made possible by engagement.

Institutionalizing "Multicultural America"

After three years of pilot classes, English 150, "Multicultural America," gained university approval. In the next two years, faculty in other departments joined the effort and soon we had Anthropology 150, History 150, and Sociology 150, each of which accomplishes common ends through specific disciplinary means. Along with Jay and Jones, the faculty and teaching assistants teaching the core classes include a senior white male anthropologist, a Filipino assistant professor of sociology, an associate professor of Native American literature, the university's first African American history professor, and a Korean-born doctoral student in English (Cultures and Communities Program, 2005). We meet together to review syllabi and assignments, share suggestions for readings and videos and, most importantly, to argue and debate key concepts and methods. These interdisciplinary conversations have been among the most rewarding intellectual aspects of the program for many of the instructors involved, have created a close-knit network across departments, and have ensured that students in the certificate program get a truly coherent foundation experience.

Our strategy for institutionalizing the Cultures and Communities core course took a page from the University of California–Berkeley model, in that we spread the opportunity for the course among a number of departments rather than relying on one department for the class or trying to create our own curricular area that would compete for student enrollments with established courses. If we succeeded, then we could also avoid teaching the class in large lecture format, since we could get enough "seats" per semester if we had multiple sections in a number of departments. Our ability to involve more departments depended on having sufficient funds to initially "buy out" faculty instructional time, especially for team teaching. Through our faculty fellowship and mini-grant programs, we assembled a cadre of interested faculty who could then be recruited to propose a core class in their own department. Departments like the arrangement because it adds new classes and student bodies to their rosters, satisfying the professional goals of the faculty and better meeting student needs. Cultures and Communities benefits because the core program allows us to sponsor curricular changes that increase the attention to diversity and expand the opportunities for community engagement. And the university can point to it as a campus-wide effort to improve the freshman-sophomore experience, a long-neglected area at major research universities.

Taking the Class Into the Community

During the two years we worked on the core course, Associate Professor of Anthropology Cheryl Ajirotutu was pioneering another new class with potential to be a model for other faculty. This course is deeply embedded in community engagement with an African American neighborhood just a few miles from campus. Ajiortutu had become involved with Cultures and Communities through one of our mini-grants. We hoped that the mini-grants would draw faculty into community engagement pedagogy by providing them with released time for research, course development, and community outreach. We made six to eight Faculty Fellowship awards annually, and from these continued our work with a number of professors who received the title Senior Faculty Associate, as well as an enduring affiliation with CC and funds set aside to support their activities. Often individual departments do not have the extra dollars to help faculty with such activities, so dedicating part of our budget in this manner earned us the goodwill of department chairs and the ongoing contribution of dedicated professors like Ajirotutu.

Parallel to the Faculty Fellowship program is our Community-University Partnership Mini-Grant program which provides small seed funds (typically $1,500–$3,000) to enable collaborations between university faculty or staff and their community partners. One of the first of these went to a proposal linking Ajirotutu's freshman seminar in "Oral Traditions" with the Walnut Way community, centered in the most historic of Milwaukee's African American neighborhoods. The Walnut Way Conservation Corporation had been established by residents to revitalize their community through economic, social, and educational activities. In a series of meetings with the Walnut Way board and residents, Ajirotutu designed a course in which students conduct oral histories of the residents, documenting the life of the neighborhood and contributing to the analytic history of race relations and urban change in Milwaukee.

In the first weeks of the semester, Ajirotutu immerses her students in the study of anthropological approaches to oral history and instruction in use of audio and video equipment. She complements this disciplinary examination of best practices with screening parts of *The Autobiography of Miss Jane Pittman* (Rosenberg, Christiansen, & Korty, 1974), which depicts an interviewer taking down the tale of an elderly black woman whose life encapsulates much of African American history from slavery to the present. Students also attend orientation events in the neighborhood, such as volunteering to plant new vegetable and flower gardens in vacant lots. In collaboration with the Walnut Way advisory board, a series of appointments for oral interviews is set up. Students, accompanied by an instructional assistant, travel to the homes of the residents, where they are often greeted with food as well as talk. Over the next few weeks, they write and revise their oral histories, thus gaining valuable skills in civic awareness, intercultural communication, composition, and critical thinking essential to general education.

At the end of each semester, the course holds two public forums, one on campus and one in the community, at which students read their narratives to an audience, which includes most of their subjects, to whom they then present a copy of their work. These are moving ceremonies that cement the reciprocal collaboration of the community and the university and illustrate how our community partners function as teachers and sources of knowledge. Students regularly testify to how their community engagement and the personal relationships they create transform and deepen their academic knowledge. Since they are freshmen, many also find that this experience is vital to their evaluation of possible career choices and plans of study, with a number expressing increased interest in civic service. In 2004, the forums were videotaped and broadcast locally on the UWM access channel, thus disseminating the university's work to the community.

Much more could be written about CC courses that connect with Milwaukee's neighborhoods and civic institutions. A revised introduction to the visual arts course now has a multicultural emphasis and takes students into the streets to create installation pieces about changing cultural identities in our city. One of the History 150 sections concentrates on "Multicultural Milwaukee" and is developing service-learning sites at places such as the Black Historical Society. Engagement with Milwaukee's fast-growing Hmong community is a feature of "American Life Stories," a freshman seminar that is enriched by CC-sponsored public events, such as a reading by three Hmong creative writers and a public forum on current challenges in the Hmong cultural adjustment to life in the United States. The geography department, led by Assistant Professor Nik Heynen, is pioneering a new "Introduction to Environmental Geography" that has service-learning students out in the city and surrounding areas learning first-hand about how science and sociocultural factors interact in environmental policy issues.

Our experiences with these courses tend to confirm the "Principal Findings" of the Higher Education Research Institute's report on *How Service Learning Affects Students* (Astin, Vogelgesang, Ikeda, & Yee, 2000), based on data from more than 22,000 undergraduates studied in the late 1990s. The University of California–Los Angeles data show that academically-based service participation: 1) has positive effects on outcome measures such as GPA, writing skills, and critical thinking; 2) deepens commitment to activism and promoting racial understanding; 3) increases leadership skills; 4) heightens a sense of civic responsibility and awareness of one's personal values; and 5) influences choice of a service career or plans to participate in service after college. The survey also confirmed that performing service as part of a course, rather than as a volunteer, adds significantly to the benefits of the experience, depending on the pedagogy of the course. Classes in which discussion, written reflection, and personal faculty support were characteristic of the pedagogy resulted in greater benefits: "Both the quantitative and qualitative results suggest that providing students with an opportunity to *process* the service experience with each other is a powerful component of both community service and service learning" (Astin et al., p. 2).

Student and Faculty Responses

How are students responding to the certificate program option for general education? Though it is too early to draw conclusions, some anecdotal evidence is worth offering. In meetings with our student services coordinator, who advises certificate students, a repeated theme emerged. Students at the junior or even senior level were coming in to sign up for the certificate because they had already completed many of the classes required. They explained that previously there had been no way for them to "capture" this interdisciplinary pattern of course work on their transcript or resume, or to document their academic service work and experience with cultural diversity. These "early adopters" were high achievers with GPAs averaging 3.5 and above who saw the certificate as a valuable asset in putting together their tool kit for future success. Many had also done volunteer, internship, or service placements numerous times, and had been looking for a way to connect these experiences to their academic program.

As we begin to reach out to the freshmen and sophomores, the target group in our original plan, we face a number of challenges typical of large universities, especially those situated in metropolitan areas. A high proportion of our students work 20 hours or more per week, which means they are already "engaged with the community," though not usually in positions requiring civic service. Initially these students may find the logistics of engagement onerous, since they barely have time to get to campus, find parking, run to class, and then get back home to children and jobs. This emphasizes the necessity of constructing academic service-learning and engagement opportunities with substantial attention to their relevance to the individual learning outcomes of the syllabus and the course. Students will quickly become turned off by assignments where they are doing menial tasks which, though helpful to the agency, do not advance the student's understanding of the topic they are studying in anthropology or accounting, English or dance (the "Why am I wasting my time making copies?" phenomenon). In the absence of regular, directed, and reviewed critical reflection writings, engagement activities may drift further and further from relevance to the course and fail to contribute meaningfully to what the student should be learning. Carefully crafted activities, however, do tend to enhance the student's sense of connection to the class and the university, which is crucial to student retention during the first two years.

To facilitate this kind of relevant student engagement work in Cultures and Communities courses, we turned to UWM's Institute for Service Learning (ISL), which had been founded just a year before we began piloting our classes. ISL has a mandate to assist with courses at every level, not just in the general education or liberal arts areas. Many of the best engagement activities, in fact, can be found in the professional schools, such as Health Sciences and Nursing. Nonetheless, as ISL struggled to grow the number of classes and faculty doing engagement, it began to work more closely with Cultures and Communities, especially since we had built service-learning into the certificate program. The more we collaborated, the more we saw the commonalities in our missions and the benefit that might accrue by combining forces.

Thus, in 2003 we proposed an administrative merger of the programs, so that they would operate as parallel, linked initiatives reporting to the same director and dean with flexibility about how to use their budgets to meet joint needs. Though the move does not mean a change in the broader scope of ISL, it does promise to give service-learning a boost by tying it closely to curriculum innovation in the certificate program. We believe that many of the general education classes now affiliating with CC will be good candidates for service-learning as well. Our new administrative union will help bring this opportunity to the attention of faculty more easily and fund pilot projects more efficiently. Since UWM's ISL office was an early partner in establishing Wisconsin's statewide chapter of Campus Compact, CC now is becoming involved with Campus Compact initiatives we might have missed before. The merger also establishes a stronger institutional base for CC and ISL, making them less likely to suffer during future budget crises (which are a regular feature of public education). While this arrangement may not work for every campus, it could be a useful model for those institutions hoping to infuse community engagement into their core curriculum. Our ISL comes equipped with more than 70 community agencies ready for placements, and its staff is highly knowledgeable about these opportunities and able to advise faculty on which might best suit their syllabi. With a service-learning office in place to undertake most of these logistical jobs, the faculty member can concentrate on syllabus design and academic learning goals. Such an arrangement makes it far easier to persuade faculty to give service-learning a try, since it does not make an unreasonable demand on their time.

Time is always an issue when infusing community engagement into the syllabus of a given course. Faculty have usually worked out a careful, week-by-week plan that they already feel gives students only a glimpse into the complexity of the subject matter. Giving up some of that time for service-learning and its requisite reflection assignments is not something faculty relish. Hence, many resist service-learning because they "can't make time for it." We have found a few ways to address this stubborn issue. One solution is simply to persuade faculty that replacing one reading or paper assignment or exam with the service-learning component will achieve their learning goals at least as well, if not better. This usually works only after some extensive review of the syllabus and creative discussion about the overall objectives of the course. It also helps if there are service-learning agency placements already established and of demonstrated quality.

A second solution is to use flexibility in the scheduling of the class and to use online discussion forums and writing assignments. In fall of 2003, for example, we taught the English department version of the core online once a week, from 4:30–7:10 p.m. Though nominally this required the same amount of seat time, in reality it saved time for students in the form of transportation and parking. This setup left more time and flexible hours for completing the service-learning minimum of 15 hours onsite during the semester. Use of Internet courseware also makes reflection activities easier through use of discussion forums accessible 24 hours a day, 7 days a week.

A third solution is the creation of a one-credit service-learning "add-on" for faculty to use at their discretion. If an instructor wishes to assign engagement that really pushes students beyond the normal workload, then they can use the one-credit add-on to ensure that students get proper credit for their work.

Conclusions and the Future

In 2001 and 2002, Pennsylvania State University sponsored two symposia on general education with invited representatives from nine research universities around the United States. In the follow-up report, organizers reiterated a classic vision of liberal education as preparation for democratic citizenship:

> As a social institution, American higher education, particularly public education, is vested with responsibilities for the maintenance and progress of the democracy in which it is situated. While it has embraced missions of research and graduate education, the research university recognizes a basic obligation to foster a reflective, informed, thoughtfully engaged citizenry, capable of discerning what serves justice and the common good. (Pennsylvania State University, 2002, p. 5)

Many of the recommendations in the Penn State report are for actions we have tried to undertake at UWM through the Cultures and Communities initiative: putting tenure-line faculty into the classes, creating coherent links among offerings, challenging the lecture-course model, advocating interdisciplinary approaches, infusing concerns for diversity and social justice, and introducing service or community engagement components. But since CC is a small program (so far), and since it has not replaced the standard general education requirements (yet), its campus-wide impact remains small. This is due in part to a number of shortcomings that the Pennsylvania State University (2002) report describes as disturbingly typical of other campuses. No one person is responsible for the general education program at UWM; there is no administrative figure, dean, vice provost, or faculty committee assessing its outcomes or promoting it among faculty and students. We do have two administrators, a deputy chancellor and an assistant chancellor, assigned to community engagement and partnerships. They have been generous in support of CC, but we have had to invent and market the connection of general education to community engagement mostly on our own, without the correspondent support of an analogous administrative office. The campus administration and departments continue to focus primarily on research, the graduate programs, and degrees in the majors.

Though the Pennsylvania State University (2002) report focuses on general education rather than community engagement, the latter agenda can be articulated well using the report's own conclusions. When we first began, we saw the current general education program as an Achilles heel we could exploit, as a weakness that made for an opportunity. Now that we wish to grow our program and disseminate its ideas more widely, we have come to realize that there continues to be latent power, and potential, in the campus's unfulfilled commitment to general education. There is much that could be done working with advisors, department chairs, faculty governance committees, student life staff, and the university's marketing wing if we wish to put our version of an engaged, diverse general education at the center of our mission and practice. Many on campus have, in fact, been resistant to the push for more multiculturalism and community engagement, seeing these as a distraction from the core liberal arts mission of the university. But the neglect of the general education program suggests that commitment to this core mission is more rhetoric than reality, as energy remains disproportionately invested in disciplinary research specializations, while the general education program languishes in obscurity.

Our recommendation to colleagues elsewhere, however, is to seize upon the general education curriculum as an opportunity for campus-wide reform, no matter how rhetorical or half-hearted the institution's current commitment to it may be. There may very well be a vacuum to be filled. Public and community support can be rallied for efforts to get the university to take its public mission and obligation to diversity seriously. These are agendas well-understood by civic leaders, regents, local politicians, and state officials, who can be allies in curriculum reform. Any campus wishing to make progress in renovating its general education curriculum, in our view, will have to abandon the distribution model based on the divisions of the sciences, humanities, and arts, and replace it with some kind of meaningful set of specified content areas and experiences.

This will require a debate about the learning goals and objectives for the general education program, as well as discussions of how seriously the university takes the task of educating students for citizenship in a diverse democracy and globalized society. It will also mean trying to move faculty away from the "banking" model of pedagogy, in which "content" is delivered irrespective of the identity, background, training, cultural competence, or learning style of individual students, or without reflection on the relation of the content to specific pedagogical theories and practices. In

terms of diversity, campus leaders will have to embrace critical multiculturalism and hold deans, department heads, and faculty accountable for
meeting serious goals for achieving educational equity. In regard to campus
partnerships, a grassroots effort will be required to make community
members true collaborators in long-term relationships. These relationships, in turn, can be catalysts for faculty development and provide crucial
political support for progressive change on campus.

A general education program focused on critical multiculturalism and
community engagement, we believe, has the potential to revitalize the mission
of the university, reconnect the campus to the world, and reinvigorate the academic experience of both students and faculty. Though some may brand this
idealistic, we think in the end this agenda will win out against the vocational-
ism and ivory tower parochialism found on too many campuses today.

Endnotes

1) In retrospect, perhaps the most important structural key to the success of the Cultures and Communities Program Office was the decision by Chancellor Nancy Zimpher
to create a separate funding structure for The Milwaukee Idea initiatives. These funds
are set aside in accounts that are independent of the budgets of the various schools and
colleges. Thus the initiatives have considerable autonomy and form a horizontal matrix
for campus innovation that cuts through the vertical martrix of the usual administrative
hierarchy of department heads, deans, and central administrative officers.

2) The many reports and publications of the Association of American Colleges and
Universities have been especially helpful, as is its *Diversity Web* page
(http://www.diversityweb.org). Particularly relevant is Debra Humphrey's 1997
report, *General Education and American Commitments: A National Report on Diversity Courses and Requirements* (Washington, DC: AAC&U). My thanks to AAC&U
Senior Vice President Caryn McTighe Musil for her counsel and support, and to
William Harvey, vice president and director of the American Council on Education's
Center for Advancement of Racial and Ethnic Equity, who invited our participation
in ACE's biannual conferences on "Educating All of One Nation."

3) Interestingly, the otherwise admirable "Vision Statement" for the federal Corporation for National and Community Service nowhere expresses an awareness of racial
injustice or the need for a multicultural analysis of service issues; see http://www.national
service.org/about/vision.html. For a fine introduction to the issues, see O'Grady, C. R.
(2000). Integrating service learning and multicultural education: An overview. In C. R.
O'Grady (Ed.), *Integrating service learning and multicultural education in colleges and
universities* (pp. 1–20). Mahwah, NJ: Lawrence Erlbaum Associates.

4) We highly recommend Johnson's book for all instructors looking for a way to get students thinking beyond their initial resistances.

5) Among the videos available, *The Angry Eye* (Elliott & Elliott Eyes, Inc., 2001) uses college students, and particularly challenges insistences on "color-blindness"; *Blue-Eyed* (Claus Strigel & Bertram Verhaag, 1995) is a 90-minute feature including footage from the original elementary school experiment as well as a workshop with adults; and *Stolen Eye* (Annamax Media, LTD & Angry Eye Production, Inc., 2003) conducts the experiment with whites and aboriginals in Australia, giving white privilege a global cast.

References

Association of American Colleges and Universities. (2000). *AAC&U Survey on Diversity Requirements: Overview of Survey Data.* Retrieved July 26, 2005, from http://www.aacu.org/divsurvey/irvineoverview.cfm

Astin, A. W., Vogelgesang, L. J., Ikeda, E. K., & Yee, J. A. (2000). *How service learning affects students.* Los Angeles, CA: University of California, Higher Education Research Institute.

Borsuk, A. J., & Sykes, L., Jr. (2001, March). City population lowest since 1940: Minorities outnumber whites in city for first time. *Milwaukee Journal Sentinel.* Retrieved February 21, 2005, from http://www.jsonline.com/news/census2000/mar01/race09030801.asp

Brown, W., & Ling, A. (2003). *Imagining America: Stories from the promised land: A multicultural anthology of American fiction* (Rev. ed.). New York: Persea Books.

Brown, T., Jay, G., & Terrell, D. (2002). Planting a new kind of teacher: The Cultures and Communities/MPS experiment. *Metropolitan Universities: An International Forum, 13*(4), 33–42.

Cultures and Communities Program. *Multicultural America.* Retrieved July 22, 2005, from http://www.cc.uwm.edu

Curtis, M. J. (2002, May). Pilot diversity program builds insight and understanding. *George Street Journal: A Publication for the Brown University Community.* Retrieved July 11, 2005, from http://www.brown.edu/Administration/George_Street_Journal/vol26/26GSJ28a.html

Humphreys, D. (1997). *General education and American commitments: A national report on diversity courses and requirements.* Washington, DC: Association of American Colleges and Universities.

Jay, G. (with Jones, S. E.). Whiteness studies and the multicultural literature classroom. *MELUS, 30*(2), 99–121.

Johnson, A. G. (2001). *Privilege, power, and difference.* Boston, MA: McGraw-Hill.

May, S. (Ed.) (1999). *Critical multiculturalism: Rethinking multicultural and antiracist education.* London, England: Falmer Press.

McIntosh, P. (1997).White privilege and male privilege: A personal account of coming to see correspondences through work in Women's Studies. In R. Delgado & J. Stefancic (Eds.), *Critical white studies: Looking behind the mirror* (pp. 291–299). Philadelphia, PA: Temple University Press.

McTighe Musil, C. (1997). Foreword. In D. Humphreys, *General education and American commitments: A national report on diversity courses and requirements* (pp. ix–xii). Washington, DC: Association of American Colleges and Universities.

Milwaukee Public Schools. (2003). *Annual child enumeration: Summary by age–ethnic totals.* Retrieved July 25, 2005, from http://www.milwaukee.k12.wi.us/fileBroker.php/8973/Census-Bk-03-P3.pdf

Occidental College. (2005) *Mission Statement.* Retrieved July 25, 2005, from http://www.oxy.edu/x2640.xml

Nieto, S. (2000). Foreword. In C. R. O'Grady (Ed.), *Integrating service learning and multicultural education in colleges and universities* (pp. ix–xii). Mahwah, NJ: Lawrence Erlbaum Associates.

Pabst, G. (2004, June 4). Number of Asians, Latinos surge: Growth expected to affect schools, economy. *Milwaukee Journal Sentinel.* Retrieved February 21, 2005, from http://www.jsonline.com/news/metro/jun04/236771.asp

Pennsylvania State University. (2002). *Students in the balance: General education in the research university.* Retrieved July 22, 2005, from the Pennsylvania State University, Division of Undergraduate Studies web site: http://www.psu.edu/dus/StudentsintheBalance.pdf

Rico, B. R., & Mano, S. (Eds.). (2000). *American mosaic: Multicultural readings in context* (3rd ed.). Boston, MA: Houghton Mifflin.

Rosenberg, R., & Christiansen, R. (Producers), & Korty, J. (Director). (1974). *The Autobiography of Miss Jane Pittman* [Motion Picture]. (Available on DVD from Sony Music, 550 Madison Avenue, New York, NY 10022-3211.)

Smith, D. G., & Associates. (1997). *Diversity works: The emerging picture of how students benefit.* Washington, DC: Association of American Colleges and Universities.

Takaki, R. (1993). *A different mirror: A history of multicultural America.* Boston, MA: Back Bay Books.

University of Wisconsin–Milwaukee. (2002). *Fact Book.* Milwaukee, WI: Author.

8 The How and Why of the Scholarship of Engagement

David N. Cox

Central to a discussion of a "new kind of university" is the meaning of scholarship. As Boyer (1990) observed in discussing the role of undergraduate higher education in society, "One of the most crucial issues—the one that goes to the core of academic life—relates to the meaning of scholarship itself. Scholarship is not an esoteric appendage; it is at the heart of what the profession is all about" (p. 1). If something is "new" about universities, that newness has to include changes in the understanding of scholarship.

As the title of this chapter suggests, a form of that newness may be found in the concept of the scholarship of engagement: what it is, how it is different, and what issues it raises for engaging faculty in meaningful scholarship across all disciplines.

The Scholarship of Engagement: What Is It?

The American Heritage Dictionary (2000) identifies scholarship as the methods, discipline, or attainments of a scholar; knowledge resulting from study and research; or financial aid for education. Focusing on its meaning related to contributions to knowledge, Boyer's (1990) *Scholarship Reconsidered* has broadened the understanding of the term to include four dimensions—discovery, integration, application, and teaching. Discovery involves adding to the stock of human knowledge. Integration involves making connections across disciplines that lead to new understandings. Application involves turning that knowledge into use by addressing real-world problems. Teaching involves passing knowledge or understandings on to others. Key to the concept of the scholarship of engagement is *how* those dimensions are accomplished.

The conduct of each dimension of scholarship—discovery, integration, application, and teaching—involves a series of actions. Broadly, they include: setting the goals for the scholarship; selecting the means and methods for carrying out the scholarship; applying those means and methods; reflection on the results of that application; and dissemination of those results.

Goal setting for discovery and integration involves choosing and framing the question to be answered. Goal setting for application involves defining and selecting the problem to be solved. For teaching it involves choosing the issues about which information is to be transferred.

Selecting means and methods for discovery and integration involves choosing the design for the inquiry and obtaining the tools required to carry out that design. The means and methods step for application involves selecting the intervention or set of interventions to be applied. For instruction, selection involves choosing the media, materials, and pedagogy to be used in transferring the knowledge.

Applying those means and methods involves just that—carrying out the design for discovery and integration, employing the intervention or interventions for application, and using the selected media and materials in the pedagogy for instruction.

Reflection for discovery and integration involves analysis and critique of the findings. Reflection for application and teaching involves assessment of the impact and outcomes of the intervention and instruction.

Dissemination of the results may take a number of forms for each of the types of scholarship. Dissemination may occur through print in journals, books, monographs, reports, or newsletters; electronically, through radio, television, or computer transmissions including web pages; in demonstrations such as site visits and poster displays; or orally in speeches and presentations, personal and professional networks, or neighborhood conversations.

The point regarding engagement is found in Boyer's (1997) definition of the scholarship of engagement. According to Boyer, the scholarship of engagement is scholarship activities that connect the university with people and places outside the campus and which, in the end, direct the work of the academy toward more humane ends. Contact, of course, can take many forms. It can be incidental and passive, or it can be regular and active. It can be one-directional or interactive, formal or informal. More recently, the notion of the scholarship of engagement builds on Boyer's definition by including active and interactive contact between people inside and external to the academy across the range of actions involved in scholarship—from setting goals, and selecting and applying means and methods, to reflection and dissemination. It is that *interaction* across the range of scholarship activities that distinguishes the contact involved in the scholarship of engagement.

Using this definition of the dynamic interaction inherent in the scholarship of engagement, it is possible to determine what is engagement and what is not. So, for example, Louis Pasteur making the connection between sewage and disease while walking city streets in the 1800s led to scholarship in the form of discovery and application. His resulting search for an intervention to treat a real-world problem shaped the questions he asked leading to the discovery of the germ theory of disease (Stokes, 1997). There is also a long history of contact with persons and places outside the academy in the form of dissemination through the transfer of technical expertise by agricultural agents connected to land-grant universities. In neither of these cases, however, were persons outside of the academy actively involved in any of the scholarship activities. They were not involved in shaping the questions, choosing or executing the means, or reflecting on the results. Moreover, dissemination was one-directional, knowledge transferred from expert to client. Thus while connected in one sense of the term, absent interaction in the processes of scholarship, these examples do not represent the scholarship of engagement.

In contrast, Chicago residents of the Renacer West Side neighborhood and faculty and students at the University of Illinois–Chicago worked together in designing the means to increase employment opportunities for the residents. They did not accomplish their short-term goal of increased employment by residents at the university, but collective reflection by residents, faculty, and students led to discovery and development of a longer-term application that expanded employment opportunities beyond the neighborhood (Mayfield & Lucas, 2000). Residents of colonias in south Texas—rural communities and neighborhoods bordering Mexico, which require sufficient infrastructure and other basic services (U.S. Department of Housing and Urban Development, 2000)—participated as partners with faculty members and students at the University of Texas–Austin in implementing and reflecting on the impact of a plan for enhancing public service infrastructure for colonias in the area (Wilson & Guajardo, 2000). Community residents in East Saint Louis, Illinois, in the 1990s were instrumental in reframing discovery and application questions being pursued by faculty members and students at the University of Illinois at Urbana-Champaign. The result was the creation of knowledge more relevant to the problems of the community (Reardon, 2000). And in a West Philadelphia neighborhood, community residents, public school and city officials, and faculty members and students at the University of Pennsylvania worked together to redesign K–12 school curricula, pedagogy, and social service programming, improving student outcomes and adding to knowledge about advancing urban school systems (Harkavy, 1999).

In sum, the scholarship of engagement, therefore, is a *set of activities*. At its core are four dimensions of scholarship—discovery, integration, application, and teaching. It becomes the scholarship of engagement through its active and interactive connection with people and places outside of the university in the activities of scholarship, setting goals, selecting means and methods, applying means and methods, reflecting on results, and dissemination of the results. Given the range of these dimensions and activities, the depth of connections may vary. At a less engaged level, the interaction may involve only one dimension of scholarship or one of a limited set of scholarship activities. At the deepest level, the interactions carry through multiple dimensions and across all of the scholarship activities. In each case, however, it is the presence of that interaction that distinguishes the scholarship of engagement.

Engaged Scholarship: How Is It Different?

Before we ask *how* the scholarship of engagement is different, we need to determine *from what* it is different. Clearly it is different from scholarship whose cues for questions and choices for instruction are driven only by the development of theory within academic disciplines. In the scholarship of engagement, in contrast, those cues are driven by and answers are produced through contact with persons and places outside of the academy.

The question could more productively be phrased: "How is the scholarship of engagement different from the scholarship currently being pursued within many American colleges and universities?" The answer to that question varies. Individual faculty, staff, and administrators within universities have been in active and interactive contact with people and places outside the academy in the conduct of scholarship for centuries. However, attention to the scholarship of engagement, particularly in urban settings, does represent a change from a model of scholarship that has dominated the academy over the past half century.

In regard to the history of engagement, Bender (1988) has shown the variety of ways universities have carried out scholarship since the Middle Ages. Two traditions have developed. In the first, those conducting scholarship within the university not only eschewed connection with the world outside the academy, but in many ways actively sought to isolate themselves from contact with and influence by the communities in which they were located. In some instances increased isolation was sought by locating universities away from urban settings to reduce the perceived corrupting influence of cities. This approach was based on the premise that external contact would corrupt the independence or objectivity of academic scholarship, and that persons outside the academy did not have the expertise to appropriately contribute to it. Disengaged rather than engaged scholarship was the goal of this tradition. The second tradition took the opposite view. Rather than separation, universities in this tradition sought to embrace the cities and communities in which they were located, believing that contact enriched the relevance and quality of scholarship.

Both of those traditions can be found in the development of higher education in the United States. Harkavy and others have described the development of the American research university, which moved away from connection to daily issues of the communities, seeking disengagement from the broader society in which they were located. Large federal and corporate investments in higher education, especially in scientific research stimulated by Cold War defense spending following World War II, rapidly increased "town/gown" separation (Harkavy, 1997). Other colleges and universities, however—often those with land-grant roots or missions focused in service or teaching—have consciously sought connection with their communities as an integral part of the conduct of their scholarship activities. Harper (1905), the first president of the University of Chicago, expressed that tradition, its rationale, and its relevance to scholarship and to communities:

> A university which will adapt itself to urban influence, which will undertake to serve as an expression of urban civilization, and which is compelled to meet the demands of an urban environment, will in the end become something essentially different from a university located in a village or small city. Such an institution in time will differentiate itself from other institutions. It will gradually take on new characteristics both outward and inward, and it will ultimately form a new type of university. (p. 158)

This "new university" is one created by the scholarship of engagement, the new emerging direction in American higher education reflected in the aims of The Milwaukee Idea, and in the following vision of scholarship.

Issues for the Scholarship of Engagement

Scholarship, and especially scholarship in urban settings that involves interactions inside and outside of the academy, represents something new in the context of the dominant form of post–World War II higher education in the United States. That is especially the case for the research university. What are some of the issues and challenges associated with the vision of that new university?

In the broader view, the scholarship of engagement can be expected to impact the role and place of higher education institutions in their communities and in society. As Boyer (1990) noted, scholarship is central to the meaning of a university. Through time, the focus of scholarship in American higher education, its role, and its meaning have changed. In the early years of the nation, the focus of scholarship was on building character and preparing students for civic and religious leadership (Tyack, 1967). In response to a rapidly industrializing nation, scholarship in the nineteenth century expanded to include practical education serving the business and technical needs of a manufacturing economy (Rudolph, 1962). The 20th century saw a shift toward research, especially science-based research, as scholarship (Gibbons, Limoges, Nowotny, Schwartzman, Scott, & Trow, 1994; Jenks & Riesman, 1968).

If faculty members and students in a higher education institution become involved in the scholarship of engagement—especially in the ways that Harper (1905) proposed—that institution and what it produces will be different. It will address different questions, use alternative methods, and transfer knowledge to new and broader populations. In so doing, it will have a significantly different impact on the community and society in which it is located. The questions it addresses in discovery and integration, and the interventions chosen for application will be influenced by the concerns and perspectives of the community, not just the advancement of theory for theory's sake.

The concerns of persons outside of the academy will often require the production of knowledge that transcends any single disciplinary specialty. Thus another difference will be broader participation by persons across disciplines. A further difference will be involvement in the exchange of the scholarship of teaching to broader audiences than just students and faculty members within the institution to diverse learning communities, including P–12 school districts and professional learners. Given these differences, a range of issues for higher education institutions, faculty members, students, and the communities with whom they are engaged are emerging regarding the implications of this *new* university (Cox & Pearce, 2004).

The Demands of Real-World Discovery

One issue for faculty members and higher education institutions is whether processes associated with the scholarship of engagement will divert resources from the primary purposes of higher education. Some claim a primary purpose of higher education, and particularly research universities, is to further knowledge by advancing theory. Questions addressed in the scholarship of discovery and integration, in particular, are to be directed by the gaps and inconsistencies in theory. Only through such directed scholarship can knowledge best be generated.

In contrast, real-world concerns shape the direction of questions addressed and knowledge created through the scholarship of engagement. Real-world concerns are dynamic, frequently subject to change. As a consequence, according to this view, the scholarship of inquiry, integration, application, and teaching shaped in response to those concerns will be subject to continual change. The resulting shift of attention from one area of concern to another will slow the development of theory in any particular field. At its worst, it can lead to intellectual and institutional dilettantism.

Advocates of the scholarship of engagement offer a set of responses. One is that much current theory-driven scholarship is failing to meet the mission and responsibility of higher education because of its lack of relevance to the pressing issues of communities and humankind (Harkavy, 1997). Another is that disconnected scholarship can become intellectually arid; it exists only for the personal gratification of the author (Stokes, 1997). A third argues that the claim that engagement comes at the cost of the development of theory is a false dichotomy. In this view, engagement is simply another means of stimulating questions for extending theory. Appropriate reflection on the results will always enrich rather than restrict the development of theory (Rice, 1996).

Engagement and the Tradition of Objectivity

Another issue for faculty members and higher education institutions concerns the implications of the scholarship of engagement on the intellectual traditions of higher education. Those traditions include a commitment to objectivity and independence in inquiry and thinking, a unique contribution of higher education in society (Brucker, 1988). The concern is that interactions involved in the scholarship of engagement can compromise that objectivity and independence. Through engagement, for example, persons outside of the academy become involved in setting the priorities for scholarship being produced by the academy. To the extent that they do so, the resulting scholarship will reflect the concerns and therefore the values of those individuals, not the disinterested choices of faculty within the academy. A concern to some is that engagement will compromise higher education's objectivity in the choice of the content of its scholarship.

A second concern is that the partnerships that define engaged scholarship may create personal attachments that create dependencies. These may range from dependencies for information for scholarship to financial obligations in support of the scholarship. Personal attachments can create affective dependencies, producing the same effects. Persons dependent on one another will be less critical of what each has done and how they have done it. What is chosen for scholarship as well as how that scholarship is conducted can be affected. Objectivity and independence in scholarship are compromised. The result is a sacrifice of higher education's intellectual integrity.

One response to this view is that no scholarship can be considered truly "value free" or objective. The questions pursued for discovery or integrations, interventions employed for application, or knowledge to be transferred in teaching all involve choices. If the question for the scholarship of discovery, for example, is driven by theory, choices are required to select a theory to be explored and in spending the time and resources to expand that theory. Those choices will be driven by values, whether the persons making the choices are inside or outside the academy. Rather than inappropriately imposing values external to the academy on scholarship, the scholarship of engagement exerts a healthy influence by helping scholarship to address the issues facing the communities and society that higher education is to serve.

Likewise, proponents of the scholarship of engagement question the independence of much of the scholarship produced by faculty members and students through the years. As we have observed, federal investments supporting "Big Science" have dramatically expanded our understanding of physical phenomena over the past 50 years (Harkavy, 1997). The rationale for much of that funding has been for national defense. The effect has been to create multiple interdependencies between funders and universities shaping the questions that are asked, the applications developed, and what is taught. Much of what is seen as independent scholarship is, in reality, not fully independent, but scholarship dramatically influenced by the priorities of external funders.

The point is not that it is inappropriate for priorities external to the university to shape scholarship. It may well be that scholarship justified as support for our nation's defense and protection of democracy is appropriate. The real question is what larger values and purposes are being served by the scholarship? If they are appropriate, the scholarship is appropriate and independence on the part of the scholar is not an issue. Engagement does not change that equation. Instead, it can be positive when it leads to scholarship contributing to the social, civic, economic, and personal health of a community and society.

Assessing the Scholarship of Engagement

Another set of issues around the scholarship of engagement concerns challenges in assessing the quality of such scholarship. A set of conventions has developed within the higher education community for assessing academic quality. The scholarship of engagement is seen to pose several challenges to those conventions, especially around documentation and external objective review.

Documentation makes scholarship visible. External objective review provides independent assessment of the quality and contribution of the scholarship. Common forms for documentation of the scholarship of discovery and integration are journal articles, books and book chapters, and monographs. Common forms for documentation of the scholarship of application are articles, books, monographs, and reports. Common forms for documentation and assessment of the scholarship of teaching are measures of student outcomes, and peer and student evaluations. The common form of external objective review is review by anonymous peers. Peers apply the standards of their area of expertise to determine the relevance of the question being addressed, the appropriateness of the methods selected and applied to address the question, and the contributions of the resulting knowledge.

One challenge posed by the scholarship of engagement is in determining what to document and how to document it (Driscoll & Lynton, 1999). Just as with any other form of scholarship, the scholarship of engagement requires documentation regarding its activities. Has the right question been asked? Has there been an appropriate application of theory and methods in addressing the question? Have the results been properly analyzed? Do the results make a significant contribution to knowledge?

Differences occur, however, as a result of engagement (Driscoll & Lynton, 1999; Glassick, Huber, & Maeroff, 1997). The relevance of the scholarship frequently extends beyond a particular discipline or field of expertise. Not only does the scholarship matter to a discipline, it matters to the external community or society, to students, to the university, and to the faculty member, raising the challenge of determining how to document the contributions of the scholarship to the various interests. Articles and other publications are used to assess conventional scholarship and communicate contributions to disciplines. Student outcomes and surveys may be used to assess contributions to teaching. But there are fewer conventions in knowing what to include as contributions to the external people and places and how those contributions are to be documented and assessed. For the scholarship of application, for example, must the application succeed in order for the scholarship to be judged as having quality? If it fails but contributes to discovery, is that enough to consider it as having quality? If it were to cause harm to a community but contribute to discovery, is that quality scholarship or failure?

Other challenges of documentation of the scholarship of engagement follow from the broader array of participants in and recipients of the scholarship. Simply put, the greater number of participants and recipients adds to the time and therefore cost required to document contributions.

That can be a burden to busy scholars working under the financial constraints of university budgets or community grants. Often the results of the engagement activity are newly created networks and relationships. Measuring something as amorphous as a new social network can be a challenge.

As there are challenges to documentation, so also there are challenges for assessment. Since the contributions extend beyond the academy, we need to determine the appropriate peers to assess the scholarship contributions to external people and places. Are scholars only those within the academy, or should they include persons on the outside? Of individuals outside the university, who are those most qualified—the participants in the engaged scholarship or anonymous external reviewers? If the contributions cross disciplines, who within any particular discipline is best able to assess the scholarship involving another discipline? And what are the appropriate standards for reviewers—and who determines them? As previously noted, for example, how does one assess the results of engaged scholarship if the aim of the activity for the community fails or harms them, but the process of the activity leads to significant gains in knowledge and instruction for faculty and students within the university?

Proponents of the scholarship of engagement have readily acknowledged these challenges to the assessment of quality. Rather than seeing them as insurmountable, however, a number of scholars and initiatives are underway to address them. Glassick et al. (1997) and Driscoll and Lynton (1999) have produced models and guidelines for documentation and assessment. Supported by funding from the Kellogg Foundation, the National Review Board on the Scholarship of Engagement was created in 2000 to provide panels of experienced experts to review scholarship of engagement portfolios. National education associations are sponsoring conferences, workshops, and publications aimed at developing standards for documentation, criteria of assessment, and technical assistance for assessment.

Questions of Expectations

Finally, the scholarship of engagement is raising questions about what is to be expected from faculty members and disciplines within the university. Regarding faculty members, if the scholarship of engagement is good for the university and the community, should all faculty members be expected to practice it? Given the time involved in interaction, is involvement in the scholarship of engagement more appropriate during some phases of a faculty member's career than others? Specifically, is it more appropriate as a post-tenure than pre-tenure activity? But, if the scholarship of engagement is good for scholarship and the community, why must participation in it be delayed during a faculty member's early formative professional years? And, if all faculty members are not expected to be engaged in the scholarship, can equitable standards be developed and applied to evaluate faculty members pursuing different forms of scholarship?

Academic disciplines also are asking whether the scholarship of engagement is more appropriate for some disciplines than others. Given the issues of communities and the type of knowledge that they create and transmit, it is generally agreed that engagement is a reasonable fit for the social sciences. The same can be said for the arts, education, health care, and business. The question is whether or where engagement is appropriate for other disciplines, such as the mathematical sciences. It may not be intuitively obvious that people external to the academy would be likely to interpret their concerns in ways that would contribute to advances in the scholarship of discovery or integration in advanced mathematics. There are circumstances of engagement, however, between faculty members and students in the mathematics sciences, and persons in the external community in the scholarship of application and teaching. Thus the answer for some disciplines may depend on the dimension of scholarship involved in the engagement.

Regarding the larger question of whether all faculty members should be expected to participate in engaged scholarship, the solution should be found in the institution's mission. Since the mission of most institutions includes the advancement of knowledge relevant to serving society, the answer is therefore one of balance. It is appropriate for some of the institution's work to be principally focused on advancing theory while other areas are shaped by engagement. One of the most important changes in higher education in the United States today remains the search for that balance. Indeed, this book provides an excellent description of our continuing search for balance as we explore more deeply the scholarship of engagement and its role in defining the new university.

References

The American heritage dictionary of the English language (4th ed.). (2000). New York, NY: Houghton Mifflin.

Bender, T. (Ed.). (1988). *The university and the city: From medieval origins to the present.* New York, NY: Oxford University Press.

Boyer, E. L. (1990). *Scholarship reconsidered: Priorities of the professoriate.* Princeton, NJ: The Carnegie Foundation for the Advancement of Teaching.

Boyer, E. L. (1997). *Ernest L. Boyer: Selected speeches, 1979–1995* (L. M. Green, Ed.). Princeton, NJ: The Carnegie Foundation for the Advancement of Teaching.

Brucker, G. (1988). Renaissance Florence: Who needs a university? In T. Bender (Ed.), *The university and the city: From medieval origins to the present* (pp. 47–58). New York, NY: Oxford University Press.

Cox, D. N., & Pearce, M. (2004). The future for economically distressed community-higher education partnerships. In D. Maurrasse (Ed.), *A future for everyone: Innovative social responsibility and community partnerships* (pp. 235–247). New York, NY: Routledge.

Driscoll, A., & Lynton, E. A. (1999). *Making outreach visible: A guide to documenting professional service and outreach.* Washington, DC: American Association for Higher Education.

Gibbons, M., Limoges, C., Nowotny, H., Schwartzman, S., Scott, P., & Trow, M. (1994). *The new production of knowledge: The dynamics of science and research in contemporary societies.* Thousand Oaks, CA: Sage Publications.

Glassick, C. E., Huber, M. T., & Maeroff, G. I. (1997). *Scholarship assessed: Evaluation of the professoriate.* San Francisco, CA: Jossey-Bass.

Harkavy, I. (1997). The demands of the times and the American research university. *Journal of Planning Literature, 11*(3), 333–336.

Harkavy, I. (1999). School-community-university partnerships: Effectively integrating community building and education reform. *Universities and Community Schools, 1*(2), 7–24.

Harper, W. R. (1905). *The trend in higher education.* Chicago, IL: University of Chicago Press.

Jencks, C., & Riesman, D. (1968). *The academic revolution.* New York, NY: Doubleday.

Mayfield, L., & Lucas, E. P., Jr. (2000). Mutual awareness, mutual respect: The community and the university interact. *Cityscape: A Journal of Policy Development and Research, 5*(1), 173–184.

Reardon, K. M. (2000). An experiential approach to creating an effective community-university partnership: The East St. Louis Action Research project. *Cityscape: A Journal of Policy Development and Research, 5*(1), 59–74.

Rice, R. E. (1996). *Making a place for the new American scholar force.* Washington, DC: American Association for Higher Education.

Rudolph, F. (1962). *The American college and university: A history.* New York, NY: Alfred A. Knopf.

Stokes, D. (1997). *Pasteur's quadrant: Basic science and technological innovation.* Washington, DC: Brookings Institution.

Tyack, D. (1967). *Turning points in American educational history.* Waltham, MA: Blaisdell.

U.S. Department of Housing and Urban Development. (2000). *What are colonias?* Retrieved June 22, 2005, from http://www.hud.gov/groups/frmwrkcoln/whatcol.cfm

Wilson, R. H., & Guajardo, M. (2000). Capacity building and governance in El Cenizo. *Cityscape: A Journal of Policy Development and Research, 5*(1), 101–123.

9 The Scholarship of Teaching and Learning in the Engaged University

Anthony Ciccone

The concept of the engaged university challenges all of us in higher education to understand our professional roles in new ways. Perhaps the most difficult role to rethink in this light is our teaching. If the faculty's commitment to research at least recognizes the possibility that this work may take place in the context of social needs, and if the faculty's traditional commitment to professional service is at least a close relation to engagement, the connections between teaching and engagement are not immediately obvious. What do teaching and learning look like at the engaged university? How does the evolving relationship between university and community reflect and affect a new relationship between teacher and learner? How can the insights gained in reformulating each of these relationships benefit all the partners? And finally, how can faculty development practices contribute to the institutionalization of engagement?

The Scholarship of Teaching and Learning

The task of helping faculty to incorporate engagement into their instructional practices and to exploit the possibilities for enhancing student learning has been made somewhat easier by higher education's recent renewed interest in effective teaching and learning, crystallizing in the developing notion of the scholarship of teaching and learning (SoTL). Our new way of conceiving of all faculty work—discovery, integration, application, and teaching—in the engagement context finds its roots in Boyer's (1990) *Scholarship Reconsidered*. By expanding the definition of scholarly work, Boyer laid the groundwork for individuals and institutions to recognize the potential scholarly nature of both "service" and "teaching." Just as important, however, his work challenged us to understand how all our roles must interconnect if higher education is to serve the needs of its disciplines, its students, and its communities. As a result, faculty developers find themselves with a new organizing framework to help faculty and staff assess the value of their work—that is, its effect on student learning and community needs—and a new way to design the work, as systematic inquiry based on meaningful partnerships. The "creation/dissemination" model for accomplishing the university's teaching and service missions can at last be modified according to a coherent set of principles, to the benefit of students, community, and, some would argue, disciplinary scholarship itself. Others have traced the evolution of the service role to its current essential place in the engaged university and examined the benefits of its new formulation for disciplinary and interdisciplinary research, curriculum development, and community service.

The University of Wisconsin–Milwaukee (UWM) has responded with new programs and courses that connect its disciplines to the study of real people and communities even as they prepare students to work as effective partners with these communities (see Chapters 10 and 11). This new curriculum has often entailed new pedagogies, especially service-learning. The very name of this pedagogy conveys the essence of engagement—learning while serving and serving while learning. Through structured workshops on topics such as curriculum design, effective assignments, and alternative forms of assessment, faculty developers have helped instructors learn to exploit the potential of service-learning. Furthermore, service-learning pedagogy itself has become the object of scholarly investigation at UWM. Funding from UWM's Center for Instructional and Professional Development (CIPD) has supported work by David Clark (English), a UWM Center Scholar in Teaching and Learning, that examines the political and ideological learning outcomes experienced by students in service-learning projects and by Greg Jay, Virginia Kuhn, and Soyoung Park, who have created and tested assessment tools for evaluating cross-cultural learning in the innovative Cultures and Communities Certificate Program.

Faculty Development and Engagement

As our understanding of teaching and learning has evolved, so have our approaches to faculty development. How has this evolution both prepared us for and influenced the design of the engaged university? A brief history will help us understand the current place of SoTL and the principles it shares with the concept of engagement. It will also enable us to place the UWM experience in its national and local contexts.

Gaff and Simpson (1994) present a cogent history of faculty development efforts in American higher education. In the 1960s and 1970s, the focus of professional development for institutions and individuals was clearly on what instructors needed to *know* in their discipline to be effective researchers and teachers. Faculty development was focused primarily on the individual faculty member and emphasized sabbaticals, research support (often including support for degree completion), and released time to develop the content of new courses.

In the 1970s and early 1980s, the emphasis gradually shifted to what instructors needed to *do* in the classroom. Faculty development thus entered the "improving teaching" phase, offering workshops on innovative practice and course design that involved the earliest versions of instructional software, better lecturing and discussion techniques, overheads, and video. Here, the emphasis was on the development of technique and format, often with the underlying assumption that "one size fits all."

During the curricular reform era of the 1980s, emphasis shifted toward what *students* needed to *know* as institutions undertook general education reform and created programs in fields such as ethnic studies, area studies, and women's studies. Curriculum development became a new form of focused faculty development as institutions brought instructors together to design new courses within defined program goals or to encourage inclusion of new materials and perspectives in existing courses. Faculty developers argued, often successfully, for the inclusion of new pedagogies to complement these new perspectives.

The confluence of changing student demographics and expanding curriculum led faculty and institutions in the 1990s to examine more closely what students need to *do* inside and outside the classroom to achieve success. Faculty developers helped instructors to understand the connection between student engagement and student learning, and provided support for institution-wide student-learning initiatives, such as writing across the curriculum, infusing diversity into the curriculum, freshman-year programs, learning communities, undergraduate research, supplemental instruction, or peer mentoring. At many institutions, faculty developers joined forces with learning technology centers to make certain that instructional technology was linked directly to improving student learning.

During much of this time, individual disciplines, education, and cognitive science continued to develop more sophisticated notions of disciplinary knowledge, instructional practice, and the process of understanding. In the disciplines, new standards or definitions of student learning were crafted (e.g., American Council on the Teaching of Foreign Languages Oral Proficiency Guidelines for foreign languages) and new (or recycled) teaching methods based on these changes were designed. Faculty developers thus sought ways to bring these ideas to departments and programs and to translate them into learning goals, pedagogy, and effective assessment.

Continued advances in the cognitive and learning sciences have challenged higher education to move beyond the content delivery philosophy of pedagogy to define learning more precisely. Increases in the numbers of adult students and returning professionals led higher education to examine theories of adult learning and to apply their insights to college teaching and learning. Faculty developers thus introduced college instructors to Bloom's (1956) taxonomy, learning styles research, and theories of moral and intellectual development (Perry, 1970; Belenky, Clichy, Goldberger, & Tarule, 1986), and designed programs that examined the nature of adaptive expertise, the importance of prior knowledge, the nature of "deep understanding," and the novice-expert continuum (Wiggins & McTighe, 1998; Bransford, Brown, & Cocking, 2000).

Throughout this evolution, evaluating effectiveness has been a constant focus, although it has taken many different forms. More recently, in response to internal needs and outside calls for accountability, institutions and individual faculty members have become increasingly interested in understanding exactly what takes place in the college classroom. Faculty developers thus worked to help faculty design and implement classroom assessment techniques (Angelo & Cross, 1993) and prepare them for new roles in curricular/learning reforms that enrich the student experience (e.g., service-learning, undergraduate research, first-year, and capstone courses).

The concept of the scholarship of teaching and learning, first elaborated by Boyer and later expanded upon by Shulman (2004a, 2004b) and others, is built upon this evolution. McKinney (2004) provides an excellent history of the theory and practice of SoTL work, as well as a clear summary of current definitions and points of disagreement about the nature of the work. For our purposes, we can use a definition that includes the most salient features of SoTL. In its most succinct form, SoTL can be defined as systematic, scholarly inquiry into student learning that advances the practice of teaching. It characterizes what is often called *engaged pedagogy*. As *systematic inquiry*, SoTL work involves posing interesting questions that require the gathering of data, evidence, and information. Since it is *scholarly*, it uses the appropriate methods of the discipline to meet accepted standards of evidence. Its object of study is *student learning;* the value of its results are defined by how it *advances* our understanding of learning in different contexts and how it *adds to* a body of knowledge (one's own and that of others). In so doing, it improves the practice (methods, philosophy, assessment) of teaching, now understood as the orchestration of learning.

Thus, SoTL work asks interesting and useful questions, in a methodologically appropriate way, in order to understand student learning better, gather useful evidence about its characteristics, and advance our knowledge of how we can best facilitate it. This quest for pedagogical content knowledge (Shulman, 1986) suggests a new relationship among instructor, student, and faculty developer built on an engaged pedagogy whose core values are reflective practice and collaborative inquiry.

The Mirror Relationships of Engagement and Learning

This new relationship among instructor, student, and faculty developer mirrors the relationship between the engaged, learner-centered university and its community partners. In effect, engaged pedagogy and engaged research/service share many commonalities. Both relationships start with the recognition that each partner has a set of skills and experiences that are essential to the shared enterprise of creating new and effective knowledge. SoTL work relies on learning about the learner in order to examine how he or she comes to understanding. The engaged university relies on learning about its partners in order to examine how to determine meaningful action.

Both relationships are problem-driven, as determined by the goals and issues of the learner and the community. In this way, the scholarship of teaching and learning and the scholarship of engagement reflect the institution's intellectual and social location within a community of learners. In a seminal article on the scholarship of teaching, Bass (1999) argued for a problem-based approach to teaching and learning issues. His understanding of a "problem" in teaching and learning parallels the use of the term in "problem-based learning," that is, not as something to be "fixed," but rather as a complex set of factors requiring systematic description, data gathering, intervention, assessment, and reflection. Not surprisingly, the scholarship of engagement and the scholarship of teaching and learning use problem-based learning as both an intervention to improve student learning and a methodology for discovering new insights for the classroom and the community.

In both relationships, partners implement and nurture a process of shared inquiry and reflective practice. SoTL work requires attention to the learner's needs, but the learner must also engage in inquiry and reflection about what facilitates understanding for him or her. Moreover, in both relationships, what is learned is not limited to a set of predetermined facts, principles, or theories that one partner transmits to the other. Understanding is created as learner and community partner not only apply what has already been discovered by others, but test the value of these previous discoveries for the current context. Indeed, both relationships also recognize that neither the learner nor the community is a monolithic concept; thus, teacher and institution remain flexible in the teaching and outreach strategies they use with their partners. The SoTL perspective defines success as greater learning for a greater number of students; the scholarship of engagement perspective defines success as advances in all sectors of the community.

Finally, both relationships recognize that the responsibilities of each partner do not overlap completely. Not everything that the teacher or the institution needs to do will have a direct impact on the learner or community, but when it does, each shares the responsibility for design, implementation, and assessment. Thus, SoTL work is part of a renewed *engaged pedagogy* that connects instructor to student and institution to community through the shared goal of increasing learning in all its aspects: what the student or community partner learns, what the instructor or institution learns, and what all come to understand about the teaching/learning process.

UWM's Response

How has faculty development at UWM responded to this commitment to engaged pedagogy? How have these efforts contributed to institutionalizing the concept and practices of the engaged university?

Where faculty development in the past was essentially teaching-centered, it is now learning-centered. The organizing principle for most, if not all, of our work is now understanding learning—what it is, how it takes place, and how it relates to certain pedagogical practices. This principle has replaced the "deficit model" and the "technique model"; understanding difficulties in teaching is now merely the entry into a larger, more interesting discussion of how learning can be facilitated in a particular context, without blaming any of the partners. As Bass (1999) helped us understand, *problematizing* teaching and learning issues—that is, making these issues objects of systematic inquiry—often leads to more important insights and better solutions than treating them as *problems* needing some sort of remediation.

In our work with faculty at UWM, the staff of CIPD and its faculty advisory committee have designed a wide variety of strategies and programs that support engaged pedagogy. Mid-course evaluations/focus groups provide instructors with the basis for inquiry into student learning and help them to gather information about a current situation. This information often leads to more reflective approaches to improving the learning environment. *Dialogues in Diversity*,[1] a set of research-based resources and workshops, accomplishes a similar goal for programs and departments interested in understanding and responding to issues in this area.

Individual faculty make the transition from asking teaching questions to asking learning questions in a variety of ways based on interest, available time, and necessary resources. Faculty development at UWM now includes reading groups, classroom assessment cohorts, student-faculty partnerships, Freshman Seminar retreats, and Center Scholars in Teaching and Learning. Reading groups focus on the more philosophical and conceptual aspects of the teaching/learning process, framed in the work of thinkers such as Palmer (1998) and Brookfield (1995), as well as in the research on learning. Classroom assessment cohorts use information from their own classroom experiences to design and test focused interventions in areas such as assignment design and syllabus planning. Faculty often find their way to this type of work by attending workshops such as Beyond Anecdotal

Evidence—presented to UWM faculty by the Center for Instructional and Professional Development—where participants learn how to ask good questions and gather evidence about student learning.

The Student-Faculty Partnerships project teams instructors and students as co-investigators of learning issues, such as how students understand and use feedback in revising writing assignments and how students work effectively in online courses. This kind of collaboration mirrors the researcher/community partner pairing. Students participate fully in the design of the methodology and data gathering, present their findings, and become more engaged in their own learning. Freshman Seminar retreats, a joint College of Letters and Science and CIPD project, assists instructors in the creation of learning-centered courses that use engaged pedagogy to counter our 30–33% student-attrition rate from freshman to sophomore year.

For some faculty this initiation into learning questions leads them to consider larger issues that require more extensive study. The Center Scholars Program provides support for individual and team projects that investigate learning in areas, including online courses, curriculum design, and pedagogical practice. The projects produce results that are useful to colleagues in other disciplines, but more importantly, they advance the institution's knowledge of the effectiveness of its own instructional practices.

In this sense, the Center Scholars work is at the core of the institution; the engaged university continually studies itself. Thus, faculty development inherently involves working with departments on assessment of student learning outcomes. Integrally involved in the campus accreditation renewal, CIPD helps departments and programs design goals, assessments, and ways to use data to make changes. More importantly, it encourages systematic inquiry and critical reflection on assessment practice itself. A "culture of assessment" is a crucial goal for any institution, but even more so for one that aspires to engagement in an environment of competing needs and diminishing resources.

As The Milwaukee Idea took shape on the UWM campus, opening new ways to connect the university to the larger community through research, curriculum, and service, it was essential that faculty development help the institution understand and adapt to its new roles. Thus, CIPD and The Milwaukee Idea joined forces to present two important conferences: The Scholarship of Teaching and Learning: Implications for the Engaged University (2001) and Voices of Scholarship: A Campus Conversation

(2002). At the first conference, participants learned about the work of the newly formed Center Scholars Program, examined the role of SoTL work in technology and graduate student/adjunct faculty professional development, and discussed the effect of SoTL work on faculty roles and rewards and the Carnegie Reclassification initiative.

In 2002 a team of faculty and staff participated in a series of discussions that included readings on the scholarship of teaching and learning and the scholarship of engagement, attended the national American Association for Higher Education conference, and organized a conference that addressed questions such as: What are the essential characteristics of scholarship? Can these characteristics apply to teaching and service? How can we assess and reward faculty for their engagement work? Due to these efforts, the SoTL perspective now informs the discussion of more campus issues, from student retention in large lecture courses to institutional accreditation. Indeed, faculty scholarship in teaching and learning and community engagement will be an essential part of UWM's accreditation self-study.

If the engaged *research* university connects to its social context through the scholarship of its faculty and staff, it also connects to its pedagogical context through engagement with other Wisconsin institutions and national initiatives. In the University of Wisconsin System, this means working with and for the Office of Instructional and Professional Development in designing programs that foster engaged pedagogy throughout the state. This partnership has led to the formation of a University of Wisconsin System Leadership Site in the Scholarship of Teaching and Learning, one of only a dozen such entities recognized by the Carnegie Academy for the Scholarship of Teaching and Learning/American Association for Higher Education national initiative.

While the nature of the engaged university will continue to be defined and argued, the concept is clearly here to stay. Engagement in all its forms and combinations—students, faculty, administration, community, state and national associations—will ultimately become one of the important ways institutions of higher education define their value. Faculty development will be in the forefront of the discussion as it continues to evolve within and exert influence on America's universities and colleges.

Endnote

1) For more information about the *Dialogues in Diversity* program at UWM, see http://www3.uwm.edu/employeedev/mydevelopment/longview.cfm?eventid=463

References

Angelo, T. A., & Cross, K. P. (1993). *Classroom assessment techniques: A handbook for college teachers* (2nd ed.). San Francisco, CA: Jossey-Bass,

Bass, R. (1999). The scholarship of teaching: What's the problem? *Inventio, 1*(1), 1–10.

Belenky, M. F., Clichy, B. M., Goldberger, N. R., & Tarule, J. M. (1986). *Women's ways of knowing: The development of self, voice, and mind.* New York, NY: Basic Books.

Bloom, B. S. (Ed.). (1956). *Taxonomy of educational objectives: Book 1. Cognitive domain.* New York, NY: Longman.

Boyer, E. L. (1990). *Scholarship reconsidered: Priorities of the professoriate.* Princeton, NJ: The Carnegie Foundation for the Advancement of Teaching.

Bransford, J. D., Brown, A. L., & Cocking, R. R. (Eds.). (2000). *How people learn: Brain, mind, experience, and school* (Expanded ed.). Washington, DC: National Academy Press.

Brookfield, S. D. (1995). *Becoming a critically reflective teacher.* San Francisco, CA: Jossey-Bass.

Gaff, J. G., & Simpson, R. D. (1994). Faculty development in the United States. *Innovative higher education, 18*(3), 167–176.

McKinney, K. (2004) The scholarship of teaching and learning: Past lessons, current challenges, and future visions. In C. M. Wehlburg & S. Chadwick-Blossey (Eds.), *To improve the academy: Vol. 22. Resources for faculty, instructional, and organizational development* (pp. 3–19). Bolton, MA: Anker.

Palmer, P. J. (1998). *The courage to teach: Exploring the inner landscape of a teacher's life.* San Francisco, CA: Jossey-Bass.

Perry, W. G. (1970). *Forms of intellectual and ethical development in the college years: A scheme.* New York, NY: Holt, Rinehart and Winston.

Shulman, L. S. (1986). Those who understand: Knowledge growth in teaching. *Educational Researcher, 15*(2), 4–14.

Shulman, L. S. (2004a). *Teaching as community property: Essays on higher education.* San Francisco, CA: Jossey-Bass.

Shulman, L. S. (2004b). *The wisdom of practice: Essays on teaching, learning, and learning to teach.* San Francisco, CA: Jossey-Bass.

Wiggins, G., & McTighe, J. (1998). *Understanding by design.* Alexandria, VA: Association for Supervision and Curriculum Development.

Resources

ACTFL Oral Proficiency Guidelines. http://www.actfl.org

Center for Instructional and Professional Development, University of Wisconsin–Milwaukee. http://www.uwm.edu/Dept/CIPD

The Milwaukee Idea, University of Wisconsin–Milwaukee. http://www.uwm.edu/MilwaukeeIdea

PART IV

Innovative Approaches to Engagement

10

All-University Engagement in Education Reform: The Milwaukee Partnership Academy

*Marleen C. Pugach, Linda M. Post, and
Alfonzo Thurman*

An urban university that takes its commitment to the community seriously must be engaged in improving the quality of the local public schools. The logic for this level of engagement is unequivocal. In urban communities, the quality of potential university students depends largely on the quality of the local P–12 (preschool through 12th grade) schools. If students are successful learners in elementary, middle, and high school, they are more likely to attend post-secondary institutions and be successful in them. Well-educated, successful post-secondary students will be better candidates for the local workforce and, as effective members of the workforce, they contribute to strengthening the economy of the urban community. This is especially true in large metropolitan areas where students tend to matriculate at local community colleges and universities, then remain in the area upon graduation. In other words, the public schools are the pipeline not only for the university, but for the local workforce itself.

Simply put, improving the quality of teaching and learning is the business of the university, the public schools, and the community at large, and it is only when all of these stakeholders form a serious, long-term, action-oriented partnership at the system level that substantial reform can take place. This level of collective responsibility increases the potential for real change to occur and creates a sense of public, shared accountability for that

149

change. This is the underlying rationale for a new concept of what it means for a university to be engaged in improving the quality of education in the local urban schools and drives how such engagement is being defined at the University of Wisconsin–Milwaukee (UWM).

How Partnerships Can Drive System-to-System Reform

What does it mean for a university to be engaged deeply in P–12 education? Historically there has been a connection between universities and colleges that prepare teachers and the local schools. Typically these relationships have been defined in one of three ways. First, students in teacher education programs spend time in the public schools for early field experience and for student teaching. Teacher education program faculty and staff try to identify the "best" schools and "best" placements for their students. Second, public schools can call on individual faculty members to provide expert advice in topics such as curriculum, social and emotional development, assessment, special education, bilingual education, and classroom and school organization—in short, traditional service to the schools. Third, university faculty who wish to conduct research seek permission from the local district to conduct studies on various aspects of education. But these connections, however strong in many communities, are not designed as a systemic approach to improving the quality of teaching and learning. Instead, they are geared toward filling an immediate need for an individual, a school, or a program.

In the 1980s a different trend emerged, one that began to redefine the relationship between teacher education programs and public schools. This trend was based on forming partnerships between colleges or universities and a small number of public school sites that came to be known as *professional development schools* (PDS). Launched by the Holmes Group (1986)—now the Holmes Partnership—a consortium of research universities committed to redesigning the preparation of teachers, professional development schools are designed to parallel the concept of a teaching hospital, where prospective teachers work with talented veteran teachers for the simultaneous reform of teaching and teacher education. The design of a PDS is such that only a small number of schools are so designated. In this model, involvement is usually limited to the school or college of education, which invests human and fiscal resources in various ways to contribute to the improvement of the specific school sites with which they partner, and to make them exemplary locations at which to prepare new teachers. (See the National Council for Accreditation of Teacher Education's web site for standards for professional development schools: http://www.ncate.org/documents/pdsStandards.pdf.)

The PDS concept challenged schools and colleges of education to become engaged with the local schools more substantially than ever before. Nevertheless, the potential of the PDS model is limited in scope. While it is meant to result in the improvement of teacher education, its design is such that it cannot result in systemic reform across the schools because the model cannot go to scale in large school districts. In other words, strong partnerships between teacher education programs and individual P–12 schools are not enough.

Obviously, improving the quality of teacher education is a critical element in improving the quality of schools. In isolation, however, these efforts for improvement cannot span the central players and constituencies who are fundamental to the operation of the schools in which teachers learn to teach and therefore cannot hope to have a sustained effect. Instead, efforts to create a stronger force of new teachers must intersect with major school district and teachers' union initiatives. For urban school districts that partner with urban universities, there is an additional sense of urgency, driven by the economic and social challenges of metropolitan environments, to improve the educational experience and success of students in *all* urban schools, not only those in a few schools.

UWM is committed to preparing and retaining teachers who are both disposed and able to teach effectively in urban classrooms that have low-income and racial and ethnic minority students. Acknowledging the interdependence between UWM and the Milwaukee Public Schools (MPS) is central to our goal of systemic reform. Over the past 15 years, consistent with our urban mission, UWM has been the largest provider of new teachers for the approximately 165 schools in Milwaukee. For the past three years, UWM has provided MPS with 43% of new early-childhood, 40% of new elementary and middle school, and 27% of new high school teachers. In actuality, 67% of staff across all positions in MPS have one or more degrees and/or certifications from UWM. The quality of teaching and learning in MPS is dependent upon the quality of preparation UWM provides to future MPS teachers and the ability of MPS to provide the support needed to retain high-quality teachers throughout their careers.

Driving the system-to-system partnership described in this chapter, then, is an authentic problem in our community that requires the coordinated, aligned efforts of each of the partners who commit to this work. The goal is not to tinker around the edges, but rather to roll up our collective sleeves and work together to address what has seemed like an insurmountable challenge, namely, improving the quality of teaching and learning in local schools.

The Milwaukee Partnership Academy as the Vehicle for System-to-System Reform

Our commitment to engaging with the community to improve education in Milwaukee's urban schools is guided by the Milwaukee Partnership Academy (MPA), founded in 1999. The genesis of the MPA was a federal grant designed to bring together the school district and UWM. Although the grant provided the initial impetus to meet, the leadership held to the idea that their collective power was much more productive than any organization's individual power. This led to the ongoing commitment and expansion of the partnership.

Every two weeks the MPA brings together major leaders in the community, including: the chancellor of UWM; the superintendent of MPS; the executive director of the Milwaukee Teachers' Education Association, the local teachers' union; the president of the MPS Board of School Directors; the president of the Milwaukee Area Technical College; the president of the local chamber of commerce; the mayor of the City of Milwaukee; the chair of the education committee of the Greater Milwaukee Committee; the president of the Private Industry Council; and the president of the Helen Bader Foundation, a major local philanthropic organization. The MPA is designated as an urban P–16 council, representing the interests of education from early childhood through the end of the baccalaureate degree. The stakeholders represent this entire spectrum of education in our community.

The regular presence of these leaders, who command attention and resources and hold power in our community, is fundamental to the joint commitment to institutionalize, stabilize, and sustain the partnership and thus to provide stability to education reform in Milwaukee's urban schools.

The visible participation of high-level leaders provides credibility to the importance of the MPA within the community.

The goal of the MPA is to ensure that every child is on grade level in reading, writing, and mathematics. This goal depends centrally upon the quality of teaching in the schools. Therefore, it also depends on the structures, supports, and the culture within which teaching and schooling take place. In the summer of 2001 the MPA Executive Committee crafted its first set of priorities as a means of focusing its work. Those priorities are revisited each year in an annual retreat. The goal is not to change priorities radically each year, but rather to fine tune priorities based on data from the prior year and to be responsive to changing conditions regarding their implementation. The priorities are critical to the success of the partnership because they provide a focal point for the alignment of efforts and resources. As such, they work to counteract the cycle that has been so prevalent in urban schools, namely, generating and discarding new initiatives every year. The current priorities that drive the MPA's work include:

- District-wide implementation of a comprehensive literacy and mathematics framework

- Tutoring and family literacy

- Teacher and principal quality, with an emphasis on coaching and embedded professional development

- Research, assessment, and evaluation

One of the important landmarks early in the development of the MPA was the realization that in order to effect serious reform and address these priorities in a substantive way, it would take more than regular meetings of the leaders of the partner organizations. The challenge was how to implement partnership activities both across the member institutions and vertically through them as well. A partnership that includes institutional leaders alone is not readily connected to the daily practices that impact and influence how education actually takes place. Conversely, a partnership that is located only at the level of practice (such as the professional development school model) may not command the attention of institutional leaders who must leverage resources, power, attention, institutional perspectives, and policy considerations on the goals of the partnership. The MPA created a unique three-part structure that addresses these issues and governs its work.

The Governance and Structure of the MPA

Three groups form the governing structure of the MPA: 1) the Executive Committee, 2) the Board of Directors, and 3) the Implementation Team.

The Executive Committee

As noted earlier, the Executive Committee of the MPA is composed of the leaders of the 10 key stakeholder organizations that include the superintendent of MPS, presidents and chancellors of area colleges and universities, the executive director of the Milwaukee Teachers' Education Association (MTEA), and corporate, civic, and governmental leaders.

The Executive Committee meets once a month to discuss the MPA's progress, to make decisions regarding the policies and priorities of the partnership, and to provide direction to the executive director. The second meeting they attend each month is a meeting of the full partnership board of directors described below. This is a public monthly, two-hour meeting of the full MPA and is led by one of the members of the Executive Committee. Executive Committee members do not send representatives or substitutes to these two meetings each month; rather, they have made a commitment to attend themselves. They may bring representatives and extend participation of individuals from their institutions, but the culture of the partnership is such that an expectation has been set that the chief leaders of the organizations are in the room, at the table, working on the goal of improving education in the community.

During the first two years of its existence, the MPA had no executive director and was run by informal agreement through individuals from the school district, UWM, and the teachers' union. It became clear, however, that the magnitude of the work demanded dedicated administrative leadership. In January 2003, the Executive Committee designated and filled the full-time position of executive director of the Milwaukee Partnership Academy.

The Board of Directors

The Board of Directors extends participation in the MPA laterally across the community and vertically within partner organizations. Members of the Board of Directors include broad representation from the metropolitan community—for example, leaders within the public library, the YMCA, area museums, and the zoo. The board also includes the deans of the

School of Education, College of Letters and Sciences, and the Peck School of the Arts at UWM, as well as the chairperson of the Department of Curriculum and Instruction. A formal representative of the private postsecondary institutions in the Milwaukee area is also a member of the board. In addition, there is parent and teacher representation. The board includes a broad range of affiliates, including the local foundation/donor community, as well as the ongoing, consistent presence of government officials, notably the state superintendent of public instruction, who *regularly* attends each meeting with staff. The former lieutenant governor attended while she held office.

The monthly meetings of the Board of Directors serve a central public function regarding the MPA. These meetings are designed to update the broad range of community stakeholders on the progress of the various priorities, to solicit input on and commitment to new activities, and to provide ongoing momentum for the work of the partnership. This meeting always includes a report from the superintendent of MPS and from the executive director of the MPA. Often there is a short presentation on a critical issue that helps create a common understanding of the activities that are being undertaken to meet the partnership's goals. A vital purpose of these presentations and discussions is to align the language, concepts, and resources that undergird and support the collective efforts of the partners. This meeting also provides an opportunity to honor the accomplishments that have been achieved to date and to refocus and recommit the partnership to its goal of improving the quality of education for the children of Milwaukee. Serious discussions take place, and there is a high degree of awareness that collective leadership across this range of partners is unique, providing an uncommon opportunity to make a difference for the Milwaukee community. These are open meetings, which guests frequently attend. The full MPA membership also holds an annual one-day retreat.

The Implementation Team

In the summer of 2001, the MPA Executive Committee established the Implementation Team, composed of multiple representatives from the partner organizations. The Implementation Team develops and implements the action plan to support the MPA's priorities; it is conceptualized as the "action arm" of the MPA. This team is chaired by the executive director of the MPA, who sets the agenda and keeps the work of the group on track. Work groups for each MPA priority are chaired by members of the Implementation Team. All work groups are inclusive and encourage volunteer members.

The Implementation Team consists of 12 voting members, three from each of the principal organizations in the partnership: MPS, the Milwaukee Area Technical College, the Milwaukee Teachers' Education Association, and UWM. The president of the teachers' union is one of these representatives. That said, all work has been accomplished by consensus and a vote has not yet been taken. In addition to this core group, leaders of the major departments within MPS are also members, including the director of teaching and learning, the chief academic officer, the director of assessment and accountability, the director of technology, and the director of leadership support.

The three university representatives to this team are all senior faculty who take on this work in addition to their regular university appointments. An array of other individuals also participate regularly in the work of the Implementation Team, including additional members of many of the departments in MPS listed above, additional university faculty from UWM and the local private colleges and universities, other community members, and teachers-in-residence (veteran MPS teachers on special assignment to UWM to develop their skills as teacher leaders). All of these people are deployed across the four priorities of the MPA and participate in work groups to move these priorities ahead. The Implementation Team's work groups extend participation to all interested stakeholders, and it is not uncommon for the MPA's executive director to get a call from individuals who wish to participate.

From 2001–2003 the Implementation Team met *weekly* for one half day, 12 months a year, and organized itself into work groups representing the priorities established by the MPA Executive Board. Beginning in 2003 the team changed to a biweekly meeting schedule. The meetings are divided into two parts. First there is a two-hour meeting of the full Implementation Team. This is followed by two hours for each work group associated with each of the MPA priorities. The members of the Executive Committee commonly refer to this as the place where the "real work" of the MPA gets done.

Early on in the development of the MPA, this team directly addressed the historical difficulty in sustaining improvement efforts with starting multiple initiatives that were not well connected and did not last long enough to make a sustained impact. Further, there was a sense of long-standing skepticism on the part of the teachers that any initiative could be sustained over time or that enough of the people in charge had the big picture in mind. As a result, aligning activities and keeping a focus on the MPA priorities commanded a great deal of time and energy, and communicating the purpose of the work across partner institutions and within the community has taken on major significance. "Keeping on message" became a critical goal, consistently helping others—and ourselves— understand the message.

All key activities of the district flow through the Implementation Team for ongoing direction and feedback. The goal is to keep focused on the critical priorities of the Partnership and to resist having its efforts diffused across a broad range of unrelated initiatives. Although the main function of the Implementation Team is the action agenda, the team has also become the vehicle for solving problems and addressing barriers in an immediate, timely fashion. This is possible due to the level of leadership from the various partners and stakeholders who sit on this team. Likewise, the Implementation Team meetings are now a given for all partners, and in the community it is common knowledge that if you want to interact with senior people from the partner organizations, Monday afternoon is a good time to find them—at the Implementation Team meeting.

What goes on at the formal Implementation Team meetings? Why is it necessary to meet with this level of frequency and intensity? The answers to these questions lie in the desire to have the MPA foster change in the way the partner organizations do business—by aligning initiatives and resources under the priorities set by the Executive Committee. Work groups report on their progress at each meeting, enabling the team to avoid duplication of effort and to combine efforts across work groups as needed. This is accomplished by having the full Implementation Team meet prior to work group meetings. Periodically, representatives of specific programs that have relevance for the work groups make brief presentations to the team. Large grants that are prepared by cross-institutional partners support the priorities of the MPA; progress on proposals, including the key positions and structures they require, come through the team. Also, any individual or group wishing to submit a grant that references the MPA as part of the rationale must present the proposal to the Implementation Team. The proposal must then be approved by a research subgroup of the team in order to receive a letter of support from the MPA. In addition, grants that are linked to the MPA must include individuals who contribute directly to the work of the MPA. These are all efforts to align our work, maximize resources, and reshape the view and practice of research from an individual to a collective purpose.

While it is a labor-intensive effort, the Implementation Team has become a critical source of brainstorming, action, and consensus building around the work of the MPA. The Implementation Team embodies the belief that it takes not only senior-level leadership on a community-wide basis, but also leadership at the level of those who take action on a daily basis, to make teaching and teacher education work in Milwaukee and to meet the goals of the MPA. Implementation Team members are invited to attend monthly MPA board meetings, and many members do so on a regular basis. Much of the agenda for the monthly MPA Executive Board meetings evolves directly from the ongoing progress and accomplishments of the Implementation Team. The agenda for the Implementation Team is directed by the decisions of the Executive Committee.

The Partnership and the Changing Concept of University Engagement

Given the condition of urban education both nationally and locally within Milwaukee, the focus of our partnership represents a critical issue for the community, one about which there is great urgency. As a result, the engagement embodied in the Milwaukee Partnership Academy is substantial, ongoing, and challenging. The problem the MPA is addressing, namely, the quality of education in Milwaukee, is one that cannot be expected to be solved by a short-term set of activities. Instead, to see real progress, the partners must be committed over time, for the long haul.

How the Partnership Changes Faculty Work

How does a community partnership that demands a long-term commitment and investment influence faculty and administrators' work? What is the nature of the university's commitment on a day-to-day and week-to-week basis?

As noted earlier in this chapter, many faculty members in the field of education have had longstanding commitments to local school districts. How do these relationships change in the context of an ongoing, multi-level partnership? Faculty members who work within the partnership take on a level of responsibility that differs from regular faculty work as well as from traditional school-university relationships.

Most important, the MPA is not a project with start and end dates, nor a temporary engagement. This longevity is especially challenging once the shine has worn off, once the partnership is no longer an innovation, but instead is a way of doing business over the long term. The conventional wisdom that organizational change takes several years and requires a willingness to stick to the task accurately represents our partnership. From the university side, partnerships, therefore, require faculty who are willing to see the work through, rather than dip in and out of it idiosyncratically.

Next, partnership work requires faculty who can function at a high level of collaboration. Individuals—faculty or otherwise—who participate must, in the end, make good partners. The goal of the MPA is a shared goal and participants who value individual goals over MPA goals are not likely to represent the institution well or contribute to productive outcomes. The need for collaboration and goal sharing may conflict with how faculty are socialized and how they view their roles. As a result of the need for collaboration, not all faculty can participate effectively in partnerships, nor are all invited to do so with the MPA. The majority of faculty involved in the MPA are senior-level associate or full professors who have a demonstrated track record of working collaboratively across organizations. Most of these individuals have worked with the MPA since its inception and continue to do so, providing consistency and ongoing leadership. Non-tenured faculty participate, primarily as members of work groups of the MPA Implementation Team. In this way their MPA tasks are well defined during the years when they are working to achieve tenure, but they also gain valuable experience working in the partnership and contributing directly to this collaborative effort.

Ongoing participation in this partnership has the potential to redefine the teaching, research, and service relationship. The partnership becomes the context that shapes one's teaching, research, and service as interconnected activities. The partnership provides a much different level of knowledge about local schools and classrooms, which, in turn, can translate into a different level of discourse in teacher preparation classes. New opportunities, directly connected to the partnership priorities, are constantly evolving that have implications for participation on the part of teacher education students, and the lines of communication to engage university students in relevant district activities are direct and frequent. These opportunities for working within the district raise issues about what constitutes, for example, appropriate field experience activities for UWM students and how those experiences can be of more direct benefit to MPS over time. As such, faculty and student resources at the university can be marshaled in a more aligned manner with the needs of the district.

The research needs of the partnership are extensive and provide a wide range of opportunities for faculty participation. However, this participation needs to be situated within the collaborative tenor of the MPA, as well as within its priorities. The key to making this interconnection of activities work is to align faculty expertise with the priorities and then interest faculty in those aspects in which they have the greatest interest and expertise. Research and service thus become integrated on behalf of the MPA. All faculty who participate need to find their niche within the framework of the MPA, but not all faculty have to make the commitment, for example, to the demands of the Implementation Team and its frequent meeting schedule.

The Role of the Dean of the School of Education in the Partnership

The focus on partnership is a message that is communicated from UWM's chancellor, provost, and the deans. The role of the dean of education is particularly different from preengagement years. In a survey of deans of education, Gmelch (2002) reported on the most important tasks for education deans. These tasks, ranked by importance to those surveyed, include:

- Maintaining a conducive work climate

- Fostering good teaching

- Representing the college to administration

- Recruiting and selecting chairs and faculty

- Maintaining effective communication across departments

- Preparing budgets and financial planning

- Encouraging professional development of chairs, faculty, and staff

- Evaluating chair and faculty performance

- Communicating the mission to employees and constituents

- Developing long-range college goals

The reform of public schools, particularly those in urban areas, must be a critical and focused part of the work of a dean of education. While the 10 tasks of a dean's work listed above are important, there is nothing obvious about how they encourage, support, and impact the dean's engagement with partners to improve the quality of education in the local school system. As a result of UWM's commitment to this goal, the role of the dean of education has been extended to include collaboration with the public schools and agencies that support the public schools, and leadership in both internal and external elements of university-school engagement. These critical new roles play out in a variety of specific structures, activities, and practices across constituencies. Among the most important are the following.

Partnerships for Education Council of the Deans. The dean of education also serves as the chancellor's deputy for education partnerships and, in this role, convenes a Partnership for Education Council of Deans that crosses disciplines, schools, and colleges. The Council of Deans includes the UWM deans of letters and science, art, engineering and applied sciences, architecture and urban planning, nursing, business administration, and health sciences. The Partnerships for Education Council of the Deans has deep and significant discussions about how teacher preparation and the reform of urban public schools can become a university-wide commitment and responsibility. Meetings of the Council of Deans usually include invited members of the public schools (teachers and administrators) and the executive director of the MPA to emphasize the needs of the public and to help strategize how the deans and their faculty can play a meaningful role in the reform initiatives of MPS. For some of the schools and colleges this may involve faculty working directly in schools to support MPA initiatives, such as family literacy and tutoring. For campus architecture and psychology faculty, it may include improving the school environment, particularly building smaller schools. It also may include, for example, the UWM College of Engineering and Applied Sciences putting forth its own concept of a small school in mathematics and sciences to build interest and skills related to engineering.

Metropolitan Milwaukee Area Deans of Education. On behalf of the MPA, the UWM dean of education convenes the Metropolitan Milwaukee Area Deans of Education (MMADE), which consists of UWM and the six local private higher education institutions that also prepare teachers, administrators, and other personnel for the public schools. Members of the

MMADE meet monthly during the academic year to discuss and develop ways in which all local institutions of higher education can support and assist MPS and to align their work with the priorities of the MPA. Building the capacity of MPS in the development of new teachers, administrators, and other school personnel is an important factor in the partnership with MPS. While UWM prepares more teachers for MPS than any other higher education institution in the state of Wisconsin, quality teachers for MPS is the business of all programs that provide teacher candidates hired by MPS. All members of MMADE contribute directly to the MPA through their work on the MPA Implementation Team and its various work groups.

Faculty participation across programs. Gaining UWM faculty participation in the work of the MPA has been the most challenging and rewarding of the experiences of UWM's dean of education. Having faculty who understand and are willing to participate in the community engagement aspects of the university is not left to chance. Important to participation is the recognition that the university's reward system is based on faculty work around research, teaching, and service. These three areas of work should intersect in partnering with the public schools and not be limited only to those in teacher education. Faculty in school counseling, learning and development, measurement and evaluation, foundations, educational policy, and administrative leadership have much to contribute to partnership work, not only in providing school personnel but also in helping to formulate assessment strategies for the work of the partnership. Communicating to faculty the necessity and responsibility of participating in the community engagement aspect of the university, and specifically the work of the MPA, is a key role of the UWM dean of education. Many faculty members, at both the junior and senior levels, eagerly embrace the work of the Partnership; however, to assure this participation, the dean has sought out and hired faculty who understand that this is an expectation of employment and that it is rewarded.

Faculty recruitment. As part of the faculty recruitment process, position descriptions for new faculty specify that partnership work is a job expectation. This expectation is also stressed at the department and dean's level in the hiring process. All aspects of the recruitment cycle, including search committees and the various outlets used to advertise positions, focus on the need for faculty to reflect the urban population its members serve. Specific strategies are identified to actively seek candidates of color and individuals from other categories of diversity for faculty positions. In the current dean of education's tenure, more than 40% of new faculty hires are African American, American Indian, Latino, or of Southeast Asian descent.

Rewards: merit, tenure, and promotion. The School of Education's merit, promotion, and tenure requirements must conform to the overall standards of the university. Latitude is provided within those requirements for departments, schools, and colleges to apply principles and standards specific to their disciplines and needs. Thus to be fully integrated into the work of the university, rewarding partnership work must be reflected in merit, promotion, and tenure structures. This expectation is communicated at the department, school, and university levels through the yearly performance review of each faculty in the merit distribution process. Other UWM departments, schools, and colleges give varying weight to work, such as partnering relationships and account for it within their merit, promotion, and tenure processes.

Faculty are directed to specify how their research, teaching, and service are incorporated into and impact the partnership activities of the School of Education. Funding is set aside by the dean from the merit pool to give "Dean's Merit" to those whose work most successfully impacts the partnership work of the school. The dean generally recommends to the provost and vice chancellor individual faculty members who are furthering the community engagement goals of the university for additional merit recognition. Such policies and practices make the work of the partnership real via the recognized reward system of the university.

Yearly faculty performance reviews are aligned with contract renewal, promotion, and tenure procedures. The dean of education reviews and recommends each faculty member put forward by the departments for promotion and/or tenure to the provost and vice chancellor. A key factor in the dean's review is how well the faculty member has integrated partnership work into his or her research, teaching, and service. Making the work of partnership part of this reward structure is vital in assuring that partnership work is recognized as critical to the university's mission.

The engagement of all sectors of UWM's campus and the private higher education institutions in the area, along with an aggressive plan to involve faculty and staff of the School of Education, have been instrumental in making the work of the MPA a vital element in improving MPS. The dean's role in aligning the work of the School of Education, the university, and the higher education community with the partnership is a critical factor in defining what it means to be engaged in the education community.

Impact

The most important impact of the MPA is the degree to which students in the Milwaukee Public Schools gain the knowledge and skills to be productive, contributing members of the society. Therefore, conventional measures like scores on standardized tests, attendance rates, graduation rates, and college attendance are germane to this work. Because this is an urban schools partnership, we are also concerned with improving teacher retention rates. However, there are other, more proximal impacts that support these goals in terms of changing organizational structures and supports for education across the community. Impact to date falls into four categories.

Structural Impacts Within the Schools

Structural impacts have been made to support building local capacity for improving teaching and learning and for using school-based data to shape education at each school site. (See Figure 10.1)

Figure 10.1

The Development of Shared Comprehensive Literacy and Mathematics Frameworks

The development of local learning targets, or standards, for each grade level

Implementing the position of literacy coach in each school, supported by a team of six literacy specialists at the district level, to provide job-embedded professional development, funded through internal budget reallocation of several million dollars

Implementing the position of mathematics lead teachers in every school, supported by a team of six mathematics specialists at the district level, funded by a grant from the National Science Foundation

Establishing learning teams at every school to create and sustain the conditions within the school where professionals thrive, learn, and grow in the quality of their teaching as a means of improving student learning. Learning teams are composed of the principal, the literacy coach, the mathematics teacher leaders, and a small number of other individuals

Creating leadership development opportunities for classroom teachers through a teacher-in-residence program at UWM

Creating specific roles for these leaders, for example, as members of learning teams

In 2002 and 2003, reading scores of MPS students in the elementary grades have increased. In particular, the third-grade scores in 2002 showed the highest percentage of increase of any district in the state of Wisconsin.

New Forms of Community Dialogue and Accountability Around Education

As a major community force, the partnership places the responsibility for improving education on the shoulders of the entire community working together rather than placing the burden on any single institution. It creates shared accountability in a very public forum across some of the most important and influential organizations in the community. The MPA has crafted a focused agenda, keeps this agenda front and center, and works steadily to align all activities and initiatives with its stated goal and priorities.

Public accountability for the how the greater Milwaukee community defines its commitment to education takes place through the high level of visibility of the partnership itself and the regular participation of leaders across the community. The governance and structure of the partnership, and especially the relationship between the Executive Committee and the Implementation Team, provides the context for recursive community-wide discussion and action. There is a regular opportunity, as well as an expectation, that progress on the MPA priorities will be discussed. Priorities that need special attention or that are experiencing problems all come to the table in a relatively short timeframe. Problems, and their potential solutions, become everyone's responsibility. The public nature of the partnership means that the operations of each of the partners become much more public and open for discussion. As a result, each institution—with very different ways of operating and different fundamental purposes—is challenged to rethink its way of doing business and its role in improving the quality of education.

New Funding Sources for Education

The MPA began with substantial federal grant dollars. Our goal in identifying additional sources of money, and especially grants, has been to align grant-seeking activities with the priorities of the MPA. If a grant opportunity exists that can be shaped to support the MPA agenda, it is pursued. If such opportunities cannot be shaped in this manner, they are not pursued.

The MPA itself does not receive grant funds, so the various partners submit grants related to partnership goals. This way of doing business relies on a high degree of trust among the partners. In addition to the original federal grants that supported the inception of the MPA, major grants include:

- Gates High School Redesign Grant, $17 million

- National Science Foundation Mathematics Partnership Grant, $20 million

- Carnegie Corporation of New York Teachers for a New Era Grant, $5 million

- Local foundation grants to support 14 learning teams for $10,000 a year for each of three years, with a community challenge to fund all teams at the same level

Other priority-focused grants include:

- Department of Public Instruction alignment of grants to low-performing schools that include a requirement for learning teams to meet as part of local school improvement and to support the work of the literacy coaches

- Broad Foundation and Joyce Foundation Grant to explore differentiated compensation models for teachers

- Joyce Foundation grant to conduct an external formative evaluation of school-based learning teams

The MPA continues to work directly with local and regional foundations to secure additional dollars to support this work. A measure of the MPA's impact is that funders are now starting to seek out the MPA to discuss funding opportunities.

Concluding Thoughts: On Sustainability and Stewardship

Cynics would tell us that partnerships rarely last and that, in urban schools, all innovations tend to be short-lived. If a partnership derives its strength from a single leader, the danger is that the partnership may fold when that leader leaves his or her position. Yet changes in leadership are commonplace in urban communities, and especially in urban school districts, and the MPA is not immune to these changes. Therefore, a critical measure of the strength of the MPA is whether or not it can be sustained in the face of leadership changes. To date, the MPA has weathered changes in leaders from two of the principal partners, with one additional change imminent at the time of this writing.

In the summer of 2002, when the MPA was founded, the MPS superintendent, Spence Korte, resigned, and William Andrekopolous was appointed as the new superintendent. Although initially tentative, today Superintendent Andrekopoulos and his cabinet are among the MPA's strongest supporters. The new superintendent brought to the table a set of five capacity builders for the district, which were integrated with the MPA priorities to forge a unified set of goals.

In August 2003 the chancellor of UWM and founding member of the MPA, Nancy Zimpher, announced that she would leave to assume the presidency of the University of Cincinnati. The interim chancellor stepped in to the MPA for the 2003–2004 year. During this interim, deans and faculty leaders at UWM worked together to ensure that the activities of the partnership were maintained at the highest levels. A marker of organizational change at the level of higher education emerged in the search for a new chancellor at UWM: The president of the University of Wisconsin System and members of the University of Wisconsin Board of Regents charged the search committee to identify a new chancellor who would continue to work in partnership with the Milwaukee community, particularly in partnership with the P–12 schools. The state superintendent of public instruction, who is a member of the MPA Board of Directors, represented the Board of Regents in the search, further ensuring the Partnership's sustainability at the higher-education level. Two members of the Executive Committee of the MPA were on the search committee, as well as one of the deans, who is a member of the MPA Board of Directors. The new chancellor, Carlos Santiago, took office in August 2004 and is an active participant in the MPA. We believe that the ongoing viability and vitality of the Partnership through these changes in leadership represent a major accomplishment.

A new president of the Board of School Directors for the MPS was elected in April 2004. He immediately cited the importance of working closely with the MPA as part of his new responsibilities. Finally, during the mayoral election in 2004, the local newspaper cited the new mayor's participation in the MPA as a critical issue for the next administration. Shortly after his election, the new mayor joined the Executive Committee of the MPA.

But partnerships are not sustained only at the executive level of leadership. They require ongoing stewardship—often, but not always, behind the scenes—to troubleshoot and solve problems on a day-to-day basis. Problems are part of the process of working together; we expect them and expect to deal with them (Fullan, 1993). It is common for problems to be raised and addressed at all levels: in meetings of the Executive Committee, at monthly MPA meetings, and at meetings of the Implementation Team. The practice of voicing conflicting viewpoints was established early on, especially within meetings of the Implementation Team.

In addition to these formal meetings, a small group of individuals from various levels of leadership are alert to problems that have the potential to diminish the goals of the partnership and that require such behind-the-scenes stewardship. Problems might include, for example: identifying activities within any organization that should be connected but are not; making sure everyone is "on message"; cutting through red tape in bureaucracies that are slow to change; or addressing issues that are blocking progress or implementation. When a problem calls for immediate intervention, these individuals make themselves available for immediate troubleshooting. More important, they see being "on call" to solve problems as an important responsibility and an essential part of their role within the framework and goals of the partnership.

Such behind-the-scenes stewardship can only take place in a context where there is a great deal of trust among the partners and where there are shared goals. As problems arise, criticisms may be leveled by a member of one of the organizations about a situation within another one of the partner organizations. Our foundation of trust, cultivated over time, forms a strong backdrop against which the inevitable problems and challenges can be addressed.

Examples of the specific challenges the MPA and its Executive Committee have faced over the past several years include: strengthening the funding base, building an internal and external communications infrastructure, simultaneously containing growth in the membership and building broad-based support, balancing goals and strategies with buy-in at the grassroots level (e.g., teachers and principals), and restructuring to best support addressing these issues and concerns.

The Milwaukee Partnership Academy is committed to long-term engagement across community institutions as the central means of addressing the enduring challenge: the education of its children and youth. There is no question that the level of community engagement required by this partnership redefines how universities—and their faculty—view their purpose and their work. With an eye towards sustainability and a commitment to stewardship, the MPA aims to change the fundamental relationships among its partner organizations, and indeed across the entire community.

Acknowledgements

We are indebted to all of our colleagues in the Milwaukee Partnership Academy for their commitment to working together, across a group of very different institutions, to improve the quality of teaching and learning for the students in the Milwaukee Public Schools. We also wish to acknowledge the contributions of the former chancellor of the University of Wisconsin–Milwaukee, Nancy Zimpher, and those of Ken Howey, formerly professor in UWM's School of Education, to the MPA in its formative stages. Their support and vision were essential in launching the partnership and seeing it through its first five years of existence.

References

Fullan, M. (1993). *Change forces: Probing the depths of educational reform*. London, England: Falmer Press.

Gmelch, W. H. (Ed.). (2002). *Deans' balancing acts: Education leaders and the challenges they face*. Washington, DC: American Association of Colleges for Teacher Education.

The Holmes Group. (1986). *Tomorrow's teachers*. East Lansing, MI: Author.

11

Taking the Lead From the Community: Nonprofit Management Education

Rita Hartung Cheng

This initiative to strengthen Milwaukee's nonprofit organizations is the product of an important community-wide partnership that brought UWM together with several major foundations and nonprofits in metropolitan Milwaukee. The initiative was inaugurated as the Helen Bader Institute for Nonprofit Management Education in summer 2001 and is housed on the UWM campus. During the past three years the accomplishments of the Schools and Colleges at UWM that have partnered with the community foundations to provide support for the Institute are significant. The governance model for the initiative was designed as a true partnership with the community.

—Helen Bader Institute for Nonprofit Management Education
Annual Report 2003–2004

The Milwaukee Nonprofit Community and The Milwaukee Idea

Learning to follow, not lead, was one of the toughest lessons of engagement in the initiative to create nonprofit educational offerings at the University of Wisconsin–Milwaukee (UWM). It was also one of the most rewarding. The nonprofit management initiative in Milwaukee is an example of community-university engagement that was initiated by the community and driven by the leadership and commitment of key community and university leaders. The creation of the Helen Bader Institute for Nonprofit Management at UWM was the culmination of many years of discussion and debate within the larger Milwaukee community. Unlike many similar initiatives, the university did not initiate the discussions, nor present the solution. Rather, the impetus for the collaboration came directly from the community.

Since 1994, an alliance of Milwaukee charitable foundations, led by the Helen Bader, Fay McBeath, and Greater Milwaukee Foundations, have funded technical assistance to Milwaukee area nonprofit organizations through contributions to the locally based Nonprofit Management Fund. The Nonprofit Management Fund operated by providing small grants ($5,000–$10,000) to nonprofit organizations to hire consultants to provide technical assistance to improve dimensions of management.

UWM's two graduate programs—Urban Studies, in the College of Letters and Science, and Educational Leadership, in the School of Education—traditionally served the continuing education needs of nonprofit leaders through masters and doctoral offerings. In 1998 the public administration and business administration faculty jointly developed options in their respective masters degree programs directed specifically at nonprofit managers.

Others on campus were active in community initiatives to address management training for nonprofit leaders. The Harvard University Denali Fellows program focused attention on business training for nonprofit leaders. Several UWM faculty were involved in selecting and evaluating the performance of the Milwaukee Denali fellows; however, the university was often unable to respond to additional requests for assistance. Nonprofit leaders were forced to continue dialogue on internships, continuing education, and consultation on operations issues on an ad hoc basis with individual faculty and staff across multiple schools and colleges. Indeed, although the community and university had been discussing the need for more executive nonprofit management education for some time, it was only with the arrival of Chancellor Nancy Zimpher that finding ways to improve and institutionalize these and other efforts became the focus of how UWM was to engage the community in a new and meaningful way.

With the announcement of The Milwaukee Idea and the UWM's expressed interest in creating sustainable university-community initiatives in

1998, the Milwaukee philanthropic community saw an opportunity to elevate the quantity and quality of nonprofit management education in southeastern Wisconsin through a partnership with the university. The first step to that end was a meeting of members of the philanthropic community to discuss strategies for improving the nonprofit sector in the area. The second step was a meeting with faculty and staff at UWM to explore the availability of university resources, expertise, and interest to support nonprofit management education and training. The third step was accomplished in June and September of 1999 when two sets of three focus group interviews were conducted by a Chicago-based consulting firm to gather additional information and opinions from the nonprofit community regarding nonprofit management education.

Building on the Idea

UWM's response to the invitation to participate in the community project to advance educational opportunities in nonprofit management was immediate and positive. A group of university representatives and community and foundation leaders began meeting regularly to discuss ways to achieve a higher level of awareness and support for nonprofit management and leadership education. The group became known as the Nonprofit Management Education (NME) Steering Committee and forged ahead in late 1999 to develop what would become a unique community-university partnership. UWM took an active role with four individuals on the steering committee and 12 others on work/affinity groups that also included nonprofit and foundation leaders. As a first step, the groups worked to sort through the issues, needs, and challenges of developing high-quality nonprofit management education and technical assistance. Data from the initial focus groups formed the basis for preliminary discussions.

The NME was charged with setting the planning agenda, assessing progress, and reviewing final recommendations. Over a six-month period, the committee engaged more than 85 individuals from the community and several other universities to serve in various capacities on workgroups/affinity groups. The groups sorted through the many educational options, including degree and nondegree, certificates, workshops, and technical assistance. Data on programs already offered in the area were collected in order to plan for building on existing programs. The group also collected and reviewed data from other cities to learn from successful programs and centers.

Information Gathering

In June 1999 executive directors of 65 Milwaukee-area nonprofit organizations were invited to attend interviews. The organizations were selected to represent a variety of types and sizes of nonprofit organizations. A key finding of the first set of interviews was that executives expressed stronger interest in nonprofit management education opportunities for their upper-level managers than for themselves. This finding led to a second set of three focus group interviews in September 1999. For the September interviews, 75 executive directors were requested to send a key manager to the interview; small organizations were represented by their executives. Twenty-seven people (36%) participated in the second set of interviews. In addition to the interviews, participants completed a brief organizational and personal profile.

In the June interviews, when respondents discussed their own educational needs, most reflected on their personal career transitions from direct service providers to executives and managers. Further analysis of the academic degrees of this group, as well as the certifications and other credentials they held, clarified that their education interests had not been in business management. Therefore, it was not surprising that many were concerned that their business skills were inadequate.

Comments from these focus group interviews served as powerful missives to the NME Steering Committee.

> I think most of us around the table have been here (in non-profit management) a long time. I am not going back to school now, but I have younger folks on my staff that would.

> The nonprofit sector is made up of grassroots people. To put a degree on it, I wonder if it would take out that warmth. That's what makes it work: I still have the same kind of people I want to work in the community. I know I won't make it rich, but I have to do it. I wonder if I put a degree on it, will it take the heart out of it?

> If I had someone on my staff that wanted to go to this I would like to invest in that person and this education.

Personally and professionally, because it would be good for the agency. I would hope the agency would think the same about me and about sending me. It is a partnership with the individual and the organization, which might speak to a sliding scale.

I wanted to say [that] if I were given the opportunity to be in a classroom with a group of people like this, how much stronger I would be. It would make me think that a course in nonprofit management would be definitely worth it.

1999 Focus Group Questions

1) When you need information about nonprofit management topics, where do you go?
2) What delivery systems come to mind when you hear "nonprofit management education?"
3) What are some of the competencies that executive directors need? If you were building a nonprofit management curriculum, what would be some of your course titles?
4) As a leader working in the nonprofit field, what are the nonprofit management topics or areas in which leaders like you need more education and training?
5) If an academic program were available that met your needs, what would be some of the factors that would influence your decision to participate?
6) Is a nonprofit management degree valued in your field—does it lead to better jobs and higher salaries?
7) How could local universities be more helpful in providing training and education in nonprofit management?
8) Some people question whether education programs for employees really make a difference in the effectiveness of an organization. Do you prefer programs targeted at individual learners or those targeted at whole organizations?
9) If a nonprofit management program were offered at a university, what else—in addition to regular classes—do you think the university should be doing for the nonprofit sector?
10) If you were in charge of developing a comprehensive nonprofit management program at UWM and you needed to develop a one-year plan, adding a new phase every two years, where would you start?

Creating a Plan and a Vision

From these early beginnings, The Milwaukee Idea office at UWM provided essential support services. The report from the NME's affinity, or planning, group, "Nonprofit Connections: Building Learning Organizations" was published by The Milwaukee Idea office in May 2000. Recommended activities to better utilize and expand existing programs and services and to develop new, collaborative services were outlined and formed the basis for continued discussion and deliberation by the NME. The affinity group recommendations were grouped around four goals:

- Provide practical, affordable, and flexible opportunities for practitioners, policymakers, and academics to develop skills and increase understanding of the nonprofit sector.

- Enhance training and learning opportunities in nonprofit management through undergraduate coursework, graduate degrees, certificate programs, and continuing education offerings.

- Mobilize resources, both intellectual and financial, for research and practical applications related to policy, leadership, and management issues in the nonprofit sector.

- Strengthen diversity within the nonprofit sector locally and nationally.

The NME Steering Committee continued to meet throughout the summer and fall of 2000. Under its formal charge to "enhance effective management, leadership, and governance of the nonprofit, or third sector, in the greater Milwaukee area by exploring and creating multidisciplinary-based education, technical assistance, and support systems," the group developed a vision statement to serve as a guide for collaboration and two-way interaction between the university and nonprofit community.

Vision Statement

The work of the UWM Nonprofit Management Education Center is to be a catalyst for developing a strong nonprofit and social enterprise sector that contributes significantly to a healthy community. The center's goals are to:

- Enhance the management capacity, expertise, sustainability, and creativity of the nonprofit and social enterprise sector

- Foster and advocate the common interests, support and collaborate across cultural communities, business, social services, philanthropic, and advocacy sectors
- Create meaningful participation of the nonprofit sector in the digital community
- Promote best practices, models, and expertise available throughout the global community

The center's strategy is to leverage the core strengths of both the university and the nonprofit community to create dynamic and two-way learning between various sectors, including:

- Linking practice-based research and applied learning opportunities for nonprofit organizations, foundations, and the business community
- Creating a hub and focal point for community building and knowledge sharing
- Integrating educational strategies with learning and service opportunities for both practitioners and students to support lifelong engagement in nonprofit and social enterprise.

By fall 2000 the committee recommended the formalization of an academic nonprofit center. The university agreed to act as a managing partner for the development of this center and a project manager was hired with initial funds provided by The Milwaukee Idea. UWM enthusiastically and publicly committed to developing an academically based community-campus center that would facilitate the engagement of all interested parties in degree and nondegree programs, technical assistance, and research.

Checking Each Other Out

In what was termed a "Big Bang—an explosive initiative to support nonprofit management in Milwaukee"—a diverse group of 45 individuals, including UWM faculty and staff, other academics, nonprofit executive directors, and community leaders met for a two-day design session in January 2001, at the offices of Ernst & Young's Cap Gemini Accelerated Solutions Environment. The goal of the two-day intensive workshop was to identify appropriate strategies to focus, organize, and launch an academic center to substantially enhance Milwaukee's nonprofit sectors. This event was sponsored by one of the Milwaukee funders who maintained a keen interest in the project and wanted to provide an opportunity to accelerate the work.

The group used state-of-the-art problem-solving strategies to address how to create a comprehensive center for nonprofit management education, research, and technical assistance. The planning focused on building community partnerships with diverse, multicultural institutions and constituencies. Members worked to consolidate nine months of process into two days and framed action for four areas: professional degree programs, nondegree programs, research in nonprofit management, and technical assistance. Together, the group developed a better understanding of the issues, concerns, and partnership opportunities and participated in a series of unique learning experiences that questioned personal and organizational connections to the initiative. Each participant wrestled with how to create an innovative, collaborative system to support nonprofits, and teams presented and reviewed creative ideas. The group engaged in honest dialogue, received feedback, and signed on to support the initiative as it moved forward.

The results of the Big Bang event included: agreement on an action plan to strengthen Milwaukee's nonprofit sector that featured partnerships

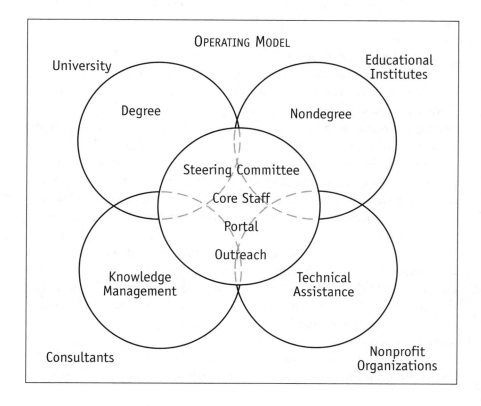

with educational and other institutions to develop for-credit and not-for-credit options; the creation of a research/information clearinghouse to link to the university and community partners; and partnerships with nonprofits and support organizations to enhance technical assistance and support to agencies. Four cluster groups were formed and charged with coming up with action plans to translate the mission and objectives of each cluster—as defined through the affinity group process and the design session in Chicago—into workable strategies that could guide implementation.

Creating a Formal Partnership

In recognition of the generous gift of $1.2 million by the Helen Bader Foundation in Milwaukee, UWM's new nonprofit management education center was officially named the Helen Bader Institute for Nonprofit Management (HBI) at a ceremony held at the university in July 2001. HBI was administratively housed in the School of Business Administration but designed to support an interdisciplinary base of faculty from multiple schools and colleges.

As the commitment in the community and university deepened, funds from The Milwaukee Idea were combined with a commitment from the School of Business Administration for the recruitment and hire of an executive director of the nonprofit center. The new executive director was recruited nationally and had considerable experience in leading nonprofit management centers. He began his work at UWM in August 2001.

With the hiring of an executive director and the official launch of a university-based center, the nonprofit management initiative was in the midst of a transition in fall 2001 from an intensive two-year planning process to the early phases of program implementation. After an eight-month action planning process carried out by the four cluster groups, the NME Steering Committee agreed to the formation of an ad hoc group of its members to review the action plans presented by the cluster groups. In February 2002 the review panel recommended approval of programs and the allocation of startup funding. The steering committee unanimously approved these recommendations and requested program staff to begin implementation.

With the submission and acceptance of their plans, the work of the cluster groups shifted focus to advising the staff on program and project implementation and providing a vehicle for ongoing community input and involvement during start-up. Cluster team members were also asked to provide advice and assistance on specific project initiatives. For example, several cluster members joined the interdisciplinary faculty group and provided valuable counsel in the planning of the credit-based programs. An advisory group was formally appointed for the noncredit certificate program. A capacity-building task force was formed to provide advice with regard to the implementation of HBI's nonprofit organizational capacity-building programs and projects. Similarly, the nonprofit technology initiative ENTECH (Empowering Nonprofits in Technology) formed a "strategy team" made up of business, government, and nonprofit representatives to assist with strategic directions and resource support.

Implementation

Implementation began in all four program areas.

Credit-Based Programs

The Graduate Certificate in Nonprofit Management was developed by the faculty and community work group in 2001–2002 and 2002–2003 by building on and expanding the number of courses offered in existing nonprofit management tracks or concentrations in UWM's MBA and MPA degree programs. The certificate is jointly sponsored by the School of Business and College of Letters and Science. (The requirements of the certificate are described in Appendix 11.1 at the end of this chapter.)

First offered in fall 2003, the certificate classes experienced enrollments of 22–25 enthusiastic students from varied backgrounds and experiences. The diversity of the students contributes to the depth of discussion and learning.

Noncredit Programs

The School of Continuing Education worked with community members to develop and deliver the noncredit professional certificate in nonprofit management. The Professional Certificate in Nonprofit Management was developed as a noncredit certificate designed for people who are committed to careers in nonprofit management and who do not seek a master's degree or graduate-level certification. The curriculum for this certificate program consists of 105 hours of classroom instruction focused on 17 competencies considered essential to effective nonprofit management performance. (For full descriptions of the certificate courses, see http://cfprod.imt.uwm .edu/sce/certificate.cfm?id=225.) The curriculum is offered through a coordinated series of noncredit workshops by the School of Continuing Education in partnership with other agencies in the Milwaukee area that provide noncredit education and training.

Knowledge Management and Capacity-Building Projects

Knowledge management and capacity-building projects have included the development and launch of ENTECH, the Nonprofit Milwaukee Portal, collaborative research projects, and funding for faculty and student research.

In September 2001, the Nonprofit Management Fund's Technology Initiative was successfully transferred to UWM and renamed ENTECH. It provides technology consulting and direct service to nonprofit organizations in Southeast Wisconsin. Since ENTECH's inception in 1999, it has worked with hundreds of tax exempt, nonprofit community service organizations to increase their management effectiveness through the use of technology.

In acknowledgement of the excellent resources and increasing collaboration of the current network of technical assistance providers in the Milwaukee community, activities focused on increasing the number of practicing consultants, expanding the number of nonprofit consultants of color, and linking these practitioners to the unique expertise and resources of the university. The technical assistance work group recommendations were formally incorporated into the knowledge management and capacity-building activities. As one of the first steps at capacity building, the Nonprofit Milwaukee Portal was conceived as a tool to develop linkages and strengthen relationships across the sector. It continues to be developed and advised by a coalition of nonprofit organizations. The portal is sponsored by HBI. Its goal is to establish an online information clearinghouse for nonprofit managers, staff, and board members that provides timely practical and theoretical knowledge and linkages to learning opportunities.

A *Consultants of Color* project was created in November 2002 in response to insights shared over the course of an intensive one-year community planning process. During that time several prominent consultants relayed personal experiences of discrimination and exclusion in the Milwaukee consulting marketplace and called on HBI to establish programming to address their concerns. The *Consultants of Color* report recommended ways to enhance the support of consultants of color by nonprofit organizations in the Greater Milwaukee area.

In December 2002 HBI joined with the Nonprofit Center of Milwaukee to assume the fiscal and operational responsibility for the annual Greater Milwaukee Nonprofit Management Excellence Awards event. The purpose of this awards luncheon is to recognize excellence in the management of nonprofit organizations in the Greater Milwaukee area. Proceeds go to the general scholarship fund of HBI at UWM. The first awards luncheon brought together hundreds of stakeholders from the nonprofit, private, and public sectors.

The *knowledge management initiative* has undertaken applied research on issues relevant to the Greater Milwaukee nonprofit sector, including a benchmark study on Social Enterprise (funded by the Helen Bader Foundation, Nonprofit Management Fund, and the United Way of Greater Milwaukee), an inventory of nonprofits led by Latinos in Milwaukee (funded by the Nonprofit Management Fund), a study of nonprofit organization governance by surveys of nonprofit executive directors and board members (funded by the Nonprofit Management Fund) and a study of the Milwaukee nonprofit arts community.

The School of Business Administration, with the financial support of the Nonprofit Management Fund, engaged a *social entrepreneur-in-residence* to provide assistance to faculty members in nonprofit management curriculum development, guest lecture in classes, and raise awareness about social enterprise both inside the university and in the community. The Nonprofit Management Fund also funded a faculty/student research project on social entrepreneurship. In addition, a *mini-grant research program* was developed and sponsored by HBI to promote research by faculty and staff at UWM with an interest in the nonprofit sector.

Reaffirming the Partnership

As the planning progressed, the university and its community stakeholders—including representatives of local foundations and nonprofit organizations of varied missions and size—determined the need to establish a

Leadership Council to serve as the principal governing body for HBI. Central to these efforts, and in the spirit of The Milwaukee Idea, was the desire to build on the collaborative spirit that characterized this initiative from the very beginning.

The governance model defines how the community and university work together to provide leadership and support for HBI and delineates those broad categories of decision-making that are shared by members of the community and those that are reserved to the university alone. At the heart of the governance agreement was a spirit of collaboration between UWM and the community, a desire to promote mutual trust and to affirm the real responsibility of the Leadership Council for HBI. To that end, the primary responsibilities of the HBI Leadership Council are to:

- Set policies and obtain necessary approvals related to the development, renewal, and adherence to the mission of HBI

- Set policies and obtain necessary approvals related to strategic planning for HBI and the evaluation of HBI programs

- Foster and sustain partnerships and other collaborative ventures as appropriate in pursuit of the mission of HBI

- Secure adequate financial resources for HBI and ensure appropriate stewardship of those resources

- Approve the annual budget for HBI

- Recommend to the chancellor of UWM the appointment and continuing service of the executive director of HBI

- Evaluate its own composition and performance and approve continuing and new members for the Leadership Council

UWM, as a public university and state agency, is responsible for the hiring, promotion, contracting, and fiscal authority for HBI. The role of the faculty in all matters of curriculum as defined in the shared governance tradition of the University of Wisconsin was also recognized.

The Leadership Council's 13 members include representatives from the university (participating schools and colleges and office of the chancellor) and of Milwaukee-area nonprofit organizations. HBI's new governing model has proven so successful that it has also been adopted for other university-community partnerships.

In addition, several traditional governance systems, advisory groups, and new administrative structures have formed within the university in response to this new type of collaboration. Each initiative of The Milwaukee Idea has a Deans' Council, made up of the deans of the schools and colleges whose faculty are likely to be significantly involved with the work of the initiative. The Deans' Council for the nonprofit management education initiative and HBI includes the deans of the School of Business Administration, College of Letters and Science, Helen Bader School of Social Welfare, School of Continuing Education, and the Peck School of the Arts. Since the business school provided most of the internal resources to support the nonprofit management initiative, including housing HBI and supporting its director, the business dean serves as the "lead" dean. The Deans' Council serves as the primary administrative oversight team for all nonprofit management education efforts on the campus.

The credit-based graduate curriculum is governed by an interdisciplinary group of faculty from the College of Letters and Science, School of Business Administration, and other programs across campus with an interest in nonprofit management. This group has oversight on all curricular decisions, admission, and student academic issues. Curricular changes must also have the approval of the faculty in the College of Letters and Science and School of Business Administration, as well as the faculty governance groups and dean of the UWM Graduate School.

In addition, the School of Continuing Education formed a Policy and Accreditation Board directed by a faculty member in the school, with membership from the community, as the governing board responsible for setting curriculum guidelines and ensuring high-quality program offerings for the noncredit professional management certificate.

Commitment to Diversity

In an effort to increase inclusiveness and gain cultural insight from people of color, HBI sponsored four informational sessions, entitled "Respectful Dialogues with a Purpose," with key individuals from Milwaukee's African American, Latino, Hmong, and Native American communities. The purpose of the dialogue sessions was to ensure that leaders and members of communities of color were given the opportunity to provide HBI with additional advice and recommendations concerning the development and implementation of critical aspects of its programming. The dialogues also addressed the needs of targeted communities who would directly benefit from future educational and technical assistance programs.

The recommendations from these discussions included:

- Use community resources where possible.

- Respond to community realities.

- Provide sequential integration of degree and nondegree programs.

- Focus on communication and connection.

- Include diversity in curriculum development and content.

- Provide financial aid.

- Hire a diverse faculty and advisors.

- Market to communities of color.

- Consider diversity in varied technology applications, research, and research dissemination.

Because one of the goals of the nonprofit initiative is to create a truly diverse community of faculty, staff, students, nonprofit leaders, and professionals who are associated with HBI, 21 standards of practice were adopted by the Leadership Council in July 2004 in areas of governance and management practice, marketing and public relations, outreach, training and development, credit education, noncredit education, knowledge management, and capacity building.

Looking Forward—Challenges and New Initiatives

The establishment of a center for nonprofit management education grew out of the university-community interactions encouraged and supported by The Milwaukee Idea. The efforts among university faculty and staff, Milwaukee foundation officials, and leaders of Milwaukee-area nonprofits have been characterized as an example of an extraordinarily high level of community engagement.

This community engagement has resulted in a number of "firsts" for UWM, including: local nonprofit leaders working closely with university faculty and administrators to ensure that educational and other programs are designed to meet the needs of nonprofit sector; local nonprofit leaders serving as full voting members of a Leadership Council for HBI; the chancellor authorizing the Leadership Council as the principal governing body of the Institute; and more than $1.7 million in extramural gifts and grants to support the array of nonprofit programs at UWM.

Today, more than five years into this initiative, the major challenges involve continuing to develop and implement the new educational, research, and organizational capacity-building programs and beginning to plan for a second phase of operations. This will require an assessment of current programming, strategic planning for the next phase, and a financial plan to sustain HBI and related programs in the future. HBI received generous startup funding from Milwaukee area foundations and internal reallocations of funding from within the university. The level of initial funding compares favorably with that of other nonprofit academic centers and programs across the country. However, the vision, mission, and strategic directions adopted for the nonprofit initiative by UWM and HBI's principal donors and other stakeholders call for an institute of broad programmatic scope and significant reach. Fundraising for the future will be a significant challenge. Another challenge is to maintain the high level of community engagement within a campus culture rich in shared governance and challenged by scarce resources.

The rewards of meeting these challenges are significant. Indeed, by partnering and recognizing the skills and programs of its stakeholders—both within and outside the university—and working to diversify and expand its revenues, UWM can continue to build and institutionalize the new nonprofit center as the focal point of a rich and viable university-community partnership.

Appendix 11.1
UWM's Graduate Certificate In Nonprofit Management

Theory and Practice of Management and Leadership in Nonprofit Sector Organizations
The scope, dimensions, and roles of nonprofit sector organizations in contemporary society will be examined with a focus on understanding the distinctive characteristics and functions of these organizations and how they interact with business and government. Students will also be introduced to the principal theories, roles, and functions of effective nonprofit management and leadership.

Accounting for Nonprofit Organizations
This course introduces students to basic accounting concepts and the basic elements of financial and managerial accounting and reporting in nonprofit organizations. It provides an in-depth treatment of the principal budgeting and other financial management techniques that are essential to managing nonprofit organizational resources efficiently and effectively.

Governance of Nonprofit Organizations
This course is designed to introduce students to the fundamentals of governance and trusteeship in nonprofit sector organizations. The course will critically examine the principal practices, processes, and models used in governing nonprofit organizations. Special attention will be paid to the ethical and moral dilemmas encountered by members of nonprofit boards of directors and trustees as they seek to carry out their roles and responsibilities in ways that are both personally and socially responsible.

Generating Revenues in Nonprofit Organizations
The principal strategies and practices used by nonprofit organizations to generate revenues will be examined. Attention will be given to how nonprofit organizations generate revenues from each of the three principal sources of those revenues: philanthropic gifts and grants, government grants and contracts, and earned income.

Human Resources Management in Nonprofit Organizations
The mobilization and management of human assets in a manner that is mission-driven is one key to effective nonprofit management. Students will learn about the challenges of managing human resources in mission-based organizations that often make use of both professionals and

volunteers. Several aspects of human resource management are examined from this perspective, including: acquisition and development of needed expertise; motivation, reward, and control; organizational justice, employee complaints, and due process; compensation systems; performance appraisal and career development, selection, and diversity; and training and managing professionals and volunteers.

PART V

Engagement:
Implications for
Sustainability

12 Funding Community-University Partnerships

Armand W. Carriere

A Brief History

Colleges and universities have had service-oriented relationships with their local, and at times not-so-local, communities for hundreds of years. In a speech he has given many times, Ira Harkavy, associate vice president and director of the Center for Community Partnerships at the University of Pennsylvania, describes the history of engagement of colleges and universities from Benjamin Franklin's time, through the development of service-based models at what have become known as the Ivy League institutions, to the establishment of the land-grant college movement. Harkavy (2003) cites 19th- and early 20th-century educators, such as Daniel Coit Gilman, the first president of The Johns Hopkins University, and John Dewey at the University of Chicago, for their ability to link the role of the university with a response to the social and community needs of the time. Harkavy arrives at the world of contemporary higher education by describing the work of his university and the close ties it has developed with the city of Philadelphia, especially with the neighborhoods immediately adjoining the West Philadelphia campus. This speech and the articles he has authored over the years have helped many of those new to the field gain a historical perspective on what seems to many to be a recent phenomenon.

It was in this contemporary world that the Office of University Partnerships (OUP) was established at the Department of Housing and Urban Development (HUD). The Community Outreach Partnership Act of 1992 authorized $7.5 million to establish a demonstration project to create Community Outreach Partnership Centers (COPCs) (Cisneros, 1996). The act authorized the HUD Secretary to make grants to public and private nonprofit institutions of higher education to assist in establishing or carrying out research and outreach activities addressing the problems of urban areas. Grants were to be used to conduct applied research on the theoretical and real problems of large and small cities, and to facilitate partnerships among institutions of higher education, local communities, and local governments to address urban problems. The enabling legislation prescribed the federal share of the grant that could be used for research and outreach and the requirement for matching funds from nonfederal sources. Other requirements included the establishment of an advisory body that would assist in identifying local needs and the strategies to address these needs, and a dissemination plan to share information with other interested parties.

The vehicle to administer the grant funds was not established until 1994. Then-HUD Secretary Henry Cisneros recognized the potential that existed among the nation's colleges and universities to make a significant contribution toward solving the problems of America's cities. Through Assistant Secretary for Policy Development and Research Michael Stegman, HUD established the Office of University Partnerships.

HUD was not the only federal agency attempting to link the campus with America's cities. At approximately the same time the Department of Education was developing the Urban Community Service (UCS) Program, whose purpose was to "encourage urban academic institutions to work with private and civic organizations to devise and implement solutions to pressing and severe problems in their urban communities" (UCS Program, 1992, p. 292). The UCS Program sought out municipal universities in metropolitan areas with a minimum population of 350,000. Eligible activities under UCS grants included planning, applied research, training, technology transfer, and other activities designed to help urban communities meet their pressing and severe problems.

The specific programming activities could include workforce preparation, health care, underperforming schools, economic development, and environmental concerns. A matching amount, equal to at least one-fourth of the UCS grant, was required. Peak funding went from $8 million in 1993 to about $10 million in 1994. Grants were for approximately $400,000 for a performance period of two to five years. The program came to an abrupt end in 1995 when only $1.5 million was made available for funding.

The Community Outreach Partnership Center program represented HUD's first efforts at true partnership programs with colleges and universities. The Historically Black Colleges and Universities (HBCU) program was functioning at HUD within the department's Office of Community Planning and Development at this time and had been for several years. However, the design and nature of the HBCU program differed from COPC's purpose of tapping the multiple resources available among college faculty and students and linking them with community partners to collaboratively work to ameliorate urban problems.

Under the first director of the Office of University Partnerships, Marcia Marker Feld, the department sought to demonstrate how colleges and universities could make a profound impact in communities that frequently shared common boundaries with the college but little else. Much has been written about the tension, mistrust, and outright hostility existing between colleges and universities and their neighbors. Among the early challenges confronting colleges and universities seeking to involve themselves with their local communities was a need to overcome the divisive issues that had developed in the community over the years.

The legislative authority creating the Community Outreach Partnership Center demonstration was purposefully broad, enabling OUP to develop the policies and guidance necessary to provide for maximum impact. Unlike the Department of Education's program, COPC sought a broader universe of applicant institutions, making the program available to accredited two- or four-year institutions serving communities which qualified under HUD's more generous definition of "urban": communities with a population of 2,500 or more. This definition stands in stark contrast to the Department of Education requirement that Urban Community Service institutions exist and operate in communities of 350,000 or more.

While several institutions selected in the first rounds of COPC funding and the communities being served would have qualified under the Department of Education criteria (e.g., the University of Illinois–Chicago, Wayne State University, and City College of New York), the involvement in later years of a more diverse array of institutions in cities large and small and the attendant success of these programs has validated the more inclusive policies developed by the creators of the COPC program. Jane Karadbil, a senior program analyst and first OUP staff person, deserves credit for establishing the foundation for the program that continues to serve well more than a decade later.

It should be noted that models of campus-community engagement were present in those earliest days, and the leaders on these campuses were helping OUP shape the COPC program. Judith Ramaley, at the time president of Portland State University (PSU), was putting PSU on the map with her commitment to turn the city of Portland and the university into an integrated community of learning. Barbara Holland, on her way to becoming perhaps the most articulate spokesperson for civic engagement on the campus, was at PSU at the same time, refining her ideas.

Other early leaders included Rex LaMore at Michigan State University, who played a major role in crafting the COPC legislation and getting it through the Congress. Elizabeth Hollander, now the executive director of Campus Compact, but then director of the Egan Center at DePaul University, and Wim Wiewal from the University of Illinois–Chicago's Great Cities Initiative, were linking their institutions with neighborhood groups in Chicago. These exceptional individuals and many more like them were helping OUP shape the COPC program in its earliest days.

Current Challenges and Trends

As the Office of University Partnerships enters its second decade of operation, a number of challenges confront it, including enhancing the work of minority-based institutions, creating opportunities for greater involvement on the part of professional schools, reconciling and addressing the different levels of support proffered by the executive office and the Congress, and determining the types of collaboration that will best serve the funder, the institution of higher education, and, most importantly, the community.

As indicated above, the Historically Black College and University Program functioned successfully within HUD for 15 years prior to being assumed into OUP's portfolio of college and university programs. Under the leadership of President Jimmy Carter, the federal government sought ways to formally support HBCUs. Subsequent administrations continued this effort, making millions of dollars available to strengthen the institutions and their surrounding communities through grants from federal agencies ranging from the Department of Agriculture to the Department of Defense.

Desires to both consolidate HUD's college and university programs and to tap into the HBCU legacy of service and commitment to the community prompted OUP to seek the transfer of the HBCU program to OUP in 2001. While the consolidation issue was important, it was the history of service to the community and the potential of applying OUP's philosophy of campus engagement to these institutions that made the transfer exciting.

Speaking more than 30 years ago on behalf of Historically Black Colleges and Universities, the Carnegie Commission on Higher Education (1971) stated, "Colleges founded for Black Americans have a special opportunity for service to their communities. They have historic contacts with their communities that have earned them a position of respect" (p. 2). The report went on to acknowledge the work of several HBCUs, including medical students from Howard University and Meharry Medical and Dental Schools providing outreach in urban and rural areas; Fisk University students providing family counseling; and Xavier-New Orleans students working with preschool children. It was this legacy that OUP sought to build upon.

While the presence and impact of HBCUs on American higher education will continue to be significant, it is the proliferation and development of Hispanic-Serving Institutions (HSIs) and their potential impact on the communities they serve that will garner the most attention in the next several years. Because the Latino population is the fastest growing minority in the United States, it is anticipated that in the next three to five years there will be as many as 78 institutions achieving U.S. Department of Education–designated Hispanic-Serving Institution status (Hispanic Association of Colleges and Universities, 2005). And while historically these institutions have been located predominantly in the Southwest and West, the coming years will find the designation being applied to institutions in the Midwest, Southeast, and Northeast.

As this universe of Latino institutions continues to grow and, along with other minority-based institutions, becomes more aware of funding opportunities through agencies like HUD, a challenge confronting OUP will be the relative competitiveness of applications for funding. Set-aside programs, such as grant programs specifically targeting a particular category of minority-based institutions, have helped ensure a funding stream to eligible institutions. It has been a different scenario, however, when the success of minority-based institutions applying for Community Outreach Partnership Center (COPC) grants is examined. While the Office of University Partnerships has paid greater attention to increasing awareness among minority institutions in the last three years, the absence of these institutions from each year's list of awardees continues to present a challenge. Of the total 238 COPC grants awarded from 1994–2003, only 19 have gone to minority-based institutions, or approximately 8%, according to U.S. Department of Housing and Urban Development (2003) records. This percentage, while consistent with the overall presence of minority-based institutions in the universe of two- and four-year institutions (approximately 8%), is troubling because of what we know to be the unique contributions these institutions can make to their communities. In most instances the essential elements for successful community partnerships are present in these unsuccessful applications: a sympathetic administration; a dedicated faculty, many of whom are from the communities to be served; students who also come from neighborhoods and communities served by the college and who desire to "give back" to the community; and viable community- and faith-based organizations that are ready and willing to collaborate with their local college or university.

What is missing from these situations frequently comes down to issues of capacity, the capacity to craft a competitive application, and the internal capacity to strategically plan and implement a grant. Unlike larger and better-funded institutions, minority-based institutions, especially smaller public or private colleges, lack staff and resources dedicated to seeking out funding opportunities and crafting competitive proposals. And even when this resource is present, the needs of the college or university are such that all development or institutional advancement efforts must focus on the institution itself. Programs that look outward may be a luxury the institution cannot afford.

Even when institutions receive awards, issues of implementing the program(s) outlined in a successful proposal can arise. Again, the realities of understaffed institutions or institutions where key administrators, by necessity, wear multiple hats, create problems of capacity, making optimal performance and continued funding difficult at best.

HUD's role, therefore, is to recognize these limitations and work with minority-based institutions to enhance their grant-making and grant-management capacity. In 2003 Congress acknowledged this need by earmarking $2 million for technical assistance to HBCUs from the appropriated $10 million for HUD's HBCU program. HUD/OUP has been mandated by Congress to deliver technical assistance to current and potential HBCU grantees in an effort to educate them in the essentials of a competitive application and to provide the necessary guidance to make better use of current and potential HUD funding. Similar language in future spending authorizations for other minority-based programs would be appropriate.

Newly formed advocacy groups, including the Association of Community and Higher Education Partnerships, and more established organizations like the White House Initiatives on Minority-Based Institutions and the Hispanic Association of Colleges and Universities have taken an active role in assisting OUP in reaching minority-based institutions. OUP should continue to work with these groups and with other groups who represent these rapidly developing institutions.

Mentoring relationships or the provision of what is known as cross-site technical assistance has enabled OUP to match established (i.e., successful) grantees with new grantees or not-yet-successful applicants with positive results. Scores on competitive applications go up in succeeding years, frequently to the fundable level, based on the provision of this technical assistance.

While OUP gears up to provide external forms of assistance to potential applicants or struggling grantees, it faces a formidable internal challenge on the campus of many minority-based institutions—the challenge of the "What's in it for us?" attitude. Unlike most other federally-supported programs targeting minority institutions, none of OUP's funds (with the exception of Tribal College funding) can be used for the direct benefit of the institution. While majority institutions may have the luxury of dedicating staff time and institutional resources to off-campus activities, many minority-based colleges and universities must focus their time and attention on internal matters. Funding that can support faculty salaries, student enrollment, or on-campus construction will appear, in the short-term, much more attractive and useful than funding that must be directed off campus.

Fortunately, a growing number of minority-based institutions have recognized the long-term benefit to be derived from tapping HUD/OUP funding and engaging with their local communities in mutually beneficial activities. These grants enable institutions to put into practice the vision contained in the institutional mission statement, and they allow the institution, through service-learning activities and community-based research, to bring its curriculum to the community and enjoy the resultant mutual benefits. Institutions ranging from Lehman College in the Bronx, The University of Texas–Pan American on the Texas-Mexico border, Winston-Salem State University in North Carolina, and the University of Alaska–Fairbanks, all minority-based institutions and all recognizing the long-term benefits of campus-community engagement, have become models for other institutions, large and small, in the pantheon of American higher education.

Involvement of Professional Schools

As the flagship program within the Office of University Partnerships, the Community Outreach Partnership Center program has traditionally attempted to ensure an integrated, multidisciplined approach to efforts on behalf of the community. Program guidance has called for a minimum of three distinct areas of programming. The rationale for such an approach should be clear: It attempts to secure a broader buy-in on the part of the institution, thereby increasing the chances of outreach being "institutionalized," and the approach provides the basis for a comprehensive response to community problems—no one intervention is likely to solve what are complex, interrelated social and economic issues.

During COPC's early history the multidisciplined approach successfully engaged a variety of curricula and departments, the leading departments typically from the arts and sciences. While there were notable exceptions (the School of Architecture at the University of Nebraska–Lincoln or the Medical College of the University of California–San Diego), most applications were prepared and ultimately directed by faculty from within the arts and sciences.

In 2003 HUD Assistant Secretary for Policy, Development, and Research Alberto Trevino directed OUP to allocate $2 million of the $7 million COPC appropriation to award demonstration grants to Schools of Architecture and Schools of Planning. With a background in planning and architecture, Assistant Secretary Trevino saw great potential in channeling the resources of such departments to issues of affordable housing and community planning.

While the policy guiding COPC over its first nine years had described a multidisciplined approach to community engagement, COPC's enabling legislation as indicated earlier was extremely broad and would allow for this "single purpose" approach. Included, therefore, in the 2003 Notice of Funding Availability was a call for proposals from schools of architecture and schools of planning. Unlike the traditional COPC application, the proposals for this demonstration program could be for a single purpose, such as affordable housing design for the architects, a 10–25 year community plan for the planners. Validating Assistant Secretary Trevino's program plan and vision, the response to the call for proposals was outstanding, both in terms of numbers of applications and the enthusiasm of the applicants. Five grants (the maximum number available) of $400,000 each were ultimately awarded. The results of these three-year grants are not known at the time of this writing and, for a number of reasons, the decision was made in 2004 to defer further funding of this initiative:

- The champion of this variation of the COPC theme, Assistant Secretary Trevino, is no longer with the department.

- Given the level of funding for COPC over the past three years, taking $2 million off the top of a $7 million budget cuts deeply into the muscle of the basic COPC grant program.

- There remains the compelling argument for a multidisciplined approach for contributing to community revitalization.

There is no denying, however, the quality and sincerity of the responses from these professional schools. Whether or not this deferment is repeated in the near future, it is incumbent upon OUP to find ways to encourage the inclusion of professional schools in a more broadly based institutional response to community betterment. Business, law, engineering, and other professional schools possess the resources to make major contributions to community development. Through organizations like Campus Compact, handbooks have been developed to aid faculty in professional and technical schools in developing service-learning curricula.

By working closely with professional associations, including Campus Compact, OUP can encourage greater involvement of professional and technical schools in the desired comprehensive approach to community engagement. Close attention should also be paid to the success of the recent demonstration grantees and the success of single-purpose institutions like the Medical College of Wisconsin or the University of Texas Health Science Center that have skillfully put together a comprehensive approach within the context of a specifically focused institution.

Support for COPC

The Office of University Partnerships, and in particular the Community Outreach Partnership Center program, has enjoyed consistently strong support from whichever administration is in power. The program continues to receive approximately the same level of funding as it did when it originated. For each of the past five years, the administration has put forth an annual budget of $8 million for COPC. Other programs within OUP's portfolio, particularly the minority-based programs, have enjoyed similar administration support. Unfortunately, at least for the COPC program, administration's support is not always matched by support from Capitol Hill. For the past several years COPC has teetered on the brink of elimination, requiring eleventh-hour heroics in Congress to maintain its presence in the budget. While these last-minute actions on COPC's behalf manage to save the program each year, it has been at a funding level lower than the administration's request.

It is interesting to note that this brinksmanship approach to funding has not been applied to other OUP programs. On the contrary, Congress has frequently funded some of OUP's programs at amounts higher than the administration requests. While the OUP is certainly pleased with this tacit endorsement and generous level of support for other programs, it remains a mystery why COPC faces such opposition each year from its appropriators. The answer may be that OUP and its supporters place a greater emphasis on the use of marketing. We have yet to "sell" effectively the success of COPC and what programs like this bring to the community. The Initiative for a Competitive Inner City (2002), a national, not-for-profit organization founded in 1994 by Harvard Business School Professor Michael E. Porter to focus new thinking about the business potential of inner cities, produced a publication highlighting the economic impact of selected institutions of higher education on their respective communities. It was no coincidence that among the institutions featured, Howard University, the University of Pennsylvania, and Virginia Commonwealth University were all COPC grantees. While all the COPC-funded work of these institutions does not instantly translate into economic impact, the efforts do represent a commitment on the part of the institution to play a major collaborative role in community development. It is exactly this kind of information that must be shared with Congress.

Highlighting this kind of success only begins to address the benefits to be derived from such partnerships. As Harkavy (2003) stated in his presentation at the National and Community Service Coalition Policy Dialogue and Annual Meeting, "The future of American Democracy will be determined by the extent to which Americans are contributing, creative, democratic citizens." Campus-community partnerships provide these opportunities for students and community partners to engage constructively in programs that enhance the well-being of all involved.

COPC's future may be tied to an ability to build upon this link of civic engagement and creative democracy. It may be in the best interest of the COPC program to explore relationships with organizations like the Institute for Liberal Education and Civic Engagement, a collaborative effort joining Campus Compact and the Association of American Colleges and Universities. The institute was established in January 2003 to support leadership and scholarship on the intellectual and educational connections between civic engagement and liberal learning.

Clearly, OUP cannot lose sight of HUD's mission. We are not, to be sure, the Department of Education, nor are we the Corporation for National and Community Service, agencies that can take a broader view of educational issues. HUD is an agency that must first and foremost focus on the challenges and problems of America's cities. In a speech to Congress on March 2, 1965, announcing the establishment of the Department of Housing and Urban Development, President Lyndon B. Johnson (1965) may have presciently identified a role for COPC-like programs and the involvement of colleges and universities when he stated, "We need more thought and wisdom as we painfully struggle to identify the ills, the dangers, and the cures for the American city." Partnerships among HUD and OUP and groups like the Institute for Liberal Education and Civic Engagement may enable OUP to demonstrate more forcefully tangible contributions to community betterment and urban revitalization while assuming a catalytic role in enhancing greater degrees of citizenship among today's students.

Administrations—Republican or Democrat—have recognized the value of the COPC program. It is essential that we establish new alliances to strengthen the program and its image with a continually skeptical Congress.

The Terms of Engagement

A willingness on the part of Congress and the administration to fund the work of colleges and universities in their communities is one part of the picture. An equally important piece is the willingness of institutions of higher education and their adjoining communities to commit to this kind of work.

The 21st century begins with colleges and universities throughout the country confronting what are frequently referred to as "draconian" budget cuts resulting in fewer classes offered, faculty and staff layoffs, reduced financial aid, higher tuition, and even delays in opening new campuses. It is an environment that requires belt tightening and keen concentration on what are considered to be the essentials of higher education. An environment, in other words, that may not be conducive to supporting outreach in the community. This could prove problematic for programs like COPC.

Since its inception, the COPC program has emphasized two key points: impact on the community and impact on the campus. It is this dual approach to outcomes in both centers of activity that distinguishes COPC from other government programs in general and other OUP programs in particular. Since impact on the campus is a primary goal of the program, HUD and OUP funding has been made contingent upon evidence of an institution's commitment to supplement the COPC grant with internally and externally generated resources. Absent this investment, COPC could easily be viewed as more federal soft money that may or may not enable the institution to follow through on the goals and objectives described in the grant proposal.

Through the late 1990s and into the first years of the 21st century, COPC applicants embraced this leveraging concept and secured generous matching amounts from within the institution and from community partners. The successful COPC applicant typically generates 150% of the amount of the federal grant, or approximately $600,000. Much of this leveraged amount comes from within the institution in the form of released faculty time, office and meeting space, equipment, and cash.

A sizeable matching contribution can speak both to the immediate quality of the program as well as to the prospects for sustainability or institutionalization. COPC grants have always been viewed as "seed money," that is, funding to establish a program on the campus but with the tacit understanding that long-term viability would come from other sources of support. While the earliest days of COPC described a rather naïve goal of a single HUD grant providing this foundation for long-term commitment, the most recent funding policies—for example, a second round of funding called a New Directions grant—continue to place the long-term responsibility squarely on the shoulders of the institution and its community partners.

Complications arise when shifting focus to the economic realities of current higher education. All of the problems confronting college campuses described earlier can impact an institution's initial or sustained commitment to outreach. Released time for faculty is more difficult to come by, tuition increases and less financial aid impact students' time for volunteering, and discretionary cash that might have supported off-campus work dries up. As significant as these problems are at majority institutions, they can be even more exasperating at minority-based colleges, many of which, even in better times, struggle with financial solvency and institutional capacity.

The community side of the campus-community equation is also suffering. Reasonable people can disagree on the relative merits of federal tax cuts, but it is clear that local and state governments are assuming a greater fiscal burden than in past years. Like institutions of higher education, municipal and state governments must concentrate on what they deem to be essential services, resulting in a reluctance to enter into partnership agreements with local colleges and universities regardless of the potential benefit. While California may be the poster child for fiscal crisis, lower-case versions of this predicament are being played out across the country.

With resources on the campus and in the community drying up, HUD must face the challenge of maintaining the rationale for local support and buy-in, while not making the requirement so burdensome that no one will apply. It is incumbent on OUP to showcase models of effective leveraging. For example, Mercer University in Macon, Georgia, a private, liberal arts college, has done an extraordinary job leveraging COPC dollars with public and nonprofit funding. Grants from a variety of sources, including the Knight Foundation, the Jimmy and Rosalyn Carter Partnership Award, the

Corporation for National and Community Service, the 21st Century Fund, and the Federal Home Loan Bank have enabled Mercer University to continue and expand outreach work in Macon.

The economic fortunes of the country will undoubtedly turn around and this will translate into hiring faculty, increasing financial aid, and opening new campuses. Until that transition is complete, however, colleges and universities will struggle with the dilemma of fulfilling their roles as good citizens in the community, while carrying out what they may perceive as the core mission of the institution—teaching and research. OUP is just one of the many organizations committed to helping institutions understand that these roles are not mutually exclusive.

The on-campus sustainability of COPC-like outreach programs hinges not only on this continuing financial support but also on how the institution views and values faculty involvement in outreach activities. OUP has attempted to influence the weight given to community service as a contributing factor in rank, tenure, and promotion decisions by requiring that applicants speak to this issue in the COPC application. Even though it might only be a small ripple in a large pool, it does compel institutions to consider this aspect of professional development.

In an effort to link the COPC program with academic purposes, the creators of the program included an applied research component. Mandatory at first, though later made optional to accommodate applications from community colleges and other institutions with limited research capability, the applied research component provided the foundation for the ensuing outreach activities. In order to maintain the outreach focus, however, the crafters of the COPC program wisely placed a cap on how much of the total funding could be used to support research. A conscious effort was made to avoid involving the community in yet another research project.

Applied research continues to be a part of most successful COPC applications. With the emergence of community-based research as an accepted form of scholarship, the case to include successful outreach into the community in rank, tenure, and promotion decisions would seem to be getting stronger. Strand, Marullo, Cutforth, Stoecker, and Donohoe (2003) strongly support this effort, describing the value of community-based research in the educational process and providing a thoughtfully considered "how to" for interested faculty. The authors leave no doubt that exciting scholarship is a product of this approach to education.

Decisions to engage actively in the community even in an age of cut-backs, if not originating at the top of the institutional hierarchy, must ulti-mately be supported by the highest level of academic administrators. Early academic leaders helped establish the current models of excellence. New leaders are emerging to continue the movement in the new century, put-ting their own mark on the work of linking their institutions with the community. Examples of this new, emerging leadership include Nancy Zimpher, president of the University of Cincinnati; Sister Kathleen Ross, president of Heritage University; Ricardo Romo, president of the Univer-sity of Texas–San Antonio; John Bassett of Clark University; and Beverly Daniel Tatum, president of Spelman College. These educators and many more like them have established themselves as champions of the campus-community engagement movement. OUP is privileged to be playing a small role in helping these academic leaders as they work to link the cam-pus with the community.

Funding Decisions

As colleges and universities work to overcome the obstacles described in this chapter and to establish themselves as serious partners in the work of community development, the role of the government—in this case, the Department of Housing and Urban Development—should be re-exam-ined. As described earlier, HUD/OUP has seen its role as one of providing "seed money." It is interesting to note that COPC grants in the earliest days of the Office of University Partnerships were for a performance period of two years. However, two years into the program, OUP made the first of what would be a series of acknowledgements that two years was not enough time to establish these programs on the campus or in the commu-nity, so grantees were encouraged to apply for a one-year "institutionaliza-tion" grant. This additional year of funding was an attempt to establish outreach programs more firmly on the campus.

In its fourth year of operation OUP determined that the "institution-alization" year should be built into the original grant to provide a full three years of funding. Even with this additional year, the grant-making princi-ple employed by OUP continued to describe a "once and done" approach to individual applicants, meaning one grant was all an institution could ex-pect from HUD. During these first years, a consistent point of contention existed among proponents of the one-grant-and-out approach and institutions that felt multiple rounds of funding were appropriate and necessary. Given that proponents of the one-grant approach included HUD/OUP administrators, this was something of a one-sided argument.

In 1999, however, a compromise of sorts was reached when OUP instituted a new funding vehicle called the COPC New Directions grant. Institutions that had previously received a COPC grant and had met HUD-formulated program and administrative requirements could return for a second round of funding. In an effort to broaden the scope of the partnership activity the institution was asked to either do new activities in the same community where the original grant operated, or provide their existing programs in a different community. These New Directions grants were for a two-year performance period. By getting new campus resources and/or new community partners involved, chances to more firmly establish, or institutionalize, the programs increased. Institutions involved with the COPC program can now anticipate, in a best-case scenario, a period of five years of funding.

But the nagging question continues to surface: Is five years enough time to establish the required on-campus infrastructure and marshal the resources necessary to adequately support these programs? Can service-learning be introduced to the pedagogy in sufficient quality and quantity to make an impact on the curriculum? Can a culture of service and civic engagement be put in place and encouraged to flourish in three to five years? And most importantly, can community partners become empowered in three to five years to the point where they come to the table as equal participants in programs designed to improve their communities?

There are no simple answers to these questions. Circumstances differ on each campus, economic conditions change, charismatic leaders come and go, and governmental funding priorities change. Given these unknown factors, it is safe to say that an arbitrary limit on the number of grants an institution may receive is not in the best interest of the program.

What, then, would be in the best interest of the institutions and the community? There are advocates for what could be termed the entitlement model—continual funding for as long as the institution could show it was achieving results. Rex LaMore, director of the Community and Economic Development program at Michigan State University and one of the creators of the original COPC legislation, would compare this type of funding to the support provided to state extension services that have served rural communities for more than 100 years (personal communication, May 9, 2003). State land-grant colleges and universities get funding each year to provide valuable and much-needed services to predominantly rural areas. LaMore sees in this approach a model for urban service. Adopting this model to the universe of potential COPC applicants (e.g., private colleges, community colleges, and professional schools) would be problematic, but it nonetheless puts a funding option on the table.

Entitlement funding, even if a model could be developed that addresses the diversity of institutions that make up COPC, presents another problem. With a limited annual budget of $7–8 million, continually making funding available to the same institutions would for all intents and purposes exclude most other institutions from participating in the program. One of the truly exciting aspects of the development of the Office of University Partnerships over the past 10 years has been the increased interest on the part of widely diverse institutions of higher education. The first COPC grants were awarded to what could be referred to as the "usual suspects," such as University of California–Berkeley, Yale University, and Big Ten institutions. More recent years have seen greater involvement on the part of regional state campuses, private institutions, and, to a more limited degree, minority-based institutions. Without a limit, artificial or otherwise, on the number of grants an institution may receive, the campus-community engagement movement would have stagnated.

So if "one and done" was naïve and unrealistic, and New Directions grants only get us part of the way to institutionalization, but entitlement funding proves to be a non-starter, do any creative funding options remain? The answer may lie in more compromise. Institutions that are doing good work in the community and can show reasonable progress toward institutionalizing these programs on campus should be eligible to return for continued federal support. The current administration should be applauded for its emphasis on accountability in federal grant programs, and if a college or university can describe concrete, positive results in the community and on campus, it should be allowed to compete for additional funding beyond the New Directions award. In order to encourage new institutions to apply for COPC funding, only a portion of the annual COPC appropriation would be available for this additional funding. A sizeable portion of the budget would remain for the new applicants.

It should be pointed out that among all of OUP's grant programs, only COPC has a limit on how many grants an institution can receive. All of the minority-based grants are renewable, providing good, measurable re-sults are achieved, and specific administrative requirements are met. While the nature and focus of these programs differ from COPC's focus, the fact remains that we acknowledge their ability to continue to work on behalf of their local communities by basing future funding decisions on their past performance.

Continuing to fund successful COPC grantees would also provide OUP with models of excellence or best practices. Including in the grant award funds for dissemination of successful work (e.g., publications, con-ferences, and web sites) would serve to inform the dialogue on community engagement. The acknowledgement of these models would also help iden-tify emerging leaders in the field. I hope that reputations earned by early leaders in this field—including Holland and Harkavy—were helped in some small way by their affiliation with early COPC grants. It is exciting to contemplate the next generation of leaders.

Another compromise would involve smaller planning grants for col-leges and universities attempting to establish outreach programs on the campus and in the community. With the exception of the Historically Black College and University program, which acknowledges never-before-funded institutions with smaller grant opportunities, all of OUP's grant programs require applicants to submit an application for a fully developed program. Given the highly competitive nature of the COPC program, this puts many institutions, especially minority-based institutions, at a competi-tive disadvantage. The awarding of a smaller planning grant for one to two years would enable an institution to lay the groundwork for a more compre-hensive proposal a year or two later. It could serve to generate interest on the campus and identify resources, including faculty, students, and staff, who could contribute to this effort. At the same time, appropriate community partners could be identified and a dialogue that would lead to mutual trust and confidence among the participants could begin. Programming goals and objectives could be modest by design during this planning stage, en-abling the partnership to build upon small successes but potentially yielding more substantial benefits to the longer term collaboration.

Other forms of funding that could be considered include channeling funding through a consolidated entity, such as a state or a state university or college system. The Corporation for National and Community Service utilizes such a model with grants to states for its Learn and Serve program. The Office of University Partnerships, with its Community Development

Work Study program, has the option of directly funding a state that can then fund individual institutions of higher education within the state. On a smaller scale, OUP currently funds community college districts that, in turn, identify an institution within the district to be the main participant in the grant.

Some of these funding options would require a radical departure from HUD/OUP's traditional way of doing business. But as we enter our second decade of service, a decade that will present a new set of challenges not only for colleges and universities and their local communities, but also for the federal government, it may be time to consider other ways of supporting this initiative.

OUP is poised to enter this next decade fully committed to working with colleges and universities to enhance their role in the community. OUP's focus will always be on the campus *and* the community. HUD's mission is to serve low- to moderate-income people. The visionaries who established OUP recognized the role colleges and universities could play in addressing the problems of low-income communities. Colleges and universities immediately stepped up in dramatic fashion and brought their resources to bear on the problems of urban America. HUD/OUP will continue to be the catalyst and provide the financial resources to enable more and more colleges to take part in this important movement.

References

Carnegie Commission on Higher Education. (1971). *From isolation to mainstream: Problems of colleges founded for negroes.* New York, NY: McGraw-Hill.

Cisneros, H. (1996, December). The university and the urban challenge. *Cityscape: A Journal of Policy Development and Research* [Special Issue]. Retrieved July 15, 2005, from http://www.huduser.org/Periodicals/CITYSCPE/SPISSUE/ch1.pdf

Harkavy, I. (2003, July). *The future of service in America.* Paper presented at the annual meeting of the National and Community Service Coalition, Washington, DC.

Hispanic Association of Colleges and Universities. (2005, March). *Office of Governmental Relations report.* Washington, DC: Author.

Initiative for a Competitive Inner City, & CEOs for Cities. (2002). *Leveraging colleges and universities for urban revitalization: An action guide.* Retrieved January 15, 2005, from http://www.icic.org/vsm/bin/smRenderFS.php?PHPSESSID=4477979af0e099a84980bd7cbbe297cc&cerror=

Johnson, L. B. (1965, Mar. 2). Message from the President of the United States relative to the problems and future of the central city and its suburbs. *Congressional Record, Vol. III, Part 3*, pp. 3,908–3,912. Washington, DC: United States Printing Office.

Strand, K., Marullo, S., Cutforth, N., Stoecker, R., & Donohoe, P. (2003). *Community-based research and higher education: Principles and practices.* San Francisco, CA: Jossey-Bass.

Urban Community Service Program. (1992). *Archived information.* Retrieved July 25, 2005, from the Department of Education web site: http://www.ed.gov/pubs/Biennial/538.html

U.S. Department of Housing and Urban Development. (2003). *Office of University Partnerships, Community Outreach Partnership Center grant files, 1994–2003.* Washington, DC: Author.

13 Weaving Engagement Into the Fabric of Campus Administration

John Wanat

A lthough universities have long been connected to the larger society in many ways, the specific term "engagement" is relatively new to the conversation in higher education. While most major universities promote their tripartite missions of research, teaching, and service, in practice their efforts and attention have centered on teaching and scholarship, making service an afterthought. For the typical faculty member, the usual concept of service is either to one's discipline or to one's department or college. Only recently among some universities has the concept of service been expanded to mean service to the larger community and labeled as "engagement."

The concept of service to the larger community as part of university mission has assumed various forms in the past. In America's earliest private colleges the mission was to prepare ministers and teachers, so the connection to the broader, believing community was clear. Later, with the passage of the Morrill Acts, public higher education was mandated to address issues faced by the agricultural and industrial sectors of society. One branch of higher education was transformed in the course of the middle 20th century when American public higher education concentrated its scholarly focus as it moved toward the model of the German research university. Funded by large infusions of federal support and fueled by the large growth in college-age students, public higher education grew, was accorded respect, and afforded some respectful distance. In this process, public higher education was able to loosen—or at least was not bound to—its prior connections to the larger community. The ivory tower was firmly established. But in some largely urban universities, the reconnection of the university with the larger set of communities was growing and causing both celebration and stress.

Some of this change has evolved from within academia. Not all faculty view their roles and careers as centered on pure scholarship. Especially in professional schools, there is a long and intimate relationship with the outside world, whether it is providing skilled and educated workers or offering research that can improve the professional or disciplinary tools available to dentists, engineers, lawyers, nurses, teachers, or musicians. But increasingly, there is pressure from those who provide the ever decreasing pool of funds to universities. These forces want to determine what universities should be doing and what faculty should be delivering. Some of these relationships are mutually beneficial. Others are not yet well defined.

This chapter explores the administrative implications of the rediscovery—in some universities—of the newly reemphasized role of engagement with communities outside pure academe. It begins with a look at the ownership of universities and the dominant cultures within them. It then explores how these cultures challenge and stress the issues of faculty recruitment, promotion and tenure, grants and contracts, fundraising and student service. The goal is to delineate some of the dynamics underlying the engagement tension/evolution and to explore some of the ways university leadership can foster engagement.

The Central Question: Who Owns a University?

The administration of the engaged university is strongly affected by who claims and exerts ownership of the university. While we typically think of groups inside the university—such as faculty and students—claiming ownership, those outside the university who feel that they have a claim on the institution increasingly put pressures on the campus to accommodate their interests, leading to campus-leadership issues.

The idealized world of a university is a picture of a collection of faculty working at the forefront of their disciplines on topics of their choosing and communicating that knowledge to students who are committed to the discipline. Academic freedom is central to this conception of a university. Faculty are thought to be the driving force in a university with the administration and all other resources at their disposal. Thus, faculty are often thought to be the theoretical owners of a university. If they want to see themselves as engaged, it will happen. If they see themselves in splendid isolation from the issues and problems of the current world, that will come to pass. In reality, however, many groups conflict with faculty over control. But regardless of the realpolitik, faculty do comprise the center and the soul of the university.

In all universities there is a board of regents, trustees, visitors, overseers, or other superior body that has ultimate legal authority over the university. Since this group controls the purse, they clearly have a say in what happens. Students claim some control both because they are the ultimate consumers of the educational process and also pay some part of the costs. Thus, they too have a legitimate claim on owning the university. (Their parents, who often pay tuition, claim ownership as well.) In some church-affiliated institutions, there are officers outside the institution that assert legitimate ownership of the university.

In public higher education, elected political officers claim to own the university on behalf of the general citizenry. Especially since the original charter of public institutions is typically grounded in legislation, governmental officers think they should have control. Since they annually appropriate funds for the university, they also claim control, although their legitimacy is questioned by some members of the academy.

Special groups in society also claim ownership. They may be primary-school parents who feel that K–12 teachers from the university are not adequately prepared for their students, business firms that want employees who fit immediately and seamlessly into their organizations, disadvantaged groups that want entry into and success in college, corporations that want access to university-generated intellectual property, social-welfare groups that want university resources dedicated to the solution of the societal problems afflicting their clients, hospitals that want university priorities shifted to favor the increased production of healthcare workers, donors who want significant university commitments to follow their gifts, those on the margins of society who want access to the mainstream, and those in the mainstream who want to stay there.

Does it matter who claims and exerts ownership? Yes, it does. But it is very clear that participation, ownership, and leadership all constitute disputed territory. Cohen and March (1986) characterize universities as splendid examples of the garbage-can model of organizations. Unlike the traditional, hierarchical organization model, the garbage-can model is characterized in part by unclear technologies, sporadic involvement by participants, and lack of agreement on goals. In addition to the tensions among the various groups outlined earlier, none of those groups is absolutely monolithic in composition or perspective.

Back to the questions of ownership and control—because universities can be such powerful engines of change and stabilizing forces in society, everyone at some time or another wants to control them or at least benefit from their capabilities. Caught in the middle of these various claimants is the university leadership, which in some cases is viewed as its administration. More frequently than not, this group feels quite explicitly the tensions among the various claimants to the legitimate ownership of the university. To administration, claims of ownership are real and important, as well as the substance of much of their daily work. How the administrative leadership acts can decidedly influence whether and how engagement can be furthered.

Administration of Engagement

Each of the potentially conflicting claimants of ownership of a university has a slightly different perspective on engagement—indeed, there is unlikely to be agreement even within each of the constituent groups themselves. And none of these perspectives automatically converges. To understand how the interests of these various legitimate owners play out, the dynamics in a few areas will be discussed. Specific areas of tension are:

- Faculty recruitment and expectations of new faculty

- Promotion, tenure, and conflicting criteria

- Grants and contracts, and relations to corporate interests

- Fundraising and relations to donors

- Student service, especially to special populations

Faculty Recruitment and Engagement

Since universities are institutions that completely depend on and are defined by their human capital, how they choose their members significantly affects how they operate. Turnover among faculty is generally low in universities, with more departures occurring in the early years of faculty careers. And due to the recent period of economic stringency faced by higher education, faculty are not eager or even able to change institutions. The relatively few hiring opportunities therefore affect how the university acts long into the future. Change in composition is usually slow and modest, meaning that change in orientation and acceptance or embracing of engagement will not be rapid.

The one area that faculty absolutely do control in a university is admission to their ranks. In most institutions, faculty lines, whether new or replacement, are defined by the subdisciplinary research or teaching needs. The scenario is that the departments of sociology, chemistry, or education are left to their own devices to choose the candidates when there is a need for a demographer, organic chemist, or curriculum specialist. All too frequently, the department seeks to clone the previous incumbent of the position. If the opening is a new position, the norms of the department related to scholarship and teaching will typically prevail, once the general decision is made in what area to recruit. Professional stature accrues to those who excel and keep current in the field, whether through books, monographs, grants, performances, or exhibitions. Peer acclamation is the coin of the realm, and it usually comes from succeeding at the game according to the current rules, which do not usually recognize engagement as a primary or even a desirable characteristic. Especially for those hired as untenured assistant professors, the expectations and reward systems may not be conducive to the new faculty member who wants to include the scholarship of engagement in his or her professional profile.

How then, do college or university leaders encourage the hiring of faculty who will espouse engagement? The easiest way is to concentrate on new positions and to offer resources to colleges or departments to recruit engaged scholars and teachers. To the extent that funds can be secured for departments to hire scholars and teachers of engagement, there is hope. But even the offer of a gift horse, so to speak, does not guarantee acceptance. At the University of Wisconsin–Milwaukee, for example, when new state funds were secured for positions that were specifically targeted to support The Milwaukee Idea of university involvement in the communities, some faculty felt that those positions were "stolen" from the replacement needs of the traditional kinds of curricular and scholarly activity. Further, the current dearth of resources in higher education can make the addition of engaged faculty a moderately difficult and costly option.

A second approach to encouraging engagement is to reduce the problems the new faculty member might experience by defining the recruitment to be at a tenured rank so that the new recruit is not expected to serve two masters—the traditional model of disinterested scholarship and teaching on the one hand, and the engaged scholar and teacher on the other. With the pressure of meeting tenure expectations removed, the new faculty member has an independence that permits a less-than-traditional career approach.

Promotion and Tenure for the Engaged Scholar

Whatever the avenue the engaged scholar and teacher takes into the university, unless hired as a full professor, he or she will eventually be considered for promotion and tenure by his or her peers on campus. On an annual basis, moreover, there will be reviews for the purpose of salary increases. What criteria will be applied? How can the administration facilitate consideration of faculty who are engaged scholars and teachers?

One way to encourage the reward of engaged scholars and teachers is to create a culture and a climate in which engagement is respected. This is more common in professional schools and colleges, and much can be learned from them in this regard. Connections with outside groups, be they clients or professional organizations, will make the faculty member's outside activities more acceptable. Nursing faculty understand that their colleagues who are interested in community health must work with outside groups, and they understand that serving client groups *and* academic reference groups is not only possible but essential to their success as scholars and teachers in community health nursing. These faculty understand that their field is not owned only by faculty in a university but also by the healthcare providers and the health consumers in the community. In comparison, a faculty member who provides valuable assistance to a local tenants' rights group may not get that activity easily accepted as valuable for purposes of promotion or salary increases. In disciplines such as business, involvement in the real world of commerce can be accepted as an indication of acceptance by a user community, but compensation for that frequently comes directly from the benefiting company when it pays the faculty member as a consultant.

So, how do academics get activities that are tied to "outsiders" accepted? Academics can still earn the respect and acceptance of their peers by taking their engaged experience and converting it into something that meets scholarly standards. The scholarly disciplines, however, retain their ownership of the quality standards. Disciplinary peers may not accept the word of the tenants' rights organization when it says that, "Professor Smith provided valuable assistance in addressing an important social issue." They want Professor Smith's insights from the consultation with the tenants' rights organization put into a form that can be generalized or that is otherwise insightful enough to merit publication in a refereed academic outlet. Academic leaders should therefore push engaged faculty to share the fruits of their involvement in the relevant communities through academic publication outlets. This, however, can present other difficulties when the top academic journals avoid the more applied or engaged areas for publication.

Grants, Contracts, and Corporate Interests

Another way to reward engagement is through grants. Funding agencies are often well disposed to support engagement, because communities want to see the university help solve problems that the community sees as important, not just those problems that the academy internally defines as important. Since investigators must pass through various filters to convince funding agencies that ideas merit consideration—filters that can include peer review by other academics—the awarding of funds can be an indicator of quality. To the extent that academic leaders can emphasize the importance of getting grants for the scholarship of engagement and can assist faculty in securing such grants, they can help to reward engagement efforts.

At the same time, the use of external grants, contracts, and corporate relationships can pose a potential conflict of interest for the engaged university. Although external approbation expressed through monetary awards does provide some legitimacy to engaged scholarship and teaching, concerns do arise inside the university, more in some disciplines than others. Again, those in the professional schools and those in the sciences generally salute the award of funds from recognized and prestigious foundations and federal agencies. Such grants address major societal issues and are difficult to attain, which satisfies both a social conscience and a sense of elitism that appeals to many academics. Others see external funding as buying the free and independent spirit of the academic. Being "bought" does not sit well with some in the university who feel their integrity being compromised when someone else is paying for, and potentially directing, their efforts.

Bok (2003) has written extensively about the dangers that the "commercialization" of higher education can pose for the academy and of the need to protect the integrity of research in the face of high-stakes patent opportunities. Who owns the time and allegiance of the university investigator is the crux of legitimacy, whether a faculty member's allegiance is to a profit-making corporation funding research on the latest miracle drug or to a community nonprofit organization whose mission to serve the public good shapes the research agenda.

These are legitimate concerns for engaged faculty, because grant and contract funding can affect the core values of the academy. Corporate demands that proprietary information be kept confidential are in conflict with the free exchange of information characteristic of academic inquiry. Especially where this affects graduate students' degree progress, imposition of constraints on publication should not be acceptable. University leaders must protect academic values by establishing clear rules outlining conflicts of interests for faculty, and, as Bok (2003) also advises, making sure that the university's own financial ties do not compromise institutional values: "When rules are unclear and always subject to negotiation, money will prevail over principle much of the time" (p. 156).

Freedom of inquiry is a great protection for the scholar involved in activities not supported by the dominant culture. Campus leadership should emphasize the rights of the engaged scholar and teacher to pursue her or his interests, regardless of whether the scholarship and teaching are the dominant orthodoxy of the discipline and university.

Fundraising and Relations With Donors

Proportionately, and sometimes absolutely, public tax support for university operations has been steadily decreasing over the last few decades. This means public university leadership has looked increasingly to private donors to make up the difference. This presents both dangers and benefits for the engaged university. Gifts frequently come with strings attached—strings that affect university finances and priorities. Almost all gifts are earmarked for particular purposes—whether for a professor of Baltic languages or for a scholarship for redheaded accounting majors (regardless of the fact that there may be no demand for Estonian language instruction or there are already adequate scholarships in accounting).

Many gifts have financial strings that may result in the expenditure of university resources. Endowed professorships, for example, do not always generate enough return to pay the full costs of a senior faculty member's salary and benefits. Frequently, a university spends as much as the donor contributes for a professorship in an area that is essentially specified by the donor. The opportunity costs of accepting such gifts can be substantial. If there is a need for a professor of art history, but the money must be channeled to the professor of Estonian, faculty will feel that their role in setting academic priorities has been diminished.

Donor gifts provide potential benefits for the engaged institution. Regardless of any strings, real or imagined, donations reflect a commitment to the university. They indicate a demonstrable link between members of the larger community and the institution. Even modest donations can advance academic goals and prepare the steppingstone for donors to support the institution in the broader public setting or the political arena as well. The continued legitimacy that the donor communities manifest in making gifts—especially in support of engaged discovery or learning—strengthens a university and can support its transformation into the new kind of university it seeks to become.

How can campus leaders help advance engagement through gift giving? If an endowed chair is dedicated to the scholarship of engagement, the faculty member holding the chair has the prestige, the freedom, and even the mandate to press engagement. If there are contributions to support specific programs of service-learning, engaged teaching can prosper. Campus leaders clearly can assist in soliciting gifts that further engagement.

The University of Missouri–St. Louis provides a useful example. As former Chancellor Blanche Touhill (2004) describes, the interests of a university donor in supporting engaged faculty has led to the formation of the Des Lee Collaborative, with 35 endowed chairs totaling more than $20 million, supporting engaged community-university collaborations. As a university leader, she was able to connect the donor wishes to existing university engagement efforts and to leverage initial endowments to encourage other donors to enlarge the program.

Serving Students

Clearly, universities are dedicated to serving students. Traditionally, faculty have decided how that will be done in the classroom, the laboratory, and the studio. But changes have occurred as faculty explore new pedagogy—

often enlivened by experiential and service-learning—and as students demand new methods of instruction and new subjects to study. Traditional disciplines have transformed themselves or given birth to new disciplines, seen in the growth of such fields as urban studies, labor studies, women's studies, and minority studies over the last 30 years. Where there have been faculty pressing for such fields, there have also been students urging instruction and scholarship in those areas.

The demands do not always come directly from students. Communities also want graduates who understand the multicultural world in which they live and work. They require individuals who are prepared to help solve the problems of poverty, pollution, transportation, healthcare, and other public policy issues.

One way in which administrators can respond to these changing program demands is to create centers for research, training, and dissemination in the areas of concern. Once again, the challenge to administration is to find the resources, internally or externally, for such centers and to justify their priority to the rest of the campus. Ideally, the centers are jump-started with one-time campus funding with the expectation that the center will generate enough grants and contracts to sustain themselves thereafter.

How does the campus leadership involve itself in student calls for more engagement? Since all courses, majors, programs, and departments in universities at some time must be endorsed or formally approved by faculty, responsiveness to student demands requires collaboration with faculty. Helping to create a climate supportive of nontraditional approaches is a basic administrative responsibility—supported through specific institutional policies and reinforced by consistent and visible administrative practices of mentoring, modeling, and good, old-fashioned cheerleading. It is also important to locate, mentor, and support champions among the faculty who will take on the responsibility of shepherding the courses and programs through the consultative and approval processes common to all universities.

What Have We Learned?

Simply put, engagement scholarship and teaching, especially in urban, public research universities, is not part of today's canon. Engagement is still the domain of a moderately small number of people in the university who see its potential. Since many disparate groups claim some ownership of universities, all have claimed some control over who is given legitimacy, what is done, what is rewarded, and what should be recognized. Compounded by the tradition of shared governance, this field of contested ownership makes it difficult for campus administration to quickly or easily encourage engagement.

Universities are large, complex, and slow-moving enterprises. Indeed, some defenders would argue that that very conservatism is the secret of their continued existence and even their success. Since the demands for change come from so many directions, there is a tendency for the academy to dig in and outwait the newcomers.

Administrators are at the center of much of the adjustment being demanded. In their roles as institutional innovators, motivators, and shock absorbers, they are expected to change the climate, encourage the faculty, and find the resources needed to make engagement happen. While the world of administrators is constrained, they can and should take some important steps. They can foster an environment of tolerance. Without that open climate, built on the traditional notions of academic freedom, acceptance of anything that deviates from the orthodox notions of ivory tower academia will not occur. They can recognize and reward faculty who are engaged and who can provide leadership to others. Administrators can also reach out to community partners, bringing them into advisory roles at all levels of the institution.

Engagement is easier to accept if it carries some kind of peer approbation. This is most acceptable from outside institutions, such as respectable funding agencies and renowned foundations. Encouraging engaged scholarship in refereed outlets will help the institution as a whole to transform its hiring, tenuring, and promotion decisions.

But perhaps the one area in which administrators are expected to play a major role is in providing resources. They can support faculty in trying to secure grants, gifts, and contracts, and in informing the university community about them.

Creating a new kind of university is not for the faint of heart. But for administrators willing to take leadership roles, the potential to transform their institutions is immense.

References

Bok, D. (2003). *Universities in the marketplace: The commercialization of higher education*. Princeton, NJ: Princeton University Press.

Cohen, M., & March, J. (1986). *Leadership and ambiguity: The American college president* (2nd ed.). Boston, MA: Harvard Business School Press.

Touhill, B. (2004). The Des Lee Collaborative Vision: Institutionalizing community engagement at the University of Missouri–St. Louis. In N. L. Zimpher & K. R. Howey (Eds.), *University leadership in urban school renewal* (pp. 249–266). Westport, CT: Praeger.

14 Institutionalizing Engagement: What Can Presidents Do?

Nancy L. Zimpher

My goal, as the new chancellor at the University of Wisconsin–Milwaukee in 1998, evolved from an articulated rationale for university engagement, resonating for both campus and community, as follows: *Embrace the opportunities for applied and collaborative research, the potential for enhanced student learning and community connections, university transformation and prestige, and fulfillment of civic responsibility.* This chapter presents the opportunity to explore further my personal journey toward engagement, the requisite leadership skills needed to achieve it, and the likely pitfalls or barriers to attaining a truly engaged university.

While the case can, and should, be made for matching institutional priorities with the local context in which institutions reside, there are some enduring observations that I have distilled over several leadership opportunities that frame my perspective on engagement. Last articulated in the concluding chapter of *A Time for Boldness: A Story of Institutional Change* (Zimpher, Percy, & Brukardt, 2002), these five properties of leadership take on new meaning each and every day that I continue to serve in a leadership role. I reiterate them here to provide a basis for the claim that "engagement" is, in the words of business gurus Collins and Porras (1994), a quintessentially "big hairy audacious goal" (p. 91). They are as follows:

- *Vision trumps everything.* Organizations are most effective when a well-articulated and ambitious vision exists of the future, reflecting the rich traditions of the past as well as aspirations for the future.

- *Vision is derived at the hands of many.* Institutions can be inclusive of the various interests and constituencies on the campus and in the community, and still align these diverse interests in a coherent vision of the future.

- *Collective vision can only derive from collective action.* Institutions must create a targeted set of actions (not too many; not too few), and then hold themselves accountable for results.

- *Institutions must ensure that they have the pocketbook for their aspirations.* Inability to offer incentives for participation in the vision is a recipe for failure.

- And of course, *vision requires persistence and constancy of message.*

I recall in the early days of my administration at the University of Wisconsin–Milwaukee (UWM), calling the university community to the engagement mission: "Our goal is nothing less than to change forever the quality of our life together by joining the urban renaissance of Milwaukee and transforming ourselves as Milwaukee's and someday the nation's premier urban university." Such a call to arms certainly met the "ambitious vision" criterion. It also set the stage for a collaborative effort to define engagement through a set of strategic actions and revenue-generating efforts, through what ultimately came to be called "The Milwaukee Idea."

This chapter seeks to answer these three questions: First, how did I, as a new chancellor, think my way into this articulated call to action? Second, what specific lessons have been learned, not only from my UWM days, but also from a couple of years as president of another urban research university, the University of Cincinnati, that might be helpful to other presidents and chancellors? And third, what are the pitfalls or barriers that challenge such an ambitious leadership agenda?

Acting My Way Into Engagement

There are many pathways to the university presidency. While mine is not unique, I am sure, it does carry with it several opportunities to clarify my personal commitment to engagement. Perhaps the most obvious has been my field of study. I am an educator by training. I began my undergraduate studies as an English major, but like many in my day, I decided to add a teaching credential in order to fortify my prospects on the job market. Through an array of teaching assignments, from the high-performing suburbs of Washington, DC, to the foothills of the Ozarks, I learned firsthand that teaching was in and of itself an "engaged profession." It is simply not possible to enter a classroom without factoring in the context from which the children and youth I taught had come. As every teacher knows, some children come to school ready to learn and others enter the room hungry, tired, sick, lonely, or scared, but always curious. So families matter to classroom teachers; neighborhoods matter; economic profiles matter; and all of these ingredients temper a child's capacity to grow and learn.

From my teaching experience, I went on to become a teacher education professor and ultimately the key administrator who placed a large college of education's students in their clinical field experiences. This responsibility opened for me the opportunity to work with district superintendents, building principals, teachers and their professional organizations, parents, and of course, more students. I experienced over the course of many years the nature and bureaucracy of the urban school district and the concomitant challenges thereof. Having served in universities situated in three mid-sized urban cities, I know firsthand the profile of America's urban school district: high levels of poverty with roughly two-thirds of the students on free or reduced lunch; high levels of illiteracy amongst their parents, many of whom are single moms and dads; high attrition rates, with roughly 50% of the students in these urban districts failing to graduate from high school. And in every case, the large local metropolitan public university was doing much to help prepare high school students to enter college and be successful.

Thus a fundamental early lesson in my personal journey toward engagement was the necessary symbiotic relationship between elementary and secondary schools and colleges and universities. Undoubtedly my background explains why I have spent so much of my presidential role advocating for a seamless educational system wherein schools and universities come to understand and embrace the reciprocal responsibilities necessary to help every child succeed. This early engagement with the educational community undoubtedly helped prepare me for an even broader forum for institutional engagement in neighborhood revitalization.

Such an opportunity presented itself when The Ohio State University (OSU) launched an ambitious neighborhood renewal effort in its adjacent neighborhoods, commonly referred to as "east of High." Just across the major boundary street of the university, High Street, sprawled a set of neighborhoods where poverty was high and home ownership low, where crime disturbingly encroached on the life space of thousands of students who lived in these neighborhoods, and where collaborative opportunities to move the economics of the neighborhood were in short supply. Thus in 1995, OSU incorporated Campus Partners for Community Urban Redevelopment as a nonprofit community redevelopment corporation to promote improvements to the neighborhoods around the university. While the charge of this new nonprofit organization was highly ambitious, including its intent to prepare a comprehensive revitalization plan and implementation program for this "University District," and with the partnership of the city and numerous neighborhood development organizations already in operation in the neighborhoods, campus activity was energized as well.

Complementary to the work of the incorporated nonprofit organization was a newly formed and "loosely coupled" group of campus departments, whose intent was to serve as a consultant to Campus Partners in the area of human services; and to research and develop recommendations in the areas of public education, health and well-being, social services, and employment. As then-dean of OSU's College of Education, I led this emerging organization, configured from an already existing Interprofessional Commission. Over a period of about five years, the Campus Collaborative, as it was called, engaged more than 40 existing campus units (colleges, departments, and academic areas), raised $2.7 million in external funding, generated more than 40 seed grants and 70 outreach and engagement initiatives (engaging almost 600 faculty, staff, students, and community residents), and graduated 40 community participants from a construction trade training program. In short, involvement in this significant effort for university personnel to "join hands and walk across the street"—a big move for any university learning its way into engagement—was an early lesson in my academic leadership development.

These two remarkable opportunities, one to engage with public urban education and the other to take a leadership role in neighborhood revitalization, made it somewhat obvious to me that this is the way universities are supposed to behave. It should not be surprising then, upon arriving at UWM and sensing immediately the hunger of the greater metropolitan Milwaukee community for UWM to become more engaged, that I would assert this as a major transformative agenda for the campus.

There was, of course, more to UWM's engagement initiative than was obvious to the casual observer. For starters, UWM was a relatively hidden resource to the broader community. I recall a trumped up "want ad" that I invented early on as a somewhat humorous introduction in one of my speeches. It read: "Large urban university, nestled in lovely residential neighborhood . . . seeks relief from threats of invisibility in large urban nexus." How, in other words, was UWM going to become "more visible" to a city that needed to understand better the reciprocal relationship between a great city and a great university? How was UWM eventually going to convince this vibrant community that an investment in the university was also an investment in their community? My response was that only by some overt effort to engage the campus in the community could we ever expect to engage the community in the campus.

Thus The Milwaukee Idea emerged, not so much as an out-of-the-blue concept, but as a way to solidify this necessary sense of interdependency. We were also extremely fortunate that the "idea" lay dormant and ready for application in the urban context. Widely known across the state for its unique history, the University of Wisconsin was founded on the premise that "the boundaries of the university are the boundaries of the state." We drew heavily on that premise—known to all as The Wisconsin Idea—and expanded the meaning from agrarian to urban, from the state of Wisconsin to the city of Milwaukee. The rest, as they say, is history. The Milwaukee Idea became fairly widely known by the time I transitioned from Milwaukee to Cincinnati, to the point that the Cincinnati media asked me if I intended to bring The Cincinnati Idea to Ohio. Frankly, I would have loved to. But alas, The Milwaukee Idea had power at UWM because it had indigenous meaning for the city and for Wisconsin, where that riveting philosophy is as much a part of the rich history of the state as its progressive politics and Packers football.

I did, I believe, bring the spirit of The Milwaukee Idea to Cincinnati. Early in my tenure at the University of Cincinnati (UC), I was asked by the Board of Trustees to engage the university in a strategic planning process out of which we derived an ambitious academic plan for the decade ahead—a vision we refer to as UC|21. This is short for "the University of Cincinnati leading in the 21st century," an aspirational plan to "define the new urban research university." The plan is organized around six strategic goals, and at least three of them engender engagement:

- *Goal 4: Forge Key Relationships and Partnerships.* Throughout its history, UC has enjoyed a deep, reciprocal, and widespread connection to its home city of Cincinnati, not just as an intellectual resource, but also as a cultural center and an economic driver. In fact, the university had roots as a municipal university, joining the Ohio State University System first as an affiliate in 1968 and then as a full state university in 1977. Yet UC|21 pledges the university to even deeper community relationships. It reaffirms a true commitment to engagement and calls upon the university to establish and nurture partnerships with our colleagues within the university and with our local and global communities.

- *Goal 5: Establish a Sense of "Place."* UC|21 seeks to develop an environment where members of the university community and the community at large want to spend time—not just learning, but also living, playing, and staying. In this goal, we could have limited our vision to just on campus, but we chose to look off campus as well, in the surrounding neighborhoods encircling our core base. Signs in the area point to a unifying name for this conglomeration of neighborhoods just north of downtown Cincinnati: Uptown. Our commitment to building a better Uptown is a large part of our goal to create a sense of place.

- *Goal 6: Create Opportunity.* UC|21 calls upon UC to develop potential in students and also in our local and global communities, as a partner in education, in workforce development, as a catalyst for entrepreneurship, and as a partner in economic development. (See http://www.uc.edu/uc21)

The foundation for this engagement, I must point out, would not be as solid nor the consensus nearly so cohesive had it not been for the tremendous physical transformation that had been taking place on the UC campus since 1989 under the leadership of my predecessor, Joseph A. Steger. That transformation had begun to cross boundaries into the surrounding neighborhoods, and our UC|21 visioning process, particularly Goal 5, Establishing a Sense of Place, strengthened that commitment. UC has played a leading role in the formation of the Uptown Consortium, a nonprofit community development corporation dedicated to the human, social, economic, and physical improvement of Uptown Cincinnati.

Through the consortium, UC joins hands with four other of Uptown's largest employers—the Cincinnati Children's Hospital Medical Center, Cincinnati Zoo & Botanical Gardens, the Health Alliance of Greater Cincinnati, and TriHealth. Taken together, the five consortium members employ nearly 50,000 people, boast a payroll of $1.4 billion, and produce an annual economic impact of more than $3 billion. The idea is that as a consortium, we can accomplish much more in Uptown by working together than we could by working in isolation. I have been fortunate to serve as the consortium's first chair. In early 2004, my fellow consortium board members and I hired a CEO, Tony Brown, whose job it is to wake up every morning working on ways to build a better Uptown. Although some of the communities within Uptown are affluent, Uptown overall has higher unemployment rates, lower rates of homeownership, and higher rates of poverty than the city as a whole. Our hope as a consortium is to enhance the area's quality of life through engagement. We have selected five priorities, based on research with the residents in the communities, on which to focus: public safety, transportation, housing, economic development, and neighborhood services, including education, health care, and economic inclusion.

In short, a journey that began as a classroom teacher, perhaps most memorably in a two-room schoolhouse outside Rolla, Missouri, has been parlayed into a leadership role in urban education renewal, neighborhood revitalization, and institutional commitment to engagement across three major public research universities and three Midwestern cities. As such, I have come to understand that engagement sits at the very fiber of my existence. I believe fundamentally that institutions, particularly public institutions, are intended to serve the public good. These institutions are a part of the social compact wherein the public supports these institutions so that they in turn can support their local communities. I believe as well that institutional engagement is really an umbrella concept, one that engenders a commitment to high-quality teaching and learning, discovery and invention, and campus/community service. It is not a choice between teaching and research, as a third leg of a stool. Rather, engagement is the intervening variable that makes sense out of the purposes of teaching and learning, discovery and invention. It is the "essence" of the public university and its raison d'être.

Lessons Learned by an Engaged President

And so I turn to my second organizing question: What lessons have I learned about leading engagement efforts? In my public speeches I gravitate to lists of five, seven, or ten, and I cannot resist the temptation to do so again. The following are my seven leadership-for-engagement markers.

1) Pay attention to local context.

2) Acknowledge institutional capacity and self-interest.

3) Lead through vision.

4) Lead through action.

5) Assure the pocketbook for aspirations.

6) Use presidential convening power.

7) Go public and walk the brand.

Pay Attention to Local Context

Perhaps the most universal understanding among presidents is the concept of "local knowledge." One must get to know fundamentally what the local context means to a university. It begins early on as a presidential candidate comes into increasing personal contact with members of his or her board of trustees, trusted faculty, key community leaders, and well-placed alumni and donors. It extends into the ways in which a president first meets the community through speeches, meetings, and other forms of outreach. And it lands in literally every dimension of expression as the president represents the institution in a host of civic and community initiatives. Thus, the first steps toward achieving a truly engaged university grow out of well-grounded knowledge of context, including the local community, its region, and the state. For some geographically centered institutions, this may even include a tristate region or a larger geographic area, like the Midwest or Southeast region of the country. Each region has its issues and its idiosyncrasies, its history and its aspirations, best known and attended to by the president.

There are many ways to uncover the important characteristics of a community in order to determine its distinctive needs. For me, this came about quite naturally, in both Milwaukee and Cincinnati, through an entry plan we casually titled, "Day One, Week One, Month One." This plan, still operative in an evolved form almost two years later in Cincinnati, was a strategic effort to meet and greet as many significant community leaders as possible from my first day on the job and onward. This included key political figures like the governor, the mayor, city manager, and instrumental civic and corporate leaders through phone calls, follow-up visits, and eventually invitations to come to campus. Another important strategy in both cities was the willingness to speak to groups as soon into my tenure as possible, including civic organizations, corporate gatherings, small groups of realtors, investors, and women's organizations—all with the goal of articulating my personal interest in putting the community's interests at the top of the action list for both UWM and UC.

Clearly, the most important effort to engage community perspective was inviting people to discuss the future of the university in a meaningful and action-oriented way. For UWM, this was the initiative later referred to as "100 People, 100 Days," a planning process that resulted in a set of first ideas to amplify The Milwaukee Idea, ultimately resulting in more than 20 new ideas for engagement between the university and the community. At the University of Cincinnati, a similar planning process ensued, later referred to as UC|21, which also brought key civic and neighborhood leaders to the table to plan the university's future. While the character of each of these initiatives varied considerably, given the unique nature of each institution, both planning efforts reflected the institution's valuing of input from the community, and both plans assumed that collaborative plans would only go forward if significant involvement from the community were a part of each outreach initiative.

Acknowledge Institutional Capacity and Self-Interest

Like most large urban public research universities, UWM and UC have much to offer their respective communities. Since both institutions are well situated within city limits, there are many pressing issues that need and warrant a university's attention. While some would describe cities as fraught with problems, my view has always been that cities provide opportunity. What better place, one could say, to grow a comprehensive research university than in a so-called problem-rich environment? While cities can never really be viewed as a crucible, as if problems are of interest only from an intellectual value proposition, cities, with their obdurate conditions, are wonderful places in which to learn and to apply what is learned. Experts tell us that by the year 2025, more than three-quarters of the world's population will live in cities. Thus, our interest and our commitment to cities has the potential for powerful effect.

However, institutions of higher education have a tendency to deal out their expertise in bite-sized pieces. For instance, in both Milwaukee and Cincinnati, early surveys of the institutional commitment to K–12 education revealed a tremendous wealth of engagement. In both institutions, well over 150 different projects existed between local schools and colleges, departments, or individual professors. In both instances, these engagements were cross-disciplinary and served some very important needs. They were led by committed faculty and staff and, in most cases, engaged both undergraduate and graduate students in the work. But in my view, these myriad projects were "boutique" in nature; many small projects do not always scale up to solutions with holistic impact. While these institutions for years were engaged in collaborative efforts to train and retain teachers, offer professional development to principals, help high-school students with college access, support parent and social agency efforts to improve the school environment, they were not having an impact on the fundamental metrics that make a district successful. These would include higher graduation rates, less truancy, and fewer teen pregnancies and infractions with the law. So while engagement could be measured as broad-based, it is not always systemic; that is, geared to resolving the most basic achievement gaps that riddle most urban school districts. It is a leadership task to assess capacity and to stretch it.

In addition to fostering institutional capacity, leaders must also take into account institutional self-interest. I add this marker with some hesitation, because it reveals a fundamental institutional reality rarely acknowledged. That is, the work of universities in many instances requires a community relationship for self-interested reasons. First and foremost, public institutions historically rely on the public's goodwill to encourage policymakers to continue financial support for higher education. While the percentage of support supplied by state coffers has exponentially declined, particularly in the past decade, it is still the case that public institutions need public support. That support is more easily attained and sustained if the general citizenry, especially those in public policy positions, such as governors and legislators, believe the universities in question make substantial societal contributions.

Beyond the state's compact with its public universities, institutions also benefit from private fundraising in the general community in which they reside. I have found in all three cities where I have served that people contribute to an urban university not because they are alumni, but rather because they know how vital the institution is to the well-being of the city. True, many contributors are alums, but a sizable number of key civic and corporate leaders are typically educated elsewhere. They direct corporate gifts to the local institution because of the key contributions the institution makes to their community, making it easier to recruit and retain employees to their various businesses or organizations.

Just as important, the challenges urban landscapes face can be too complicated for any single agency to prevail—in stemming the tide against poverty, unemployment, illiteracy, poor health, racial tension, or low academic success. "It takes a village," and higher education is a key partner in that village mentality. So, no matter how prestigious the institution, no matter how significant national rankings are in the life space of the university, the greatest gains in institutional reputation, I believe, stem from sound working relationships with the community, opportunities to apply theory to practice in the local environment, and the community's understanding that access to a first-rate public institution is value added for that community.

Lead Through Vision

This heading might just as well read, "What do I do on Monday?" Leading engagement is not, in and of itself, difficult to imagine. But leading an institution through a major planning process that results in a vision that meaningfully incorporates engagement remains a challenging assignment. Part of the problem with a focus on engagement is one of nomenclature. It is so often said that the triadic mission of universities is in teaching, research, and service. While the words have changed a bit, thanks to the Kellogg Commission (2000) and its emphasis on engagement and Boyer's (1990) efforts to define the "scholarship of engagement," many people still view university mission as a triadic structure. A competing view is that these three legs of the institutional stool are at best a delivery mechanism. They tell us how we will serve society—through teaching and learning, discovery and inquiry, service and outreach. But they do not tell us why or in what ways we can better serve society. Nor do they frame a substantive vision for an institution going forward. Only institutional vision and strategic action can provide such definition.

The "vision thing" is key to an institution's future and to its commitment to engagement. Further, establishing institutional vision is a *process*, not a single act. At all costs, a president should avoid answering the question, "What is your vision for the university?" without the imprimatur of the larger academic community. While boards of trustees are the keepers of the institution in so many ways, they cannot arrive at an institutional mission for the campus alone, but rather as part of the campus. So, one measure of institutional mission and the strength thereof is the degree to which a broad-based conversation has occurred about the most desired future of the institution. Here, issues of research aspiration, the quality of teaching and learning, and the nature and degree of community engagement can be answered *for* the institution and *by* the institution. Clearly, this was the purpose of both UWM's "Committee of 100" initiative, which led to The Milwaukee Idea, and the recent effort of the University of Cincinnati to undergo a "Comprehensive Academic Planning Process," which resulted in UC|21.

The presidential role in creating vision is one of guide or moderator, best established by some framework for participation that helps lead a group of key institutional constituents through the visioning and planning process. In Milwaukee, the visioning process was clearly framed by the historic context of The Wisconsin Idea. While I had been unaware of this organizing framework when I initially arrived at UWM, it soon revealed itself to me during the 150th anniversary celebration of the founding of the state. From that point forward, it just seemed obvious that UWM's future should be tied inextricably to this same riveting concept. So presidential commitment to engagement was really established by my extolling a long-held value in the state and applying it to the urban context. In this very direct way, engagement became central to the visioning process at UWM as The Milwaukee Idea became synonymous with expanding the boundaries of the university to the boundaries of the community.

The Cincinnati visioning process was more challenging. There appeared to be no particular historic clarion call for engagement. Further, the visioning process was viewed by many as a balancing act between a very strategic and well-established physical facilities transformation and the need to provide, as most hoped, an umbrella academic plan to extend the physicality of the campus while also guiding greater academic achievement. Purposeful as this confluence of plans was, we still needed some point of inspiration or departure to guide our planning. We found it, happily, in the national context, best portrayed by a series of important perspectives on the university of the 21st century. Noted academic leaders were pursuing this notion (Duderstadt, 2000; Duderstadt & Womack, 2003; Rhodes, 2001; Weber & Duderstadt, 2004), and as such the concept of a new university for the 21st century began to emerge in our thinking. Herein we found specific calls for the engaged university as a 21st-century icon:

> There is little doubt that the need for and the pressure upon universities to serve the public interest will intensify. The possibilities are endless: economic development and job creation; health-care; environmental quality; the special needs of the elderly, youth, and the family; peace and international security; rural and urban decay; and the cultural arts. There is also little doubt that if higher education is to sustain both public confidence and support, it must demonstrate its capacity to be ever more socially useful and relevant to a society under stress. (Duderstadt, 2000, p. 135)

Duderstadt (2000) also writes:

> Public service must be a major institutional obligation of the American university. The public supports the university, contributes to its finance and grants it an unusual degree of institutional autonomy and freedom, in part because of the expectation that the university will contribute not just graduates and scholarship, but the broader efforts of its faculty, staff and students in addressing social needs and concerns. It is of some concern that the role of public service in higher education has not received greater attention in recent years, since this was an original mandate for many of our institutions. (p. 146)

Rhodes (2001) cautions in *The Creation of the Future:*

> Outreach and public service will succeed only to the extent that the emphasis and motives are not paternalistic but rather fraternal, based on the assumption that the

search for solutions will be a joint one, whose benefits are
mutual, in which experience is shared and in which each
partner and each institution gains through a common
commitment. (p. 205)

Again, using a presidential call to the visioning table, we used this notion of the engaged 21st-century institution as a point of departure for our
discussions.

Lead Through Action

Still, engagement requires, even demands, more than the rhetoric of a vision. It requires action. No thoughtful visioning process can escape the
scrutiny of a set of strategic goals that lead to action. What differentiates
The Milwaukee Idea from UC|21 is the comprehensive nature of the latter
and the community-focused nature of the former. This important distinction unfolds accordingly: UWM was not well exposed or valued by the
local Milwaukee community. Its presence had been taken for granted for
far too long, without a successful intervention from the campus to win the
community's attention and eventual investment. Such is simply not the
case with UC and Cincinnati. The rich history of the institution as
Cincinnati's university, created by the merger of several key educational institutions into one, gave UC a kind of legitimacy that the university did
not need to reinvent. So it was possible to commence the visioning process
with more support from the community.

To put it another way, UWM aspires to be a distinguished research university, finding through its commitment to engagement the kind of community support necessary to achieve significant research status. That is,
building the research capacity needed to follow a successful engagement
strategy. At UC the research reputation was already well established, perhaps better so than the institution's track record on engagement. So in some
respects the balancing act was the reverse. UC needed to show the community that a first-rate research institution could increase its commitment to
the community. Either way, engagement is a leverage point and can be a
successful tool in winning local support for research and teaching, or a wonderful outgrowth of academic and research success. Fundamental to this exchange is the action that provides results—the specific ideas that evolve
from a planning process that communities can point to with pride and with
a recognition that the university is truly committed to the community.

For The Milwaukee Idea, these were illustrative "first ideas"—including construction of The Milwaukee Idea house, the development of a non-profit management institution, a diversity center, and a tech transfer initiative. In contrast, the action base for UC|21 unfolds out of six strategic goals, noted earlier, and invokes partnerships that cut across goals and constituencies, from the campus to the community and back. While UC's idea generation is still in the process of becoming, these ideas show every promise of being highly integrated, interdisciplinary, and both campus- and community-based.

Assure the Pocketbook for Aspirations

Engagement is not free, or even revenue-neutral. It assumes that plans will be drawn and actions taken that actually encumber resources. Several steps must be taken to ensure that plans to better serve the community and the academic needs of the campus are included in budget allocations. Perhaps the most rewarding moment during my tenure at UWM was the success we realized in the legislative biennial budget process just two years into my tenure as chancellor. In the previous legislative session, the University of Wisconsin–Madison had been awarded an earmark for institutional growth that was intended to be replicated during the next biennium. UWM requested that the University of Wisconsin System sponsor it for such a request in tandem with the second biennial request from Madison. I am pleased to report that not only did the Madison campus succeed in its second request, but UWM succeeded as well—to the tune of an $11 million earmark for The Milwaukee Idea. While a turn of fate led to a reduction of the earmark during the second year of that biennium, this award was an important victory for the campus. It gave considerable wind to our wings and allowed many of our first ideas to be launched.

Such an earmark scenario is not likely in the near future for UC. Still, the revenues to support our ambitions are central to our growth plans. To create the kind of ambitious financing necessary to realize the full potential of UC|21 and the engagement elements of the plan, we have devised a plan to increase our revenues over the next five years by 50%. We call this plan "50 in 5!" It is an elaborate combination of strategies, including increased revenues from federal grants and contracts; increased enrollment that generates tuition dollars; more entrepreneurial activities, such as enhanced distance-learning programs; belt-tightening consolidations and efficiencies; and the kind of revenue generation that comes from increased student retention and transfer capacity. All of these strategies ensure that as the engagement ideas unfold, integrating research activities with instructional and service initiatives, we will have the revenues to support these creative and collaborative ideas.

Use Presidential Convening Power

Leadership is an incredibly powerful construct. Much has been written about the tensions that surround leadership, management, and institutional change. Some argue for charismatic leadership, others for performance metrics. But by whatever measure, leadership is central to achieving results. One attribute of leadership that has tremendous potential in aiding successful institutional engagement is the ability to bring disparate groups and potential partners to the table. Indeed, presidents have the power to design the table, call people to it and set the agenda for dialogue. I am also a strong believer that what happens next, while not totally in the control of the leader, requires strong presidential leadership to turn opportunity into results.

Presidents create the table when they call various constituencies together, in forums or gatherings, town hall meetings, or plenary sessions and in so doing make it important and meaningful for others to participate. The president can announce the topic, the time frame, invite nominations for participation, and then select from within those key representatives needed to move the agenda.

I have followed this pathway several times in my career: in reinventing the nature and scope of a college; in defining the outreach agenda of a university; and now at UC, in creating a comprehensive academic plan for the future. When called, people come. I am amazed as well that they come with great constancy of purpose. And when asked to work, they work; to meet timelines, they deliver. And when it is all said and done, more gets done than said! It has been my experience that people take ownership of the plan; they live the plan as long as the leadership continues to reinforce the centrality of the planning process to the future of the organization, and as long as they provide, as noted above, the revenues to sustain the initiative.

Go Public and Walk the Brand

Once a vision is crafted, there is a profound need to "go public." While this can take many formats, the most successful strategy I have experienced is around the presidential inaugural. There are university leaders these days who have chosen to forgo the inaugural, for good reasons (a tight revenue environment, too recent a turnover from previous administrations). On the other hand, when a new president arrives on a campus with little experience with turnover, making a statement about new leadership can be important. Further, if a body of key constituencies has worked hard to develop a vision and compelling message, what better time to put it forward than in a very public gathering?

Public gatherings such as an inaugural do something else as well: They give way to public accountability. If you invite the media to attend and document a public gathering, and in that gathering you make promises, the media will hold you to them. How wonderful! What better way to keep the organization's attention riveted on outcomes and deliverables than to have the press clamoring for results—more importantly, results that the institution is poised to deliver. Thus, the clearer the definition the leadership gives to the plan, and the more interesting the measures of success, the more interested the public will be. This wager only works, of course, when success is assumed and realized. This strategy is not for the faint of heart; but then engagement is too important to be left to any other kind of leadership context.

Going public with the engagement vision requires a carefully crafted message that goes beyond mere public promotion to become a pledge of institutional will and commitment. In this, the leader plays a critical role in carrying the message, tirelessly and unrelentingly. Some have called this kind of messaging "branding." While branding is often mistakenly perceived as a logo or graphic rendering, at both UWM and UC we have taken it to deeper levels.

Few scholars have explored the personality and leadership traits that characterize CEOs who qualify as "walking brands" (Stagaman, 2004). These are the charismatic individuals who not only represent the organization well but also exemplify to stakeholders the desired associations with the organization and its brand or brands. The association of this leader with news about an organization can elevate the value of the information to the media. Also on the plus side, the charismatic leader—Aaker (1996) uses the example of Sam Walton—can turn the impersonal, a corporation, into the personal. The result can be a connection that builds critical relationships with those stakeholders.

Not only is the academic vision of the engaged university "walkable" through the leader's activities and messages, it can and should be connoted in the graphic design of printed materials, the use of lapel pins and other insignia, or, as was the case with UCI21, the broad distribution of the plan's technical report through a miniature CD-ROM and the UCI21 web site. In light of the engagement agenda, finding ways to carry the vision and message broadly and consistently into the community is key to convincing the community that the university really is interested in reaching out.

But Will These Ideas Work in Practice?

Only time will tell if the best-laid plans actually come to fruition. Even in the success stories of universities that have sought to create sustainable, broadly institutionalized, and mission-focused engagement, there are pitfalls and barriers that warrant a cautionary note.

First, passionate leadership is a highly internalized good. Only those who truly believe in redefining universities with a strong eye toward community engagement will be able to pull off a successful engagement agenda. You cannot fake engagement; do not even try. Either believe it in your heart of hearts, or take the institution somewhere else.

Second, while presidential leadership is critically important, other champions need to be present—and most of them had better be deans. I cannot emphasize strongly enough how central deans are to engagement and institutional change strategies. Ignore the power of these key academic leaders at your peril.

And finally, build a succession plan. Once a powerful engagement agenda is launched, it cannot be put on hold while the institution transitions. Leaders must find ways to make the engagement agenda continuous, a necessary ingredient to success, so that the next leader will carry on with passion the commitment of another. While difficult to realize at times, no university president stands but on the shoulders of all who have gone before. Recognizing that, and extending the vision, are the most important elements in the long-term viability of a strong and vibrant university.

References

Aaker, D. A. (1996). *Building strong brands.* New York, NY: Free Press.

Boyer, E. L. (1990). *Scholarship reconsidered: Priorities of the professoriate.* Princeton, NJ: The Carnegie Foundation for the Advancement of Teaching.

Collins, J. C., & Porras, J. I. (1994). *Built to last: Successful habits of visionary companies.* New York, NY: HarperCollins.

Duderstadt, J. J. (2000). *A university for the 21st century.* Ann Arbor, MI: University of Michigan Press.

Duderstadt, J. J., & Womack, F. W. (2003). *The future of the public university in America: Beyond the crossroads.* Baltimore, MD: The Johns Hopkins University Press.

Kellogg Commission on the Future of State and Land-Grant Universities. (2000). *Renewing the covenant: Learning, discovery, and engagement in a new age and different world.* Washington, DC: National Association of State Universities and Land-Grant Colleges.

Rhodes, F. H. T. (2001). *The creation of the future: The role of the American university.* Ithaca, NY: Cornell University Press.

Stagaman, M. (2004). Unpublished manuscript, University of Cincinnati.

Weber, L. E., & Duderstadt, J. J. (2004). *Reinventing the research university.* New York, NY: Economica.

Zimpher, N. L., Percy, S. L., & Brukardt, M. J. (2002). *A time for boldness: A story of institutional change.* Bolton, MA: Anker.

15 The Path Ahead: What's Next for University Engagement?

Mary Jane Brukardt, Barbara Holland,
Stephen L. Percy, and Nancy L. Zimpher

More than a decade after Boyer (1994) called for America's colleges and universities to become connected institutions, "committed to improving, in a very intentional way, the human condition" (p. A48), great strides have been made to make community engagement a central focus of higher education's mission and practice at campuses across the country. As the chapters of this book illustrate, institutionalizing engagement has involved, at the macro level, national conversations about the scholarship of engagement, discovery, and learning; experiments in funding and assessment; and growing support for institutions large and small to define engagement for their own time and place. On individual campuses, such as the University of Wisconsin–Milwaukee (UWM), making engagement sustainable has required the challenging but rewarding reexamination of faculty development, student learning, and relationships with community partners.

In the spring of 2004, UWM's Milwaukee Idea partnered with the University of Cincinnati to invite a group of national engagement leaders to convene at The Johnson Foundation's Wingspread Conference Center in Wisconsin to reflect on the past decade of progress and to chart the path ahead. The 41 participants were asked to consider how engagement can be made more sustainable and fully integrated into the fabric of higher education.

While the conference attendees acknowledged the real work that has been done to support and broaden understanding of the engaged institution across public and private four- and two-year campuses, the group insisted that higher education did not need another call to action. The rationale for engagement has been articulated eloquently and broadly, and the first wave of champions has advanced the field. What is needed is not another call to "give engagement a try." Instead, the Wingspread participants argued, it is time to call the question: the question of commitment. Is higher education ready to move beyond the status quo to the possibility of radical change?

What follows is an excerpt from the final report produced by the Wingspread conferees and published by The Milwaukee Idea at the University of Wisconsin–Milwaukee. The full report is available electronically at www.milwaukeeidea.org.

Calling the Question: Is Higher Education Ready to Commit to Community Engagement?

For those who seek to measure the health of higher education in this new century, the proverbial glass may be half full or half empty. That the glass is half full is evidenced in the trend to increasing enrollment, expanding fields of study at home and abroad, and new opportunities for commercial partnerships and technology transfer. Or it may be half empty, with decreasing public support and growing competition from for-profit and international institutions. There is a third viewpoint, however, that suggests the glass may just need to be shaken up a bit—and community-university engagement may be the best way to do so.

Colleges and universities across the nation have found in community engagement a unique opportunity to renew the civic mission of higher education and to strengthen and expand the learning and discovery that has been at the foundation of the academy. Faculty and staff are energizing their scholarship and research through community collaborations, students are discovering the value of experiential and service-learning, and academic and civic leaders are finding new, mutually beneficial partnerships that unite town and gown in enriching the common good.

The Challenge of Engagement

A decade of "calls to action," begun by the Kellogg Commission's (2000) report on university engagement and *The Wingspread Declaration on Renewing the Civic Mission of the American Research University* (Boyte & Hollander, 1999), has not yet produced a flowering of transformed institutions. While 500 presidents and chancellors have signed the Campus Compact Declaration to commit higher education to the democratic ideal, and many institutions have created centers for outreach or encouraged professional faculty to partner in new and creative ways with their communities, engagement has not become the defining characteristic of higher education's mission, nor has it been embraced across disciplines, departments, and institutions.

This is not because engagement does not work—an increasing body of scholarship demonstrates overwhelmingly that it benefits both the academy and community. And it is not for lack of knowledge on how it can be implemented—case studies for institutions large and small, public and private, provide a wealth of information on how to form partnerships, integrate engagement into curriculum, and assess progress. Rather, engagement is difficult work. To be effective, it requires institution-wide effort, deep commitment at all levels, and leadership by both campus and community.

We believe engagement is the best hope for the future of higher education. A return to a mission in which the advancement of discovery, learning, and the common good is fueled by collaborative partnerships is a vision that is right for our time and for a world that looks to higher education for clear direction.

Six Promising Practices

Answering this call to commitment, however, is not easy. Those institutions that do will be distinguished by six practices that help to institutionalize engagement in sustainable ways.

1) Integrate engagement into mission.

2) Forge partnerships as the overarching framework for engagement.

3) Renew and redefine discovery and scholarship.

4) Integrate engagement into teaching and learning.

5) Recruit and support new champions.

6) Create radical institutional change.

Integrate Engagement Into Mission

If engagement is to become institutionalized, it must be recognized as central to the purpose of higher education. It cannot be just an add-on to an existing mission, but instead becomes the animating core, where "service [engagement] is a central and defining characteristic," (p. 60) as Holland (1999) wrote about her comparative study of 23 engaged institutions. University mission is where engagement must become embedded, because it is through active engagement that university mission comes alive and takes on real meaning for campus and community.

This vision of institutionally integrated engagement, while challenging, is not a new one. It has its seeds in America's colonial colleges, founded to train the pastors and teachers who would help to create the country's frontier towns and cities. It is a vision that was alive at the turn of the century, when America's leading research institutions—Columbia University, The Johns Hopkins University, and the University of Chicago—took as their central tenet that they should "make for less misery among the poor, less ignorance in the schools, less bigotry in the temple, less suffering in the hospitals, less fraud in business, less folly in politics," (Long, 1992, p. 199) as President Daniel Coit Gilman stated in his inaugural address at Johns Hopkins in 1876. And service to society as a fulfillment of its democratic mission was core to the founding purpose of the land-grant universities established by the Morrill Act of 1862.

In the century since these progressive ideals were articulated, American higher education has been smothered by what Benson and Harkavy (2004) term "traditional academic scholasticism" (p. 29), under the dominance of the research institution model and by increasing disengagement from real-world problem solving to the isolation of ever-more-specialized disciplines. This has been reinforced by a consumer society that sees education as a private benefit for graduates rather than as a public good. It is against this current—and limiting—mission for higher education that we return to the idea of the university in service to society: supporting our democratic fabric by preparing students to be active, principled citizens and by linking knowledge to the public good through engaged scholarship.

The 1999 Wingspread Declaration on Renewing the Civic Mission of the American Research University articulates the case, and to date, more than 500 presidents and chancellors from higher education have signed the Campus Compact Declaration to reexamine higher education's "commitments to the democratic ideal." We join them in reiterating that if higher education is to take its place as a leader in the life of our country and in advancing social good, we must commit ourselves to leadership in, not above or outside, the world we serve.

What does an institution with an engaged mission look like?

- Engagement is one of the defining characteristics of institutional mission. It is central to the vision the university has for itself in relationship to its teaching, research, and service. It applies across the entire institution, not only to university outreach or to the professions and disciplines for which engagement has historically been important. It will be recognized and communicated in word and deed by university leaders, faculty, staff, students, and supporters.

- What engagement means for each institution will be shaped by the unique history, assets, and needs of the institution and the community it serves. The mission of a private liberal arts college in the suburbs or a metropolitan community college will, of necessity, look different from that of a research-intensive university. But for each, engagement offers the opportunity to create a distinctive institution because it ties the academy to real problems in a real world. This means, of course, that the mission will and must evolve with the institution and with its partners.

- Renewing the mission is a collaborative act. Institutions with an engaged mission will reflect the voices of constituents on and off campus. Creating mission will be an ongoing process that involves society in a thoughtful and informed consideration of the purposes of education and how society is best served. Engagement's transforming impact on higher education will lead to the development of more responsive, adaptable modes of organizing and planning academic work in public contexts.

- Accountability for the success of the university will be shared. While higher education must embrace its responsibility for discovery, teaching, and application of knowledge, it also must evaluate its practice, its performance, and its results in relationship to and with its partners.

Forge Partnerships as the Overarching Framework

Partnerships are the currency of engagement—the medium of exchange between university and community and the measurement of an institution's level of commitment to working collaboratively. Committed engagement requires authentic or "deep" partnerships. By this we mean mutually reciprocal collaboration that is acknowledged by all participants and that generates the best outcomes for all partners. Within the partnership, "we all feel right," as one Wingspread participant described—whether we are a tenured professor, a parent, a governor, or a student.

While collaboration is as much an art as a science, recent efforts have undertaken to assess more closely what makes for successful partnerships and what defines an engaged campus. Campus Compact is currently documenting best practices of engaged institutions as part of its Indicators of Engagement project, funded by the Carnegie Corporation of New York, and has also created Benchmarks for Campus/Community Collaboration (information is available at www.compact.org/indicators/). But more needs to be done to determine how successful partnerships are created and nurtured. Wingspread participants were adamant that their work was only half complete, because the conference focus on institutionalizing engagement in the community requires equal focus on the role of the community in sustaining collaboration.

What does commitment to partnership look like?

- Partnerships are learning environments. Too often the university arrives with the answers. True partnerships are spaces within which questions are created, there is genuine reciprocal deliberation, and the work to find the answers is begun cooperatively. It is within the partnerships that expertise both inside and outside the university is valued and honored.

- Partnerships will be alive across the institution, but for each institution they must also be attached to its critical areas of interest—the academic priorities it has set. For each institution these will be different: a focus on teacher education, major investments in the professional schools, a well-earned reputation for distinguished research in a particular discipline. At the engaged institution, partnerships will be most active and supported around what the institution deems most important, priorities that are rooted in institutional history and in its unique sense of place.

- Engaged institutions will always support a spectrum of active partner-ships—shifting patterns of engagement (Bringle & Hatcher, 2002). There will be a mix of small-scale, faculty/community relationships that may involve a volunteer project that focuses on immediate needs. There will also be emerging and startup partnerships around critical is-sues identified and shaped by the partners. Service-learning opportu-nities geared to short- or long-term needs may be a hallmark of these partnerships. And there will be the "essential relationships," as Judith Ramaley calls them, the significant collaborations that are institutional priorities. P–16 partnerships, healthcare, or community revitalization efforts are examples of long-term, multidimensional, and all-university efforts that require significant leadership and investment. A rich array of such partnerships characterizes the engaged institution.

- University partnerships respect and build community capacity. The university sees the community as the source of multiple assets, not overwhelming problems. Success will be measured by the partnership, not by the research or learning goals and outcomes of the university. The university will ask, "Does this work for you?" when assessing progress.

- Authentic partnerships are best when they are not dependent on the vision of a single individual but when partnership structures offer mul-tiples ways for engagement by diverse members of the community and the university.

- Authentic partnerships involve an exchange of human and financial re-sources under the shared control of the partnership, not the university alone. This means that the university may not have a leadership or controlling role in all partnerships, even those to which it contributes significant dollars or expertise. This will necessitate creative new ways to manage and account for university resources that recognize interdis-ciplinary realities and ensure responsible but flexible stewardship.

- Effective partnerships demand reflection and continuous improve-ment by all collaborators to improve practices, policies, services, and capacity. In this regard, faculty and staff are well qualified to bring their intellectual, human, and financial resources to benefit the collab-oration.

Renew and Redefine Discovery and Scholarship

We believe it is time to move beyond the traditional tripartite mission of the academy—teaching, research, and service. We propose, instead, a new couplet—*engaged* teaching and learning, and *engaged* discovery and research scholarship—which recognizes that connections to society are integral parts of these two core functions of the contemporary college and university. This new model does not supplant the old triad, but expands it. It celebrates the historical connections the academic disciplines have to the world at large. It values all scholarship, particularly that within a context of contemporary need. Engaged research provides incredible benefits to faculty who link their work to their communities. They are able to see the impact of their research result in social good.

The nature of research and scholarship has changed significantly over the past two decades, driven, in part, by the growth of globalization, the Internet, and the computer. The questions of research—its sources of expertise, its ends, and its audiences—have been transformed beyond the narrow confines of the academy, offering limitless possibility for work that has the potential to impact our communities and the world. Michael Gibbons, secretary general of the Association of Commonwealth Universities in Great Britain, calls for multisided conversations between the research community and the practitioner community to widen horizons and improve lives (Association of Commonwealth Universities, 2001). The result will be engaged scholarship that is heterogeneous, multidimensional, and collaborative, and that serves multiple audiences and involves a range of participants, supported by new technologies and driven by advanced communications.

What does commitment to engaged discovery and scholarship look like?

- The work that has begun on redefining and reconceptualizing the scholarship of engagement must be continued and expanded. New definitions will evolve through collaborative efforts on three levels: nationally, as part of the engagement movement; within disciplines to define how engagement can be integrated into individual disciplinary traditions; and on each campus, within its schools, colleges, and, most important, departments, as a reflection of its unique culture and community of learning. The engaged university will support efforts at all three levels through ongoing dialogue and also through its financial and resource priorities. Such dialogue will be inclusive of students and the community.

- Engaged discovery and research scholarship is relevant and essential beyond the metropolitan and urban universities where it has already found a fruitful environment. Community colleges, private suburban, and research-intensive institutions have much to contribute to wide-ranging social challenges, each according to their missions and their strengths.

- Engaged discovery and scholarship will address faculty recruitment, recognition, and reward structures and the means to assess engaged discovery and scholarship. To date, the means to evaluate such scholarship has been outside the conventional mechanism of peer review. Much constructive work is being done by the Clearinghouse and National Review Board for the Scholarship of Engagement to critically assess faculty portfolios using transdisciplinary guidelines. Commitment to such scholarship will also need to recognize and create mechanisms to assess the interdisciplinary role of such efforts, its integration with teaching and learning, its problem-based rather than theory-based impetus, the nontraditional timeframes for such work, and the role of community partners and students in its outcomes. Leaders of engaged institutions must strive to make useful resources such as the Clearinghouse and National Review Board more visible within their institutions.

- New conceptions of engaged discovery and scholarship will be shaped by a recognition of the critical importance of community partners to determining research goals, setting parameters, participating in knowledge gathering, defining success, and contributing to the resources and networks needed. Determining how to structure and assess accountability will be a key concern.

- Critical to new notions of engaged research will be the involvement of deans and department chairs and other leaders within individual disciplines in expanding the conversation. Engagement offers substantial benefits to these leaders, including access to new revenue streams, improved and revitalized scholarship opportunities, and new links to teaching and learning. Their leadership is only the first step in supporting advocates at all levels of the academy to build a supportive network.

- Individual disciplines also have a vital role to play in convening and advancing national and international conversations around integrating engagement into reconceptualized notions of scholarship and discovery. Campus Compact, for example, has created institutes for engaged departments that help faculty, students, community members, and department chairs to integrate engagement more effectively.

- Opportunities for new ways of doing research and scholarship will be embedded into the mission of the institution and validated by the institution's board so that they can become a part of the culture of the institution's learning community. Engaged discovery and scholarship will not determine all academic endeavors, but it will offer new avenues for exploration by faculty determined to advance knowledge in the ways now open.

Integrate Engagement Into Teaching and Learning

If university-community partnerships can be seen as a learning environment, then engaged pedagogy within the university should be a model of the best of shared learning on which such partnerships draw. Unfortunately, at too many institutions the methods by which knowledge is communicated have not kept pace with what we know about how individuals learn and with the new technology that is transforming teaching. The principal desired outcome of citizens prepared to participate in a civil democracy requires a pedagogy and a curriculum that is collaborative, problem-based, interdisciplinary, intentional, and respectful of students as producers as well as recipients of knowledge. The community has a wealth of expertise to contribute as coeducators in this enterprise.

But the rationale for a new pedagogy and curriculum is not just that it supports and reflects the engaged mission of higher education. It also produces deeper and more productive learning—for faculty, students, and community. The growing body of research around the effectiveness of service- and experiential-based learning underlines the powerful role such pedagogy can have to enrich and extend cognitive learning.

What does commitment to engaged teaching and learning look like?

- An engaged mission is important to universities and colleges, but it will become part of the campus culture only when it is integrated into curriculum and teaching. The important collaborative understandings necessary for effective engagement must be fostered and reinforced throughout a spectrum of courses and through diverse means. To this end, engaged teaching and learning is an institutional priority across all disciplines, and is demonstrated through campus-wide service-learning, experiential learning, and interdisciplinary exploration.

- Engaged teaching is supported by the institution, through faculty and staff development programs, centers for teaching and learning, and financial support for community partnerships. Engaged teaching and learning is not intuitive—faculty require technical and instructional assistance to create active learning groups or video-anchored portfolios. While faculty and staff development is important, so also is financial recognition. Institutions must invest in a reward structure for faculty, administrators, departments, and colleges that recognizes the importance of engagement to the university.

- If we demand engaged teaching from faculty, they will require more than remedial support while on the job. Wingspread participants expressed deep concern about the inadequate state of teacher training for graduate students. Engaged teaching will require new kinds of training for graduate students that recognizes the value of collaborative, experiential learning in addition to specialization in a discipline. Such training has powerful implications for higher education overall and for its leadership.

- A defining attribute for engaged teaching and learning is the integration of multicultural understanding into the curriculum. If students and faculty are to be engaged with diverse communities, they must be prepared to acknowledge cultural context and deepen their own understanding of what they can learn and what they can contribute.

- Engagement integrates graduate and undergraduate students by facilitating peer learning at all levels. For most universities, this requires creating space and time for students at all levels to interact and learn from each other.

- Engagement integrates community-based research into learning by involving students, faculty, and community in problem-solving together. Engagement breaks down the false division between learning and discovery and provides constructive ways in which civic capacity can be encouraged.

- The engaged institution facilitates teaching and learning by community partners as well as faculty and students. This may involve creating boundary-crossing mechanisms that facilitate community-campus collaboration: team teaching, master teachers drawn from community leaders, and community teachers-in-residence who help create curriculum as well as provide instruction. (See *Crossing Boundaries* by the Joint Task Force for Urban/Metropolitan Schools, 2004.)

Recruit and Support New Champions

If engagement is to become a driving force in the transformation of higher education and the possibilities it offers society, it must be championed both in the community and on campus. The voices that have been spreading the word must be amplified by university presidents and chancellors, by community leaders, by boards of directors, by deans and department chairs, and by students, faculty, and staff who have experienced its benefits.

Presidents, chancellors, and provosts have an important role in championing engagement, not only as a result of their position at the nexus of campus and community, but also as those individuals most vested in the leadership and success of their institutions. University engagement offers new resources, creative new research directions, national leadership opportunities, and the potential to attract high-caliber students who demand learning based in experience. The task for such academic leaders is to provide the institution with a vision for an engaged university and to reflect critically on the process of moving toward it—facilitating a renewed mission, mirroring collaboration, encouraging a culture of experimentation and innovation, and communicating with audiences inside and outside the university.

New champions must also be found beyond the presidential office. Learned societies, department heads, and deans are important connecting points between disciplines and the faculty, and they are best suited for communicating the benefits of university engagement. Voices outside the academy must also share the message. Community leaders who have participated in reciprocal partnerships can add a credible call to others inside the university and throughout the community. Legislators, trustees, and other opinion leaders have networks of influence that can effectively support and enlarge engagement efforts.

What is the task for new champions of engagement?

- Engagement champions answer "Why?" They connect the often unspoken and deeply felt culture and traditions of the academy to the benefits of engagement. They demystify engagement by providing the rationale for how engagement can distinguish the institution, support faculty research, improve learning, and enrich students.

- Engagement champions hold all levels of the institution accountable by the questions they ask, by the priorities they set, by the process through which resources are allocated, and by the way activities are measured and rewarded. This requires university faculty and staff to be engaged in policies and practices that encourage, support, and reward engagement, for example through financial aid, work-study, and admissions priorities.

- Engagement champions are inclusive. They seek out and support engaged leaders at all levels (both through promotion and through strategic hiring), so that participation in engaged efforts is encouraged by a spectrum of champions—faculty, students, community members, and staff.

- Engagement champions are mentors and role models. They demonstrate different approaches to incorporating engagement into research and teaching. They partner across disciplines and departments and find ways to connect new faculty to engagement efforts.

- Engagement champions connect the institution to national leaders to provide peer mentors, new models, and assessment tools.

- Engagement champions help to free up faculty time to work on engagement agendas. Freeing up time for faculty is a major issue in promoting more engagement. Champions encourage new ways of organizing and structuring academic time while still providing students with a quality education.

- Engaged champions connect to community and campus, creating a vital link for both.

Create Radical Institutional Change

The structures and processes of the academy are both the framework for how higher education operates and metaphors for what it values. Today's hierarchical, elitist, and competitive environment not only is vastly at odds with higher education's professed ideals, but also is increasingly anachronistic in a world that values collaboration, entrepreneurship, and flexibility.

The organizing rationale for engagement holds promise to be a productive model for higher education as a whole. By encouraging networks of inquiry and learning, by developing capacity across disciplines and in community partnerships, and by sharing resources and accountability, engagement creates new relationships and ways of operating that will be essential if higher education is to thrive in this new century.

Translating the habits and patterns of engagement more broadly into the academy—renewal by transposition—requires leadership from presidents, chancellors, and provosts; tenacity and experimentation from faculty, staff, and students; patience from community partners; vision from deans, department chairs, and boards; and daring from funders and supporters. But what an inspiring alternative it offers!

How can radical change be encouraged?

- Radical change requires clear insight into current barriers. Departments and shared governance can be both enablers and barriers to institutionalizing engagement. Each institution needs to assess what is working, what confounds the ideals of the university mission, and what needs to be changed.

- Interdisciplinary relationships are a priority and should be encouraged. This may involve the creation of new structures, such as councils that link disciplines or forums that facilitate networking. Or it may involve the devolution of existing structures that confound collaboration.

- Formal and informal recognition systems will be essential to encouraging and reinforcing patterns of engagement. Such systems must be at the departmental and institutional level but also more broadly, across higher education. This will include rewarding engagement as essential to the mission of higher education through accreditation and in our national rankings.

- "Green carrots"—financial incentives—can energize reorganization and creativity, especially in regard to how programs are organized or reporting structures implemented. Dollars are important to the success of engagement and institutional investment will signal to outside funders the seriousness with which the institution intends to act.

- Community-university partnerships create new relationships with which the conventional academy has no experience. Partnerships involving large grants or shared resources require new governance structures to assure accountability. The engaged institution will support authentic structures that acknowledge the shared nature of the partnership.

- Engagement has real potential to connect higher education to critical public issues (e.g., preparation of teachers who can teach effectively in urban schools or the economic revitalization of urban cores) as well as to diverse streams of external collaboration and financial support.

- For the engaged institution, assessment and change will be a priority. Research-based, scholarly evaluation is essential to winnow the practices that do not further the institutional mission, enrich faculty and staff work, foster student learning and participation, and reinforce community collaboration.

- A rigorous allegiance to the university mission is essential. If engagement is truly its animating value, then internal structures and policies that hinder the vision will change.

- People are more likely to subscribe to a set of policies, processes, and procedures when they are part of the decision-making process. Creating high quality opportunities for all stakeholders to engage in critical decisions is an essential practice.

And So We Call the Question . . .

Is higher education ready to commit to community engagement? Is it ready for the radical, institutional change such a commitment will require?

Engagement is not a passing fad nor for the faint of heart. If the movement is to advance, leaders and practitioners throughout higher education must acknowledge what is involved in moving to the next level. We have outlined that commitment in this chapter and painted a picture of what institutions will need to do to integrate engagement in sustainable, university-wide ways. Engagement will be at the core of institutional mission. Partnerships will redefine how colleges and universities are organized and how they relate to their communities. Scholarly research and teaching will be transformed and champions nurtured to make it so.

We ask presidents and chancellors to take the lead in supporting institution-wide change, raising up new leaders, and articulating a vision for how engagement will invigorate their institutional mission. We call on provosts, deans, and department chairs to support engaged faculty, encourage interdisciplinary efforts, and expand disciplinary assessment models. We call on students to demand of higher education new pedagogy in support of learning that is connected to community and prepares citizens for our democracy. We ask members of our communities to hold higher education to high standards of partnership that can transform the academy and benefit society. And we call on funders and policy leaders to make engagement a national priority.

Creating sustainable engagement will not be easy, for it faces considerable resistance by institutional inertia, traditional definitions of scholarship, and pressures from a market-based economy. The promise of engagement, however, lies in its potential to rejuvenate the academy, redefine scholarship, and involve society in a productive conversation about the role of education in a new century. Not only is this the right time for such a conversation, it is an imperative. If higher education is to serve our students with deep learning, our faculty and staff with opportunities for integrated scholarship, and our communities with our creative and intellectual resources, it will require broad support in making possible the kinds of institutional transformation that only engagement can provide.

We call the question because university-wide, institutionalized, and sustained commitment to engagement is a necessity and a priority if American higher education is to continue its global leadership role. Engagement is higher education's larger purpose.

Participants in the Wingspread Conference on Institutionalizing University Engagement

Sharon Adams, University of Wisconsin–Milwaukee
Barbara McFadden Allen, Committee on Institutional Cooperation
Mary Jane Brukardt, Eastern Washington University
Armand W. Carriere, U.S. Department of Housing and Urban Development
Michael H. Carriere, University of Chicago
Rita Cheng, University of Wisconsin–Milwaukee
Anthony Ciccone, University of Wisconsin–Milwaukee
David Cox, University of Memphis
Jacqueline C. Dugery, Pew Partnership for Civic Change
Deborah Fagan, University of Wisconsin–Milwaukee
Bob Greenstreet, University of Wisconsin–Milwaukee
Karyn Halmstad, Mount Mary College
Ira Harkavy, University of Pennsylvania
Barbara Holland, National Service-Learning Clearinghouse
Elizabeth Hollander, Campus Compact
Kenneth R. Howey, University of Cincinnati
John P. Keating, University of Wisconsin-Parkside
Susan Kelly, Argosy University
Esther Letven, University of Wisconsin–Parkside
Marc V. Levine, University of Wisconsin–Milwaukee
Mitchel Livingston, University of Cincinnati
Robin Mayrl, Helen Bader Foundation
Jane Moore, Greater Milwaukee Foundation
Ellen Murphy, University of Wisconsin–Milwaukee
Jarad Parker, University of Wisconsin–Milwaukee
Stephen L. Percy, University of Wisconsin–Milwaukee
Anthony Perzigian, University of Cincinnati
Patrice Petro, University of Wisconsin–Milwaukee
Terry Pickeral, Educational Commission of the States
Joan Prince, University of Wisconsin–Milwaukee
Marleen Pugach, University of Wisconsin–Milwaukee
Judith A. Ramaley, The National Science Foundation
Lorilee Sandmann, University of Georgia

Thomas Schnaubelt, Wisconsin Campus Compact
Mary Kay Tetreault, Portland State University
Alfonzo Thurman, University of Wisconsin–Milwaukee
James Trostle, Trinity College
John Wanat, University of Wisconsin–Milwaukee
Nancy L. Zimpher, University of Cincinnati

References

Association of Commonwealth Universities. (2001). *Engagement as a core value for the university: A consultation document.* Retrieved July 22, 2005, from http://www.acu.ac.uk/policyandresearch/research/engagement.pdf

Benson, L., & Harkavy, I. (2002, October). *Truly engaged and truly democratic cosmopolitan civic universities, community schools, and development of the democratic good society in the 21st century.* Paper presented at the Research University as Local Citizen conference, San Diego, CA.

Boyer, E. (1994, March). Creating the new American college. *The Chronicle of Higher Education, A48.*

Boyte, H., & Hollander, E. (1999) *The Wingspread declaration on renewing the civic mission of the American research university.* Providence, RI: Campus Comact.

Bringle, R. G., & Hatcher, J. A. (2002). Campus-community partnerships: The terms of engagement. *Journal of Social Issues, 58*(3), 503–516.

Holland, B. (1999). From murky to meaningful: The role of mission in institutional change. In R. G. Bringle, R. Games, & E. A. Malloy (Eds.), *Colleges and universities as citizens* (pp. 48–73). Needham Heights, MA: Allyn & Bacon.

Joint Task Force for Urban/Metropolitan Schools. (2004). *Crossing boundaries: The urban education imperative.* Washington, DC: American Association of State Colleges and Universities and National Association of State Universities and Land-Grant Colleges.

Kellogg Commission on the Future of State and Land-Grant Universities. (2000). *Renewing the covenant: Learning, discovery, and engagement in a new age and different world.* Washington, DC: National Association of State Universities and Land-Grant Colleges.

Long, E. L. (1992). *Higher education as a moral enterprise.* Washington, DC: Georgetown University Press.

Index